T0314304

BEYOND PRIVACY

People, Practices, Politics

Edited by
Sille Obelitz Søe, Tanja Wiehn,
Rikke Frank Jørgensen, and Bjarki Valtysson

BRISTOL
UNIVERSITY
PRESS

First published in Great Britain in 2025 by

Bristol University Press
University of Bristol
1–9 Old Park Hill
Bristol
BS2 8BB
UK
t: +44 (0)117 374 6645
e: bup-info@bristol.ac.uk

Details of international sales and distribution partners are available at bristoluniversitypress.co.uk

© Bristol University Press 2025

British Library Cataloguing in Publication Data
A catalogue record for this book is available from the British Library

ISBN 978-1-5292-3968-3 hardcover
ISBN 978-1-5292-3969-0 ePub
ISBN 978-1-5292-3970-6 ePdf

The right of Sille Obelitz Søe, Tanja Wiehn, Rikke Frank Jørgensen, and Bjarki Valtysson to be identified as editors of this work has been asserted by them in accordance with the Copyright, Designs and Patents Act 1988.

Cover design: Lyn Davies Design
Front cover image: Stocksy/Wizemark
Bristol University Press uses environmentally responsible print partners.
Printed and bound in Great Britain by CPI Group (UK) Ltd, Croydon, CR0 4YY

FSC
www.fsc.org
MIX
Paper | Supporting responsible forestry
FSC® C013604

Contents

Politics

Notes on Contributors

Paško Bilić is Senior Research Associate at the Institute for Development and International Relations in Zagreb, Croatia. His recent publications include a special double issue of *Critical Sociology* (SAGE, 2023) titled *Critical Sociology of Media and Communications: Theoretical Contributions to a Disconnected Field*, which he co-edited with Thomas Allmer. Additionally, he has co-authored the book *Political Economy of Digital Monopolies* with Toni Prug and Mislav Žitko (Bristol University Press, 2021) and a book in the Croatian language titled *Sociology of Media: Routines, Technology, and Power* (Jesenski and Turk, 2020).

Taina Bucher is Professor in Media Studies at the University of Oslo, where she teaches on-screen cultures, cultural imaginaries of AI and digital infrastructures. She has published widely on algorithmic power and platform media, including the books *IF…THEN: Algorithmic Power and Politics* (Oxford University Press, 2018) and *Facebook* (Polity Press, 2021).

Greg Elmer is Bell Media Research Chair and Professor of Communication and Culture at Toronto Metropolitan University (formerly Ryerson University). Elmer has published a number of books and articles on consumer surveillance, media financialization, social media methods, and pre-emptive forms of policing and governing. His next book, co-authored with Stephen Neville, is entitled *The Politics of Media Scarcity* (Routledge, 2024). His most recent documentary film *The Canadian Delegation* screened at film festivals in Canada, the Netherlands, South Africa, and South Korea.

Rikke Frank Jørgensen is Senior Researcher at the Danish Institute for Human Rights, focusing on the intersection between technology and human rights. She is also Honary Professor of Digital Rights at University of Copenhagen. In her most recent book, *Human Rights in the Age of Platforms* (MIT Press, 2019), she examines the human rights implications of the social web, through the lens of datafication, platforms, and regulation. Besides her scholarly activities, she has worked as a special adviser within the Danish government, served on the board of European Digital Rights

(EDRI), and is currently appointed to the Danish Data Ethics Council and the government's expert group on Tech Giants.

Marjolein Lanzing is Assistant Professor of Philosophy of Technology in the Philosophy Department of the University of Amsterdam. She researches the ethical, political, and social dimensions of new technologies, in particular their implications for autonomy and social justice. In addition to her academic work, she is an enthusiastic board member of Bits of Freedom, a Dutch NGO that protects online civil liberties and digital (human) rights, as well as member of the AI Taskforce of the University of Amsterdam and the Free University of Amsterdam.

Jens-Erik Mai is Professor of Information at the University of Copenhagen. Mai's research concerns basic questions about data and information in the digital society, dealing with philosophical, ethical, cultural, and contextual dimensions of information, information and communication technology, digital media, and information and cultural institutions.

Johan Lau Munkholm received his PhD from the University of Copenhagen in 2023. He is currently employed as a postdoc at the University of Southern Denmark in the research cluster *Bio-Machines and the Question of Life*, where he works on the relationship between technology and labour in contemporary society with a focus on its aesthetic mediation in literature and art. Generally, his work revolves around questions of platform power, digital technology, and contemporary capitalism with an emphasis on cultural and political theory.

Bryce Clayton Newell is Associate Professor in the School of Journalism and Communication at the University of Oregon and was, during the writing of this chapter, a researcher at Utrecht University. He has degrees in Law (JD, University of California, Davis) and Information Science (PhD, University of Washington). His research focuses on issues of privacy, surveillance, law and technology, and the use and regulation of information technologies in society.

Beate Roessler is Professor of Philosophy and chair of the group *Philosophy and Public Affairs* at the University of Amsterdam, the Netherlands. She formerly taught philosophy at the Free University, Berlin, and at the University of Bremen, Germany, and as a Socrates Professor of Philosophy at Leiden University. She has been a fellow at the Institute for Advanced Study in Berlin, at the Centre for Agency, Value, and Ethics at Macquarie University, Sydney, and at the University of Melbourne, Law School. She was also a visiting professor at the New York University, and the Bok Fellow at the University of Pennsylvania Law School. She is a co-editor of the

European Journal of Philosophy and a member of various advisory boards. She is a member of the Göttinger Akademie der Wissenschaften, of the Academy of Europe, and of the American Academy of Arts and Sciences. Roessler has published widely on many issues in ethics and social philosophy; her publications include *Privacies: Philosophical Evaluations* (ed.; Stanford University Press, 2004); *The Value of Privacy* (Polity Press, 2005); *Social Dimensions of Privacy: Interdisciplinary Perspectives* (ed. with D. Mokrosinska; Cambridge University Press, 2015). Her book *Autonomie: ein Versuch über das gelungene Leben*, was published in 2017 (with Suhrkamp) and in English (with Polity Press) in 2022. Her current research focuses on *Being Human in the Digital World* with an edited volume coming out in 2024 with Cambridge University Press.

Sille Obelitz Søe is Associate Professor in Philosophy of Information at University of Copenhagen. Søe's research deals with conceptual questions regarding the relations between information, humans, and (digital) technologies. Her contributions to philosophy of information span from conceptualizations of information, misinformation, and disinformation, over analyses of personal information in relation to privacy in a datafied society, to analyses of the differences between humans and digital technologies in regard to surveillance practices, prediction, and knowledge production, as well as the concept of information in intelligence practices.

Karen Louise Grova Søilen is Assistant Professor at the Department of Arts and Cultural Sciences, Lund University, Sweden. Søilen's research is anchored within the recent 'cultural turn' in surveillance studies, which examines contemporary surveillance through cultural practices and imaginaries. Her research interests include the ambivalent entanglements of digital everyday life with surveillance and control, and how surveillance is perceived as bodily, emotional, and multisensory experiences. She received her PhD in Information Studies from the University of Copenhagen in 2021, and is the recipient of Surveillance Studies Network's 2020 Early Career Researcher Award.

Bjarki Valtysson is Associate Professor in the Department of Arts and Cultural Studies, University of Copenhagen, Denmark. Valtysson has published widely on cultural policies, digital culture, platforms, cultural institutions, and regulation. His most recent book is Digital Cultural Politics: From Policy to Practice (Palgrave Macmillan, 2020).

Tanja Wiehn is Assistant Professor at the Department of Communication and Arts at Roskilde University. Previously, she has been Postdoctoral Researcher at the Department of Arts and Cultural Studies at the University of Copenhagen, Denmark. In her research, she focuses on the socio-political dynamics of (synthetic) data, algorithms, machine learning, and platforms. Wiehn also investigates digital culture and artistic (research) practices through feminist epistemologies.

Simon Willmetts is Associate Professor in Intelligence and Security at Leiden University's Institute of Security and Global Affairs. His research focuses upon the impact of intelligence agencies and their practices upon wider social, political, and cultural ideas and debates.

Introduction

Sille Obelitz Søe, Tanja Wiehn,
Rikke Frank Jørgensen, and Bjarki Valtysson

Setting the stage

Putting her watch on her wrist and the phone in her bag, she was ready
to leave for work. The secret she was carrying had to be dealt with later.
She had not fully decided yet what to do about it. Maybe she should
pay the clinic a visit, just have a chat. What could be the harm in that?

Once again, he felt constrained in his work. The system did not really
fit. It spilled over into his personal life and he had trouble figuring out
exactly how it worked. It seemed to be everywhere and nowhere all
at once. At least everybody was in it together.

'What are we looking at?' he asked. 'Numbers, patterns, categories.
We need to figure out how to move forward.' They were unsure what
to make of it, what did the numbers represent? Hopefully, it wasn't
that important, it wasn't people after all.

These three snapshots are all examples of what this book is about – how
people, practices, and politics are interlinked and condition how we can
think about privacy, and to what end.

The main motivation for this anthology lies in providing a cutting-edge
scholarly discussion of privacy-related issues by moving *beyond privacy* and
thinking about its workings in different contexts. For the past few years,
we have observed how privacy is repeatedly contested and challenged by
big tech, datafication, and platform economy. When we suggest moving
beyond privacy, we are not 'leaving' privacy or in any sense devaluing its
significance. Rather, we are making a productive move to enlist it within
a broader spectrum and co-existence of concrete externalities that take
specific forms in the hands of different chapter contributors. Thus, we felt a
need to invite contributions that cut across the traditional spheres of inquiry

1

with regards to privacy, thereby initiating in-depth discussions that address broader societal issues at play.

Much discussion regarding digital technologies, new media, platforms, and information practices have centred on the protection of personal data and privacy. In the digital sphere, privacy has often been reduced to a matter of controlling the flow of personal data and consenting to the use of such data. However, the advent of big tech, the platform economy, and the widespread practices of data sharing, have challenged this dimension of privacy with its focus on individual actions, rights, and responsibilities. While recent measures, such as the GDPR in a European context, have given people more rights and means to control their personal data, and have introduced more regulation of big tech, datafication and the power of major platform providers continue to present unresolved challenges. We notice that there is a large body of work on the value and meaning of privacy (Westin, 1967; Roessler, 2005; Solove, 2008; Nissenbaum, 2010; Cohen, 2012; Koops et al, 2017), but less work on how privacy operates in specific contexts and situations. By moving and situating privacy in the different contexts of synthetic data, atmospheres, the digital state, impersonal profiles, identity, surveillance, non-domination, and capital, the chapters provide new frameworks for thinking about privacy and perceive its workings in different contexts. *Beyond Privacy* thus complicates and nuances a commitment to privacy and proposes new conceptual and theoretical directions.

Structurally, *Beyond Privacy* aims to expand discussions on privacy along three integral and intertwined levels: people, practices, and politics. From multiple disciplinary and interdisciplinary lenses, the 11 chapters therefore engage with issues that involve privacy and its various entanglements with people, practices, and politics offering new and innovative perspectives on privacy in our current datafied societies.

Beyond what?

The field of privacy studies comprises an immense body of interdisciplinary work developed over several decades. Scholars have discussed, for example: the value of privacy, including the link between privacy and freedom (Westin, 1967; Allen, 2011), privacy as a necessary condition to lead an autonomous life (Roessler, 2005), and as a condition for boundary management (Cohen, 2012); the types of privacy-related harms linked to different types of activities such as information collection and processing (Solove, 2008); the contextual norms that privacy expectations rely on (Nissenbaum, 2010); the social and intersubjective contexts of privacy (Roessler and Mokrosinska, 2015); privacy as a human right (Rengel, 2014; European Court of Human Rights, 2022) related to data protection (Bygrave, 2014; Pedersen, 2023); and many more. It is beyond the scope of this introduction to provide an account of the many discourses that have shaped the field of privacy studies over several decades.

Rather than providing yet another attempt to conceptualize privacy and its value and function at individual, social, and societal level, the collection will explore *what* privacy can and cannot do *when* connected to key concepts and challenges of contemporary society. What role does privacy play as we seek to understand and address new practices of data mining, shifting public and private boundaries, and the continuous tracking and targeting of individuals as they live, work, and socialize? (Filimowicz, 2022; Kaufmann, 2023).

By choosing the title *Beyond Privacy*, we do not attempt to leave the notion of privacy behind or somehow ignore the extensive work that has been done within the field. Our aim is to nuance the complexities in which privacy comes to operate. These are moments of concrete practices, in which the notion of privacy becomes a valuable category to think through matters, such as feminist politics, state intelligence, and the right to silence. We thus ask in the book: How can privacy challenge the processes of datafication and platformization permeating realms, institutions, and the individual? In what ways is privacy a valuable norm to formulate relevant policies and regulations? When does privacy become a placeholder in new-found market logics serving to maintain digital infrastructures and their economies? What does it mean to think beyond privacy?

Background and structure

This volume is the result of the research project *'Don't Take it Personal': Privacy and Information in an Algorithmic Age* funded by the Independent Research Fund Denmark and hosted by the University of Copenhagen and the Danish Institute for Human Rights. The project started in 2018 and, since then, we have visited and presented at various conferences and engaged with different academic communities, practitioners, regulators, agencies, and organizations that work with privacy from different angles. During these interactions, we have learned that, against all odds, privacy is, indeed, not dead. Quite the contrary. It is alive and kicking in different directions and its multiple effects are felt in numerous contexts. This volume looks further at some of these contexts and, as such, contributes to the current scholarly and theoretical framework of privacy. The interdisciplinary approach of this collection aims to make sense of the new circumstances under which privacy is understood and leveraged in current times. The analytical strength lies in the ways in which privacy is addressed by scholars well embedded within privacy studies as well as contributions that revisit privacy through the lens of other schools of thought, such as surveillance studies, information studies, political economy, and critical algorithm and data studies.

The re-evaluation of the notion of privacy constitutes a framework for further critical inquiry along the lines of new technological developments and the manifesting logics of datafication. As previously mentioned, we are interested in investigating and challenging the fundamental societal and structural issues that emerge around privacy from the perspectives of *people*, *practices*, and *politics*. The intention is to provide specific contexts to place theoretical and analytical takes on privacy, which the authors have productively embraced in various ways.

People

The chapters in this part of the book all deal with the individual – the person – and their claims to privacy. From discussions of the relational nature of privacy, to considerations of the limitations of privacy as an individual right in light of personal tracking devices, to deliberations on the right to silence, these chapters explore and renegotiate the roles and privacy rights of the individual in a networked, datafied society. An underlying theme is the blurred boundaries between the individual and (data-driven) systems.

Sille Obelitz Søe and Jens-Erik Mai set the stage for this first part of the book. In Chapter 1, Søe and Mai propose the concept of hybrid-identity as a way to understand the interrelations of privacy, secrecy, information, and systems. The premise of the chapter is that data and information obtained about people do not stay within the system or context in which they originally were obtained. Indeed, there is a risk of data leaking to other systems. Furthermore, on an individual level, data stick. They impact who we are, and who we can be, and how we can go about in the world. When perceived from this perspective, privacy becomes a question of identity formation, construction, and co-construction by me, myself, and everybody else, including the algorithmic systems that we meet. To further understand these complexities, Søe and Mai advocate for the use of the concept of hybrid-identity. According to them, hybrid-identity changes the way we understand registration of personal information in systems, it amplifies the relational nature of privacy, and it requires new conceptual attention to the notion of secrecy. Søe and Mai demonstrate how those changes occur in three different contexts: for information and categorization systems; for privacy's concern with personal information; and for the information asymmetries created by secrets.

In Chapter 2, Beate Roessler uses the magnifying glass of the private to look at recent social phenomena, such as the me-too movement, to understand a shift in the line between public and private. The chapter asks the following questions: has the power to define what is considered private been broken by the influence of social media? How do we reconcile the legitimate protection of the private sphere with the public's legitimate interest in avoiding abuse? Is the conservative framing of 'woke' as a 'cancel culture' also a setback against the liberating publication of previously private issues such as homosexuality or queer identities? Roessler proposes that the *perspective of the private* helps to better understand the inherent ambivalences, but also the discourses of power and liberation.

In Chapter 3, Marjolein Lanzing addresses the challenges and potentials of privacy as an individual right to data protection. In the chapter, Lanzing observes that privacy has been criticized for dominating the public and academic debate on the ethics of technology. Situated within the discussion of FemTech health apps, such as period and fertility trackers, the chapter points out the importance of privacy as an individual human right while showing that it is helpful to move the FemTech discussion beyond privacy-as-individual-data-protection. The chapter identifies limits to this conceptualization of privacy and claims that if we want to understand how new technologies contribute to – or undermine – people's autonomy, there is a need to recognize both the social and decisional dimensions of privacy.

Finally, Taina Bucher's contribution in Chapter 4 explores the 'right to silence' as an often-overlooked aspect of the definition of freedom of expression and freedom of information. According to Bucher, Western democracies traditionally prioritize speech as central to democratic participation, following the idea that informed citizens and freedom of expression form the touchstones of modern democratic and political theory. While media research emphasizes the power of speech, it often neglects the right *not* to speak and the right *not to absorb* or *attend to* the speech of others. Extending Westin's (1967) concept of information privacy, Bucher argues for ways that individuals determine for themselves when, how, and to what extent information about *others* is communicated to *them*. The chapter draws on artworks that explore the role of digital media for an understanding of information privacy by mobilizing politics of withdrawal, concealment, and self-care. By moving beyond traditional notions of privacy, the chapter proposes a nuanced approach to managing information flows and personal boundaries in the light of networked hyperconnectivity.

Practices

Blurred boundaries are also detectable in the practices around datafication, platformization, and use of technologies in general. The chapters in this part of the book shift the focus from individual to collective activities. The chapters deal with the practices surrounding the use of different platforms and the implications for privacy – both in terms of what it can be and what we think it is. From the embodied and felt experience of privacy in the home, to a systemic shift between state and market in providing core services to the public, and further to a critical framework for impersonal platformed media, the discussions in this part of the book are situated within a broader frame of the overall structures guiding platforms and practices in Western societies – for example, their embeddedness in economic systems.

Karen Louise Grova Søilen's chapter reflects on how privacy can be theorized as a distinct form of sphere, namely an atmosphere. Drawing on perspectives from phenomenology and aesthetics, Chapter 5 provides a conceptual framework for exploring the embodied and felt experience of privacy in everyday lived spaces. The chapter discusses two cases from contemporary surveillance culture in which domestic privacy is at stake: a series of deeply voyeuristic images taken by the artist Arne Svenson of his neighbours in their apartments in a glass building, and 'Lighthouse', an artificial intelligence (AI)-enabled home surveillance assistant that provides remote access to the smart home and its inhabitants through the user's smartphone. The chapter offers key insights into how the spatial boundaries of the home are dissolving in new ways, and how thinking about privacy as an atmosphere directs our attention to how one *feels* in an environment – and thus to the transformation of the experience of the home as a privacy space in the 21st century.

In Chapter 6, Bjarki Valtysson and Rikke Frank Jørgensen, focus on how private companies are instrumental in forming processes of public sector digitalization and thereby become key actors in shaping the digital infrastructure of the Danish welfare state. Valtysson and Jørgensen focus on the education sector and reveal how Danish digitalization strategies have, for the past two decades, encouraged increased cooperation between public and private actors. The chapter uses two recent cases that concern pupils in Danish public schools. The cases reveal several challenges when platforms and platform ecologies driven by powerful tech giants become major actors within the Danish public education system. These include opaque flows of data and citizens' privacy rights. Findings indicate that despite recent regulatory measures, tensions pertain to the still closer cooperation between private actors guided by market values and public actors guided by public interests and an obligation to protect citizens' privacy rights.

Last, in Chapter 7, Greg Elmer explores the practices underlying social media as marketing. Elmer returns to controversial German economist Werner Sombart's theorization of the early corporation as a means of rethinking predominant theories of privacy, particularly in the contemporary context of social media platforms and related digital properties. Of specific interest for the context of the chapter, is Sombart's discussion of cost accountants, professionals who aggregate and calculate all facets of a corporation to project possible future business plans and decisions. In the chapter, Elmer develops Sombart's subsequent definition of 'impersonal' capital as a means of understanding the contemporary practice of clustering online users for marketing and valuation purposes.

Politics

In this part of the collection, economic structures are tied in with politics in a more general sense, looking at the market structures governing current practices around datafication, as well as looking at the possibilities for regulation and alternatives. From the prospects of synthetic data to the use of AI and personal data in law enforcement, these chapters address the broader issues of jurisdiction and regulation across the European Union and the United States (US). An underlying theme is that of power and empowering, how privacy is challenged but at the same time holds the key to individual and collective freedom, tying the broader regulatory issues with individual rights, leading us back to people.

In Chapter 8, Paško Bilić offers a critical socio-economic perspective into the debates around privacy. He evolves a theoretical approach that critiques the underlying political economy in which privacy abuse appears. Bilić discusses how the production of 'technological forms' instrumentally merged with the social experiences of users and mediated through aggregated commodified data, becomes the underlying problem of data privacy. According to Bilić, the 'technological form' circumscribes the range of experiential possibilities orchestrated by algorithms and conducive to generating surplus value. To mitigate privacy risks, Bilić notes, more investment in public infrastructure is needed to strengthen privacy and data rights and to enable alternative environments that are excluded from commodification.

Johan Lau Munkholm and Tanja Wiehn, in Chapter 9, demonstrate what happens when privacy is reconfigured under market logics. Munkholm and Wiehn investigate the emergence and development of synthetic data as a new data privacy technology. Synthetic data are purported to reduce the labour intensity and costs of data collection while severing the connection between the individual and data in a way that satisfactorily complies with existing legal requirements. Arguing that synthetic data are a symptomatic result for a European political and regulatory discourse that foregrounds the protection of individual rights, Munkholm and Wiehn critically discuss the promotion and emergence of synthetic data. Thus, Munkholm and Wiehn underline the epistemological and political limitations of the concept of privacy.

In Chapter 10, Simon Willmetts focuses on the link between surveillance and privacy, considering the further integration of AI technologies into state and military intelligence programmes. Taking departure in the revelations brought forward by Edward Snowden, Willmetts notes how different operative definitions of surveillance were animating each side of an ensuing debate. In the chapter, Willmetts discusses that while privacy activists defined surveillance as the acquisition of data, even in unprocessed form, defenders of the intelligence community maintained that it was only once certain data were selected for analysis that surveillance took place. Willmetts explores the impact of AI upon the intelligence cycle, and the implications of this for our definitions of surveillance and privacy.

In Chapter 11, Bryce Clayton Newell draws on a Republican perspective to challenge the collection, use, and analysis of geolocation data. Newell argues for new legal frameworks that account for the sensibility of geolocation information. In the chapter, Newell summarizes how data privacy laws in the US regulate the transfer, sale, and dissemination of personal geolocation data to public law enforcement by private companies, and compares the US approach to the EU's approach. Newell situates the location-related surveillance of the state, and the laws regulating these practices, within a Republican critique and foregrounds how the data-processing practices of private companies, including data sharing with law enforcement, implicate domination and reduce the liberty of those whose data are collected and processed. Newell thus outlines how a neo-Republican theory of privacy can inform policy and scholarship related to location privacy and state surveillance.

Going where?

Together, the 11 chapters in this volume paint a picture of the vast complexities we are dealing with in today's datafied societies. With datafication, digital platforms, and market logics, boundaries are blurred to an extent not seen before. The distinctions between public and private are challenged and renegotiated in unprecedented ways. Tracking and surveillance shifts between private actors and states, and although the individual might not always be of interest to market logics and state dynamics, it is still their data which, in different ways, cater to the new technological developments. And, in some very specific and important cases, it does have implications for these individuals – the people – in the sense of who they can be, their rights, their health, and their possibilities within societies. However, in order to address these implications, we need to understand the structural levels at which these implications are manifested and made possible – the practices and the politics permeating our societies.

With this volume, we aim to start new and different conversations on privacy. Together, the chapters show that people, practices, and politics are not distinct and set apart, but rather weave into one another in different ways. The individual contributions progress, in their own way, new understandings of the role and impact of privacy in the context of institutions and datafication, as well as on an individual level. The chapters illustrate the many forms and notions of privacy across contexts, showing that it expands well beyond being an individual value and right. Even when privacy is tied more closely to the individual, it is not merely a matter of managing information. Privacy holds democratic value for the implementation of policies and regulation to protect citizens. At the same time privacy is (re-)defined by social and political practices. However, privacy is also leveraged as a placeholder for the further development of economic interests.

Considering that societies are further configured by the logic of markets, datafication, and technological innovation, thinking beyond privacy considers the many layers of this dynamic. *Beyond Privacy* thus aims to bring forth productive nuances for future research on privacy. Finally, it allows us to reassess, criticize, and ultimately formulate the meaning of privacy in the socio-political conditions under which we want to live.

Acknowledgement

This book is the final outcome of the research project *'Don't Take it Personal'. Privacy and Information in an Algorithmic Age* generously funded by Independent Research Fund Denmark (grant number 8018-00041B).

References

Allen, Anita L. (2011). *Unpopular Privacy: What Must We Hide?* New York: Oxford University Press.

Bygrave, Lee A. (2014). *Data Privacy Law: An International Perspective.* Oxford: Oxford University Press.

Cohen, Julie E. (2012). *Configuring the Networked Self: Law, Code, and the Play of Everyday Practice.* New Haven, London: Yale University Press.

European Court of Human Rights (2022). *Guide on Article 8 of the European Convention on Human Rights.* Council of Europe. Available at: https://ks.echr.coe.int/documents/d/echr-ks/guide_art_8_eng-pdf

Filimowicz, Michael (ed) (2022). *Privacy: Algorithms and Society.* London: Routledge.

Kaufmann, Mareile (2023). *Making Information Matter: Understanding Surveillance and Making a Difference.* Bristol: Bristol University Press.

Koops, Bert-Jaap, Newell, Bryce Clayton, Timan, Tjerk, Škorvánek, Ivan, Chokrevski, Tom, and Galič, Maša (2017). A typology of privacy. *University of Pennsylvania Journal of International Law,* 38(2): 483–575. Tilburg Law School Research Paper No. 09/2016.

Nissenbaum, Helen (2010). *Privacy in Context: Technology, Policy, and the Integrity of Social Life.* Stanford, CA: Stanford University Press.

Pedersen, Anja Møller (2023). *The Fundamental Rights to Privacy and Data Protection in the EU Legal Order: Reconciling privacy rights and rationales,* PhD thesis, University of Copenhagen, Faculty of Law.

Rengel, Alexandra (2014). Privacy as an international human right and the right to obscurity in cyberspace. *Groningen Journal of International Law,* 2(2). Available at SSRN: https://ssrn.com/abstract=2599271

Roessler, Beate (2005). *The Value of Privacy.* Cambridge, Malden: Polity Press.

Roessler, Beate and Mokrosinska, Dorota (eds) (2015). *Social Dimensions of Privacy: Interdisciplinary Perspectives.* Cambridge: Cambridge University Press.

Solove, Daniel (2008). *Understanding Privacy.* Cambridge, MA: Harvard University Press.

Westin, Alan (1967). *Privacy and Freedom.* New York: Atheneum Press.

People

Me, Myself, and Everybody Else: The Implications of Hybrid-Identity for Systems, Privacy, and Secrecy

Sille Obelitz Søe and Jens-Erik Mai

72 seasons. The first 18 years of our lives that form our true or false selves.

James Hetfield, 2022

Introduction

72 Seasons. The title of Metallica's 2023 album. The 72 seasons – besides being the first 18 years of our lives – refers to 'The concept that we were told "who we are" by our parents. A possible pigeonholing around what kind of personality we are. I think the most interesting part of this is the continued study of those core beliefs and how it affects our perception of the world today' (Hetfield, 2022). But, it is not only our parents who tell us 'who we are'. It is also our friends, schools, teachers, the society, algorithmically governed systems, and ourselves. We are not only told who we are, but also 'who we can be'. And that shapes our perception of the world. It shapes and co-shapes our identities – not in a split between true and false identities, or between real and digital identities, but in a hybrid and networked structure, constructed, co-constructed, negotiated, and shaped by others and ourselves (Søe and Mai, 2022).

According to Hetfield, 'Much of our adult experience is reenactment or reaction to these childhood experiences. Prisoners of childhood or breaking free of those bondages we carry' (Hetfield, 2022). This might be even more so for the children that are brought up today in Western digitalized societies, where most of their childhood memories are shared by their parents on Facebook, the public school tracks their performances through educational platforms, and their social lives are conducted through Snapchat, TikTok, Fortnite, World of Warcraft, and other social media and online games. Each of these systems form and shape one's identity, and as such 'it is difficult to change when one cannot move beyond the past. The Internet changes access to the past and this new form of access may limit the growth and development of the individual' (Ambrose, 2012: 22). That is, the systems, platforms, and categories that people interact with influence the individuals' possibilities to shape and co-construct their identities.

In a broad and inclusive sense, privacy can be understood as the state of being free from scrutiny or interference in your personal life, the ability to form your identity, both in terms of your own perception of yourself and in terms of categories and nouns others use about you, and privacy is about your ability to have your identity reflected in databases and category systems in a way that you accept and recognize. Informational privacy is often understood as the ability to control information about oneself; the idea being that if one has control over the access of information about oneself, then one enjoys privacy (Koops et al, 2017). In this way, the notions of personal information and privacy have been addressed as intertwined; as tightly connected concepts where one constrains the other. That is, current theories and discussions of privacy – specifically informational privacy – are closely related to a specific notion of personal information, with privacy being conceptualized as the ability to control and/or restrict access to personal information.

According to Koops et al (2017: 484), there are 'eight basic types of privacy (bodily, intellectual, spatial, decisional, communicational, associational, proprietary, and behavioral privacy), with an overlay of a ninth type (informational privacy) that overlaps but does not coincide, with the eight basic types'. Thus, information plays into the eight basic types of privacy, but privacy is much more than merely control over that information – and, as hinted above, we argue that identity is significant to people's control over their selves at a more basic level than the mere control of their personal information. Hence, it is necessary to go beyond control of information to unpack the notion of privacy in relation to identity formation.

We argue that people enjoy privacy when they control access to their personal life and they control the construction of their identity, regardless of how and by whom that identity is represented. This understanding of privacy is based on what we have called 'hybrid–identity' (see Søe and Mai, 2022). The central thesis in this notion of hybrid-identity is to acknowledge the networked structure of identity formation between the physical and digital realms of society and the world, as well as the leaky and greasy nature of information. In the digitized, datafied, and algorithmic age, data and information obtained about people do not stay within the system or context where they were obtained. They leak to other systems and contexts, and they stick to the individual. Thus, information collected and profiles generated within systems have consequences outside those systems. They impact who we are, and who we can be, and how we can go about in the world. It becomes a question of identity formation, construction, and co-construction by me, myself, and everybody else, including the algorithmic systems we meet. We suggest that the value of this notion of hybrid-identity is that it captures these complexities, which different data-identity metaphors such as data-double, algorithmic subjectivity, and so on do not capture, because they operate with a split identity between a physical and a digital self.

In this chapter we develop the notion of hybrid-identity further to show how it provides an accurate and contemporary understanding of identity, which has implications for how systems, privacy, and secrecy are best understood. To establish this argument, we first present some of the main features of our notion of hybrid-identity, then we dive into the relations between information and systems, information and privacy, and information and secrecy, before offering a conclusion.

Hybrid-identity

The notion of 'hybrid-identity' captures the networked structure of identity by including digital representation (data collection, profiling, and so on) as part of the world and therefore as part of what goes into the formation and construction of a person's identity. We suggest that identity is a mix of internal and external factors – social identity, personal identity, and self-identity (Lynch, 2019). All classic data-identity metaphors, on the other hand, operate with a split between the real world and the digital world, and thereby with a split between 'real' and 'digital' identities. Hybrid-identity is developed to include the digital domain in the real world by regarding digital data as part of the external factors that go into identity construction (Søe and Mai, 2022). Information, whether it be digital or not, influences identity formation and mediates identity construction and ascription. What information others have available about us influences how they see us – and how we are seen by others influences how we see ourselves (Henschke, 2017). And, it does not matter whether our personal information is registered correctly, it is part of who we are and who we can be (Koopman, 2019a, 2019b).

Hybrid-identity is a networked structure interweaving digital and lived identity, thus it is not confined to a specific sphere or system, but cuts across all spheres. Hybrid-identity is based on the idea that identity is fluid in the sense that identity formation is a complex process – a process continuously influenced and shaped by internal and external factors.

Further, hybrid–identity is interconnected with information understood as representational content.

The relation between identity and information is determined by use, in language games, embedded in forms of life and is, as such, Wittgensteinian in nature. Our identities are formed and constructed in language – through the use of nouns and categories situated in social contexts – that is, in language games (Wittgenstein, 1953/2009). Therefore, identity is not a stable or permanent feature; there is no natural sphere of 'who we are' nor does a collection of data represent who we are. Our identity is formed and constructed through language games and thereby shapes how it is possible to talk about us, which categories can be used about us, how the categories are employed, and what they mean. Our identity is developed in the interaction between others' view of us, how we regard ourselves, how we are represented in databases and systems, the accepted categories in a culture and their meanings, and how that interaction plays out in a specific context, that is in a language game situated in a form of life (to use Wittgenstein's terminology). Concepts and meaning are developed in language games which form the structure that lies beneath culture, social context, internal standards, and habits that provide the rules and conditions of possibility. The possible relations with ourselves, others, society, and the world are given within language games – and our possible identities are formed within language games.

Therefore, we argue that the digital should be seen as one external factor among many factors that go into and influence identity formation together with the individual's internal, own perceptions of self. That is, the notion of hybrid–identity emphasizes the networked structure of identity by interweaving the 'reality-based' aspects of identity and the 'digital-based' aspects of identity to form one notion of identity, *hybrid-identity*. Further, in this hybrid understanding of identity, how we understand ourselves, and how we are understood by others is co-constructed: it is a mix of how others perceive us, the role and presence we have in specific social contexts, and how we perceive and think about ourselves in those contexts. Thus, the concept of hybrid-identity is informational. How we understand ourselves and others is based on information, the information we have at hand, the information about us in systems, the information others have about us, and how we informationally perceive ourselves. Digital information (and data) is part of that information which influences identity, influences our perceptions of ourselves and others.

Therefore, hybrid–identity changes the way we understand registration of personal information in systems, it amplifies the relational nature of privacy, and it demands renewed conceptual attention to the notion of secrecy. In the following three sections we will demonstrate how those changes occur in three different contexts: for information and categorization systems, for privacy's concern with personal information, and for the information asymmetries created by secrets.

Information and systems

Modern society is built on the collection, analysis, and application of personal information. As society developed throughout the 19th and 20th centuries, and as public services grow in demand and private businesses expand, society becomes more organized and structured, and there is an explosion in information. It is a time with a focus on 'classifying and cataloguing the mushrooming recorded forms of knowledge in its various compartments' (Black, 2001: 68). There is a need to

> know about people ... to arrange social life: what they buy, and when and where, how much energy they require, where and at what times; how many people are in a given area, of what gender, age and state of health; what tastes, lifestyles and spending capacities given sectors of populations enjoy. Bluntly, *routine surveillance* is a prerequisite of effective organization. (Webster, 2014: 279–280, emphasis in original)

For society to offer modern school systems, roads, public transportation, healthcare, shopping (including the logistics), banking, telephone systems, collection of taxes, delivering mail, and so on and so on, an enormous amount of information must be collected about individuals in the community served. At the same time, 'bureaucrats provided tools for making sense of a nation's inhabitants in broad terms, using big categories like race, class, sex, state, and region and smaller categories related to health or occupation' (Bouk, 2017: 94). People are lumped together in categories based on shared characteristics, and facts are inferred based on similarities with others in the same group. It can be assumed that you are like others in your group, and that one can say something specific about you because you belong to a certain category. All members of a certain category share defining characteristics; and it is assumed that the defining, shared characteristics are objective, true, and factual information about individuals.

People are treated as 'individuals' for the purpose of developing the social organization of society in terms of assessing the need for roads, hospitals, and schools in particular areas. This understanding gives rise to statistics and allows historians to explain fundamental transitions of ordinary life. As more personal information is gathered, and more in-depth understanding of the population is developed, the notion of society as 'a mass' emerges (Bouk, 2017: 95). It allows private businesses and public agencies to develop precise understandings of individual consumers and citizens. Insurance companies, for instance, can develop business models based on analyses of the likely behaviour of individuals, banks are able to assess individuals' creditability, and universities can admit the brightest students based on intelligence tests and curves.

In the first half of the 20th century there arose a need for 'individuation', to view people not only as belonging to a group but as individuals as well. To collect the correct amount of taxes, to have a record of people's health history, and to document their schooling it is necessary to have a file on each individual. As such, the collection and processing of personal information make 'new kinds of subjectivity' possible (Bouk, 2017: 94). To be able to serve the needs of their customers and citizens, organizations must create files of the individuals they serve, to optimize that service. The telephone company needs information about who you call when and for how long to be able to send you an invoice, the local butcher needs information about your purchases to bill you, and your dentist keeps a record of the services they have provided you.

Thus, as modern society developed in the 19th and 20th centuries, we see two kinds of systems of personal information: systems of personal information that businesses and public organizations have about individual customers and citizens; and systems of personal information that are used to create statistics about society as a mass. Yet, in these systems at this point in time, there is nothing personal about the personal information used to create the records and statistics. Each piece of information is kept within its container, and it stays there – it is only used to serve a single, specific purpose, and it says nothing about the identity of the involved people.

As such, modern society is built on the collection of personal information and surveillance of citizens. This collection and use of personal information is based on the understanding that there is nothing sinister or ill-intended about the mere collection of information – it is for the greater good of the community. It is only when that social contract is broken, and people experience that the collection of their personal information is not for the greater good, but for the benefits of the few or for large private corporations, that they start questioning the use of their information. Unfortunately, it is not easy to separate surveillance for the good (welfare) from the bad (warfare) today, because any piece of personal information could be used both to benefit the greater good and to harm individuals. 'To some extent, welfare and warfare are common bedfellows, where one often justifies or necessitates the other. Monitoring of internet and mobile phone traffic and tighter security and surveillance at airports are now all commonplace; we are monitored but (so it is argued) for our own safety' (Weller, 2021: 168).

With the introduction of the computer in business and public administration in the second half of the 20th century, something significant happens to personal information; it becomes greasy (Moor, 1997) and it leaks from its containers (Lyon, 2001). While analogue personal information stays within the container (context, system) in which it was collected, digital personal information is difficult to contain. Once produced, digital information can easily slip from one container to another, from the dentist to the insurance company, from the telephone book to the pizzeria.

This greasing of information and creation of leaky containers gives rise to concerns about the potential shifts in power structures, as Langdon Winner warned in 1986:

> Those who stand to benefit most obviously are large transnational business corporations. While their 'global reach' does not arise solely from the application of information technologies, such organizations are uniquely situated to exploit the efficiency, productivity, command, and control the new electronics make available. Other notable beneficiaries of the systematic use of vast amounts of digitized information are public bureaucracies, intelligence agencies, and an ever-expanding military, organizations that would operate less effectively at their present scale were it not for the use of computer power. Ordinary people are, of course, strongly affected by the workings of these organizations and by the rapid spread of new electronic systems in banking, insurance, taxation, factory and office work, home entertainment, and the like. (Winner, 1986: 106–107)

Today, in the 21st century, the collection of information and use of computer power and digital devices is even more pervading than Winner (1986) anticipated, and the power structures do indeed seem to have shifted significantly. We live in a surveillance capitalistic (Zuboff, 2020) and expository society (Harcourt 2015), dominated by surveillance technologies infiltrating all parts of our lives (Henschke, 2017). Internet, social media, digital platforms, apps, and smartphones have become increasingly popular and pervasive in terms of how we deal with the world, ourselves, and each other. Thus, default tracking, information collection, and profile building have become an inevitable part of everyday life. Surveillance logics are the modus operandi of tech companies and government digitalization strategies (Jørgensen and Søe, 2024). The digital nature of much of the information collected and profiles generated has made the greasiness and leakiness of information even greasier and leakier.

The leaky, greasy, and datafied nature of personal information calls for a new understanding of informational representation of people in systems. When information about people leaks out of its containers and sieves into other containers or out of the digital domain and sticks to people, it has new implications for identity formation. As personal information flows in and out of systems it becomes easier for governments, intelligence agencies, and private organizations to monitor and provide services to their citizens and customers – and it becomes impossible and unrealistic for individuals to control access to their personal information. Identification and profiling do not stay within a specific system – they operate across systems and platforms, and weave through the physical and digital domains.

The representation, categorization, and identification of people in information systems inform and constrain their identities. Information in systems is not a mere reflection of people's identities. As such, the registration of personal information is not a neutral act of mere registration of objective facts or data, but an active interference that contributes to the construction of their identity. The registration of personal information in systems limits how we might possibly present ourselves and how others might perceive us, and, as such, information in systems will have an influence on our identities and our lived lives.

Information and privacy

With the increase in the collection, analysis, and application of digital personal information by businesses and public agencies, there is a concern that people's right to privacy – the right to private life, to act autonomously, to form one's identity, to control information about oneself, and to be let alone – will come under pressure.

From a conceptual, legal, or a rights perspective, the notion of privacy is much broader than merely concerns about information. Nonetheless, privacy has, from the start of the modern period, beginning with Warren and Brandeis' ([1890] 2005) notion of *the right to be let alone*, been associated with the ability to control information about oneself. Warren and Brandeis argue that privacy is concerned with the information about specific state-of-affairs, and in 1967 Westin famously suggested that, '[p]rivacy is the claim of individuals, groups, or institutions to determine for themselves when, how, and to what extent information about them is communicated to others' (Westin, 1967: 7). This basic idea, that privacy is concerned with people's ability to control their personal information, dominates thinking and conceptions of privacy (see Solove (2008) and Nissenbaum's (2010) critical reviews of the notion of privacy). The same line of thinking can be found within GDPR, which concerns people's ability to protect their personal information, understood as any information relating to them (GDPR, 2016). This results in two unfortunate understandings of privacy: (i) that privacy has mostly to do with information, and (ii) that there is a special kind of information that is 'personal information' (Søe et al, 2021).

One central, but often overlooked, aspect of the discussion of usage of personal information, is how to define and delimit 'information'. From the start of the creation of the modern information and surveillance societies (Lyon, 2001; Webster, 2014), information is understood and employed to mean true, verifiable facts. Personal information is first understood as characteristics that objectively describe a person; their sex, race, job, income, family, health, occupation, and so on. It is used to form categories. Personal information later comes to mean a person's preferences in terms of restaurants, pets, and partners, and their tastes in movies, music, and wine, and their travel patterns and whom and what they 'like' on Facebook. Personal information is now employed to mean anything that is gathered in relation to a person to form a profile of that person for the purpose of anything from marketing to intelligence practice.

Information and, in particular, personal information, has shifted in meaning from facts about a person to utterances of or about a person – utterances about me, myself, and everybody else (Søe, 2021). In the late-modern society, the meaning of (personal) information is based in language games in which the information is used and employed – the meaning of (personal) information is no longer defined and delimited as true, verifiable facts. When (personal) information is not merely facts about a person, but meaning constructed and developed in localized, contextually bound forms of life, then privacy cannot be defined as the control of personal information; because it is never possible to control the construction and development of meaning-making.

When it is accepted that it is not helpful to define privacy in the late-modern society as the ability to control information about oneself, then we need to develop an understanding of privacy that goes beyond information. Not in the sense that information is unimportant, but in the sense that privacy is not only a matter of controlling information. Privacy is a matter of identity: the possibility of developing, co-constructing, and shaping one's own identity. Hybrid-identity is a mix of internal and external factors, how you see yourself, how you are seen by others, and how you are categorized and constructed within the digital realm. Hybrid-identity weaves across the physical and the digital. Privacy influences the story about you. Thus, the role of information changes and the social contexts, relations, and practices become more important. 'Rather than being a social fact in which we should protect an individual's privacy and liberty, information (and its partner, secrecy) is thus constitutive of the individual and her social relations' (Coll, 2012: 19). Our identities are informational – and secretive – but if we only focus on the control of information when defining privacy or ascribing privacy rights, we miss the whole by focusing on its parts.

Our identity formation and construction is relational. Hybrid-identity captures that identity formation is shaped by how we see ourselves and how we are seen by others, both in real-life relations and by data in digital systems. The gaze from the outside is defining for who we can be – whether this gaze comes from a person or is mediated by technologies and information. It is the relation between us, others, and systems – the language games we play – that sets the terms for who we are and who we can be. Privacy is relational in the same way. Personal information is interrelated – information about me might also be information about you – and information about us, or related to us in some other way, is shared all the time. This sharing also takes place within language games and is, as such, relational (Søe and Mai, 2023). Thus, we need to constitute privacy as a relational concept having to do with the construction of identity by me, myself, and everybody else. In so far as privacy is concerned with protection of one's identity, the notion of hybrid-identity demonstrates that the protection of privacy is much broader than the mere control of personal information and data.

Information and secrecy

Secrecy and privacy are conceptually linked notions, in the sense that both are concerned with the idea that everyone should not have access to everything, and both notions have to do with information – the withholding of information – but both notions also have to do with something more than access and withholding of information.

Secrecy, the urge and need to keep something secret, is fundamentally human and necessary for the functioning of society. According to Coll (2012: 19), information and secrecy are partners and 'constitutive of the individual and her social relations'. As Akiko Busch (2019) beautifully puts it:

> In the woods no more than an hour, I am struck anew by invisibility, and its improvisational choreography, as a necessary condition of life. I am reminded of the grace of reticence, the power of discretion, and the possibility of being utterly private and autonomous yet deeply aware of and receptive to the world. (Busch, 2019: 4)

While secrecy is related to privacy, it is conceptually distinct, as it is not just a question of deciding who knows what about you or has access to your home, mind, or body. Whereas it is (at least in theory) possible to both enjoy privacy and yet disclose everything about yourself, as long as that decision to share is yours alone, secrecy points to a core concern in most privacy theories: the value and necessity of keeping some things hidden, as a secret.

Secrets can be understood as 'informative asymmetries' and as such they are 'in many cases ... vital for the everyday functioning of so many procedures within our society' (Capurro et al, 2012: 1). Examples of such asymmetries are trade secrets, financial secrets, intelligence operations, the inner workings of the state, negotiations, health information, intimacy, and so on – these are examples of information that is kept secret for most of us, and only shared with a select few to make societal processes and institutions function.

Although secrecy is also sometimes – maybe even often – used to hide devious behaviour and shady affairs, 'secrecy, as a social dynamic, guarantees a society social cohesion. Any social relation requires a balance between disclosure and concealment, and this balance needs to be negotiated in each social interaction' (Coll, 2012: 17), because it is also secrets that protect us from others' devious and shady behaviour. There are reasons we might want to keep our sexual orientation, social security number, bank account, maybe even our phone numbers hidden. And, sometimes we actually prefer if others keep certain types of information hidden from us; oversharing is socially awkward. There are secrets and private matters we prefer not to be told. Whether we want to share our secrets and whether we want to be confided in, often depends on whom the listener or confider is. 'Thus, the context of the social interaction defines the relevance of the informational disclosure as well as its (in)appropriateness' (Coll, 2012: 18).

Secrets are intimately linked with our datafied information society. Secrets are what surveillance and intelligence practices try to uncover, while at the same time keeping their own practices and operations secret. Thus, secrecy is a concept with a double force – a social and wicked problem as 'the secrecy that accompanies certain veillances intrudes on the boundaries of privacy, reputation, and carry with it violations of personhood' (Maret, 2016: 3). At the same time, secrets and secrecy might be constitutive of the person.

> To take something more personal: the person itself – the meaning of the original Latin notion 'persona' is 'mask'. It hides the face of the actor from the audience and is thus constitutive for the play. It hides the actor and presents the figure. Is this informative asymmetry associated with the notion 'persona' also constitutive for our being a 'person' – to keep things hidden from others and present something defined to them? Rather to be a secret than to have secrets? (Capurro et al, 2012: 1)

It is our possibilities for keeping secrets that are under pressure in our modern societies, defined by surveillance technologies and datafication. We no longer have the power to fully decide what is hidden from others. Information collection, data analytics, and profiling within digital systems bear the promise or the threat of being able to reveal our innermost desires, dreams, and hopes of and for the future. The ability to predict what we want or need tomorrow, before we know ourselves. The predictions and profiles not only tell what we want tomorrow, they also shape our longings and desires without us fully realizing. They play into our identity formation, shaping who we are and who we come to be. One may wonder whether revealing a secret somehow threatens our identity, thereby explaining why secrets and secrecy are constitutive of being a person?

Secrecy, the mystery, seems somehow to be necessary for identity. It is part of what enables us to define who we are. It gives us the power to take charge in our identity formation. The decision to show something and hide other things. We are not fully in charge of defining our identities and never will be. We have hybrid-identities shaped and co-shaped by ourselves, others, and systems (as kinds of others). But secrets and secrecy and the possibility to keep things hidden – out of reach of others, including systems and surveillance technologies – help enforce our rights to our own identities. We therefore argue that being invisible and private does not denote that one does not care or participate in the world – instead being invisible and private enables participation and the development of autonomy. It is merely another way to take in the world (Søe and Mai, 2023).

Hybrid-identity and the realization of how information, data collection, surveillance, ourselves, and others all influence identity formation, require new attention to the concept of secrecy and its constitutive nature for personhood. The notion of hybrid-identity helps unpack the notion of secrecy in a digital world by demonstrating that secrets are constituted in the interplay between various parts of a person's life and world, and is not mere withholding of access to certain information or data about the person.

Conclusion

Systems, privacy, secrecy, information, and identity. These concepts are intimately linked in today's digital society. It is possible to understand society and its need for information about citizens to provide quality and relevant services, without a conception of the relation between systems, information, privacy, secrecy, and identity. However, one cannot understand what it means to be human and have autonomy in such a society without a conception of the relation between systems, information, privacy, secrecy, and identity. It is utterly fundamental.

In the lyrics to *72 Seasons*, Metallica couples inheritance and violence in the references to identity and how it is formed, continuously returning to human wrath. And identity formation can seem almost violent in the realization of how much others and systems have to say in who we are and who we can be. Hybrid-identity with its informational character brings this to light.

From a sociological perspective, information about people is not about individual people, it only concerns the patterns and structures which information reveals about people's behaviour, needs, and preferences. As such, privacy is not a matter of concern in that context, because the processing of information is not about specific individuals, it is about society as a whole, as 'a mass' (Bouk, 2017: 95) and the patterns of behaviour, preference, or activities that can be extrapolated from that mass. The point being that the concern is not the individual people, their personal information, or their privacy – and certainly not their identity in any sense of the word. The purpose is to identify patterns of behaviour for a specific purpose; to decide whether to expand the public school, to build a new road, or to set the price for a life insurance policy.

However, personal information becomes personal as it becomes possible to say more specific things about individual people. This shift occurs with the proliferation of predictive analysis; with predictive analyses of data, it is possible to create profiles of individual users and citizens, not only as description of what people have revealed about themselves, but also as models of both societal structures and individual preferences. And this has everything to do with identity. It has to do with the construction of hybrid-identity by me, myself, and everybody else.

Acknowledgement

This chapter is written as part of the research project *'Don't Take it Personal'*: *Privacy and Information in an Algorithmic Age*, generously funded by Independent Research Fund Denmark (grant number 8018-00041B).

References

Ambrose, Meg Leta (2012). You Are What Google Says You Are: The Right to be Forgotten and Information Stewardship. *IRIE* 17: 21–30.

Black, Alistair (2001). The Victorian information society: surveillance, bureaucracy, and public librarianship in 19th-century Britain. *The Information Society*, 17(1): 63–80.

Bouk, Dan (2017). The history and political economy of personal data over the last two centuries in three acts. *Osiris*, 32(1): 85–106.

Busch, Akiko (2019). *How to Disappear: Notes on Invisibility in a Time of Transparency*. New York: Penguin Books.

Capurro, Rafael, Britz, Johannes, Hausmanninger, Thomas, Nagenborg, Michael, Nakada, Makoto, and Weil, Felix (2012). Editorial: on IRIE Vol. 17. *IRIE*, 17: 1.

Coll, Sami (2012). The social dynamics of secrecy: rethinking information and privacy through Georg Simmel. *IRIE*, 17: 15–20.

GDPR (2016). *European Union General Data Protection Regulation (GDPR)*: Regulation (EU) 2016/679 of the European Parliament and of the Council of 27 April 2016 on the protection of natural persons with regard to the processing of personal data and on the free movement of such data, and repealing Directive 95/46/EC (General Data Protection Regulation), OJ 2016 L 119/1.

Harcourt, Bernard E. (2015). *Exposed*. Cambridge, MA: Harvard University Press.

Henschke, Adam (2017). *Ethics in an Age of Surveillance: Personal Information and Virtual Identities*. Cambridge: Cambridge University Press.

Hetfield, James (2022). 'Metallica announces new album tour'. Available at: www.rfi.fr/en/people-and-entertainment/20221128-metallica-announ ces-new-album-world-tour

Jørgensen, Rikke Frank and Søe, Sille Obelitz (2024). Metaphors at work: reconciling welfare and market in Danish digitalization strategies. *Media, Culture & Society*, 46(22): 308–323.

Koopman, Colin (2019a). Information before information theory: the politics of data beyond the perspective of communication. *New Media and Society*, 21(6): 1326–1343.

Koopman, Colin (2019b). *How We Became Our Data: A Genealogy of the Informational Person*. Chicago, London: The University of Chicago Press.

Koops, Bert-Jaap, Newell, Bryce Clayton, Timan, Tjerk, Skorvanek, Ivan, Chokrevski, Tomislav, and Galič, Maša (2017). A typology of privacy. *University of Pennsylvania Journal of International Law*, 38(2): 483–575.

Lynch, Michael Patrick (2019). *Know-It-All Society: Truth and Arrogance in Political Culture*. New York, London: Liveright Publishing Corporation.

Lyon, David (2001). *Surveillance Society: Monitoring Everyday Life*. Buckingham, UK: Open University Press.

Maret, Susan (2016). The charm of secrecy: secrecy and society as secrecy studies. *Secrecy and Society*, 1(1): Article 1.

Moor, James H. (1997). Towards a theory of privacy in the information age. *Computers and Society*, 27(3): 27–32.

Nissenbaum, Helen (2010). *Privacy in Context: Technology, Policy, and the Integrity of Social Life*. Stanford, CA: Stanford University Press.

Solove, Daniel J. (2008). *Understanding Privacy*. Cambridge, MA: Harvard University Press.

Søe, Sille Obelitz (2021). A unified account of information, misinformation, and disinformation. *Synthese*, 198(6): 5929–5949.

Søe, Sille Obelitz and Mai, Jens-Erik (2023). The ethics of sharing: privacy, data, and common goods. *Digital Society*, 2(2): article 28. DOI: 10.1007/s44206-023-00057-z

Søe, Sille Obelitz and Mai, Jens-Erik (2022). Data identity: privacy and the construction of self. *Synthese*, 200(6): article 492. DOI: 10.1007/s11229-022-03968-5

Søe, Sille Obelitz, Jørgensen, Rikke Frank, and Mai, Jens-Erik (2021). What is the 'personal' in 'personal information'? *Ethics and Information Technology*, 23(4): 625–633.

Warren, Samuel D. and Brandeis, Louis D. ([1890] 2005). The Right to Privacy. In A. D. Moore (ed) *Information Ethics: Privacy, Property, and Power*, pp 209–225. Seattle, WA: University of Washington Press.

Webster, Frank (2014). *Theories of the Information Society*. Fourth edition. New York: Routledge.

Weller, Toni (2021). The Historical Ubiquity of Surveillance. In Andreas Marklund and Laura Skouvig (eds) *Histories of Surveillance from Antiquity to the Digital Era*, pp 163–179. London: Routledge.

Westin, Alan F. (1967). *Privacy and Freedom*. New York: Atheneum.

Winner, Langdon (1986). *The Whale and the Reactor: A Search for Limits in an Age of High Technology*. Chicago, IL: University of Chicago Press.

Wittgenstein, Ludwig ([1953]/2009). *Philosophical Investigations* (P. M. S. Hacker and J. Schulte (eds); G. E. M. Anscombe, P. M. S. Hacker, and J. Schulte, Trans.). Malden, Oxford: Blackwell Publishing Ltd, Wiley-Blackwell (original work published 1953).

Zuboff, Shoshana (2020). 'We Make Them Dance': Surveillance Capitalism, the Rise of Instrumentarian Power, and the Threat to Human Rights. In R. F. Jørgensen (ed) *Human Rights in the Age of Platforms*, pp 3–52. Cambridge, MA and London: The MIT Press.

2

Where Lies the Power to Define What Is Private? Some Recent Shifts of the Boundary Between the Private and the Public

Beate Roessler

Introduction

Over the last 20 years, the debates about informational privacy have made enormous progress and the awareness of how important and how endangered informational privacy is has grown vastly. This awareness of data security and the consequences of the economization of personal, private data must not be underestimated, even if this does not mean that the power of tech companies is in any way diminished by this awareness.

In the following, however, I want to expand the view on the social line between the public and the private and use the magnifying glass of the private to look at other phenomena. If we do this, we can see that the me-too movement, for instance, can be understood as having to do with a shift of the boundary between the public and the private. It is no longer Harvey Weinstein's private matter how he treats women; it is a matter of public concern. And we can realize, again, that informational privacy always has two sides: what can and do people want to hide and what can or must be made public.

I am interested not so much in the questions concerning analyses of the legal right to privacy but rather in the question of how our *idea of what should be private* and *what should be public* has changed over the last decades. In one sense, this is obvious, because of the enormous amount of data and surveillance which was unheard of and simply impossible 20 years ago. In another sense the question is not so obvious: what does it mean to have privacy, who are the people who claim privacy, what are their relations? In which way has our self-conception, our sense of identity and our idea of private relations changed?

The issue I want to pursue revolves around these supposed shifts in the separation of privacy and the public sphere: I will tie in with the discussions about the protection of privacy on the internet, but at the same time with the debates in the 1990s, in which Feminists – centrally Anita Hill, but also philosophers such as Nancy Fraser – in the context of Clarence Thomas' nomination to the Supreme Court have shown that what is considered private is not naturally or necessarily so, but is subject to the powers of definition that prevail in the public sphere.

The thesis I want to argue for is that attempts at emancipation and experiences of liberation should often be seen as shifting the boundary between private and public: the boundary must always be seen as one that is produced by power structures.

Hence, my questions are the following: what does it mean to say that the separation of the spheres has changed, shifted? How do we reconcile the legitimate protection of the private sphere with the public's legitimate interest in avoiding misuse or violation of privacy, of the domestic sphere? These are not only empirical questions; they are also conceptual and normative, and my thesis is that the perspective of the private can help to better understand the inherent ambivalences in judging social transformations, but also to understand the discourses of power and liberation. We will see later that the conservative framing of 'woke' as a cancel culture is also a setback against the emancipatory attempt to make public what previously was perceived as a private issue, such as homosexuality or transgender identities.

I want to proceed in the following steps: I will first remind you of the debates surrounding the nomination of Clarence Thomas and the accusations raised against him by Anita Hill. Nancy Fraser wrote a very helpful article on this which I will present briefly. In a second step, I want to take on a different perspective: that of one of the first European Court of Human Rights (ECHR) decisions on homosexuality. I will examine this decision and the ensuing debates. In a third step, I will take a closer look at the public sphere: how precisely are problems negotiated here, how should they be negotiated, how can we analyse the shifting line between the private and the public? I will do this in a critical discussion of Thomas Nagel's position on the neutrality of public debates and will in the discussion refer to Fraser's (and a little to Habermas') criticism of the public sphere.

Only against this background will I then come to the question of the more recent shifts between the private and public. I will focus, on the one hand, on the me-too debates, and, on the other hand, on the public presence of trans people negotiated under the title 'culture wars'. At the end I will tie the threads together and argue why the emancipatory aspects of these social and political transformations are best analysed and framed as changes in the politically drawn line between the private and the public.

Anita Hill, Clarence Thomas, the private, the public, and the power of definition

Roughly, we can say that conventions of the boundary between private and public are typically directed against women's interest in equality. A right to privacy as a right to be left alone, as a right to the protection of one's personality is *gendered*. The different coding for men and women works in such a way that in cases of conflict men are granted a far more generous protection of their private lives than women. A paradigm case of this conflict is Nancy Fraser's analysis of the hearing of Clarence Thomas before his nomination as Supreme Court judge. She demonstrated the fact of the gendered coding in a now classic study on the case of the allegations of sexual harassment made against him by Anita Hill.

Anita Hill was a professor of law at Oklahoma University and had worked as an attorney adviser to Clarence Thomas in 1982–83, when Thomas was the Chairman of the Equal Employment Opportunity Commission (EEOC). President Bush nominated Clarence Thomas to succeed Thurgood Marshall as a Supreme Court judge, although Thomas had only served for one year as a judge in the federal circuit. It is during this time at the EEOC, that Thomas, as Hill's supervisor, sexually harassed her. She claimed this in the 11 October 1991 televised hearing for the senate.

Fraser precisely analyses the hearing as well as the ensuing fights in the press about Hill's accusations and Thomas' defence strategy (I will summarize only briefly). She makes out three axes of power: sex or gender, race, and class. Fraser first shows that Thomas was much better able and much more efficient in defending his privacy than Hill because of the gendered power relations. On the one hand, he fought against being associated with privacy because this would effeminate him. On the other hand, he claimed that watching pornography had nothing to do with his public persona, that it was his private business.

Thomas' insistence that his behaviour with respect to a woman was private and had nothing whatever to do with the question of his trustworthiness was protected at the expense of Anita Hill's attempting to keep her private life out of the public discussion. These gendered conventions governing the protection of privacy blatantly exposed, Fraser argued, the reproduction of power relations and inequalities in the freedoms available to women and to men.

On the second axis, the axis of race, Fraser demonstrates another way in which Thomas successfully downsized Hill's accusations with the help of public discourse and conventions and stereotypes, in this case racist: Thomas played with his blackness and succeeded in 'owning' it in an ambiguous way, both positively by referencing black men's sexual prowess and negatively by arguing he was turned into being the victim of racial stereotypes, claiming that the hearings were a lynching. The result was, as Fraser points out, that Hill became 'in effect, functionally white' (Fraser, 1992: 604).

This was supported by the third axis constituting the public discourse, the axis of class. Thomas and his defence managed to construct Hill as bourgeois (and implicitly white), implying that he in fact was the poor working-class black and victim, thereby insinuating that Hill as the educated, ambitious successful career woman belonged to the white elite and was therefore not someone with whom one must show any solidarity.

Fraser's article is a showpiece of feminist social criticism and it is very helpful if one wants to understand the connection between the conventions governing privacy and the public sphere and the underlying patriarchal structures.

The role of gendered privacy conventions is still very much visible and lively in contemporary societies. Therefore, this criticism keeps being essential, for nothing is private in itself: privacy has to be understood as a function of convention, not of nature.

These gendered conventions explain the fact that women symbolically even nowadays belong to the bourgeois private sphere, still are supposed to have their fallback position always in the home and in the privacy of the house.

Consequently, it is not only the actual different role assignments in different social spaces (private or public) that contribute to these gendered, patriarchal conventions, but also the gender-specific coded definitions of what can be considered private and worthy of protection for individuals. This coding is essentially a power game, since it is used by men (and also women) maybe not everywhere and always any longer to keep women out of the public sphere, but to show them their place and, if need be, push them back into the private sphere.

This has not even changed fundamentally in the age of social media: although we can see that social media *can* be used to help women, especially young women, to free themselves from stereotypes and mandated forms of life (see Marwick, 2023).

The European Court's decision on homosexuality and privacy

It is almost a truism nowadays to state that the history of homosexuality is also a history of the demarcation of what is public and what is private. Since homosexuality was in most liberal democracies (to speak only of them) illegal until late in the 20th century, there was always the hidden and dangerous playing with it in public places. Marcel Proust narrates these games – although he is also completely clear about the fact that the playfulness has its cruel limits (see Proust, 1993). In order to understand the specific legalization that is pertinent in Europe, I want to have a look at especially those cases where the privacy of a person's sexual identity is at issue.

A number of prominent cases brought before the ECHR concerned domestic legislation by which homosexual conduct was prohibited or otherwise suppressed (see Roessler, 2017). One of the best known and most discussed cases is *Dudgeon v United Kingdom*, which resulted in a ruling that has occupied many legal scholars. The question to be settled by the court was 'whether the existence of criminal offences relating to homosexual conduct in private between consenting males over the age of 21, or some lesser age, constituted an interference with a person's right to respect for his private life in contravention of Article 8 of the European Convention on Human Rights' (*Dudgeon v United Kingdom*, 1981: 1). The court ruled that such legislation did indeed constitute an interference in the private life of homosexuals. But the reasoning given for this ruling – that is, the normative principle on which it relied – came in for criticism. To quote the court:

> There can be no denial that some degree of regulation of male homosexual conduct, as indeed of other forms of sexual conduct, by means of the criminal law can be justified as 'necessary in a democratic society'. The overall function served by the criminal law in this field is, … 'to preserve public order and decency [and] to protect the citizen from what is offensive or injurious'. Furthermore, this necessity for some degree of control may even extend to *consensual acts committed in private*, notably where there is call … to provide sufficient safeguards against exploitation and corruption of others, particularly those who are specially vulnerable because they are young, weak in body or mind, inexperienced, or in a state of special physical, official or economic dependence. (*Dudgeon v United Kingdom*, 1981: para 49, emphasis added)

Why was this decision so controversial (and has remained so)? On the one hand, the court's argument is quite unambiguous, since it clearly held that the concept of private life is 'a concept which covers the physical and moral integrity of the person, including his or her sexual life'. Thus, the court decided, on the one hand, that homosexual acts among consenting adults in private should be free from any interference, and also that the freedom to do so constituted a matter of human rights (see Heinze, 1995; Johnson, 2010).

Yet, on the other hand, in defending a right to homosexual conduct, the court was relying on a *traditional purely spatial distinction* between private and public and was relegating homosexual life to the secrecy of a private space. By endorsing the need for this spatial division in the interest of controlling public social practices, the court also seemed to remain committed to the notion that public homosexuality is incompatible with public morality, and that it can be coercively kept from public view. The relevant discourse here is one which views gay men as corrupting public morality due to their deviant behaviour, which should therefore be confined to private spaces (Johnson, 2010).

To fully understand the issue, we must see that a *spatial concept of privacy* is not sufficiently explanatory, and one therefore needs a different, a *dimensional* concept of privacy. This way, we have the conceptual resources to understand homosexuality as both a private matter and one that people are entitled to bring into public space. And this way, we are in a position to criticize the court's reasoning in a different and more plausible way. The right to privacy protects people within relationships, independently of whether those relationships are being lived in the private sphere or in public. Since choices concerning one's sexual identity should be seen as private choices, it is normatively most adequate to conceptualize homosexuality as being protected by decisional privacy and not a local, domestic idea of privacy. The court – and the discourse relating to it – does not realize that the critique of a hitherto wrong understanding of privacy shifts the boundaries between private and public in a different way than a purely spatial concept of privacy can comprehend. However, this is precisely the central insight that we need in order to see the emancipatory force of the struggle of homosexuals who insist on not being reduced to a 'private affair' (Roessler, 2017).

Power in public discourses? Neutral versus critical democratic public spheres

Where does the struggle for power and about the meaning of concepts take place? Both in the case of Fraser and Hill as well as in the case of the ECHR, we have seen that what is crucial is the question *where* and *how* the dividing lines between the private and the public are debated and negotiated. In order to understand this better, it seems helpful to go back to a theory by Thomas Nagel about the 'neutrality of the public sphere', which was written during the so-called Clinton affair and the ensuing public discussion of the president's sex affairs in the 1990s.

Nagel's objective is to defend a stance of 'cultural liberalism', an attitude that neither takes (excessive) note of private, intimate, or personal matters in others, nor makes public an inappropriate amount of one's own personal affairs; in other words, a stance that is in general able to distinguish competently between what belongs in public and what does not. Such attitudes, abilities, and conventions are vitally necessary not only for liberal culture, but for the continued existence of human civilization in general: civilized social life is only possible if, in principle at least, we keep 'our lustful, aggressive, greedy, anxious, or self-obsessed feelings' to ourselves, or so he argues (see Nagel, 2002: 3; explicitly on Thomas and Hill, p 23).

The separation of the private and the public is regulated by conventions that inform us of what is to count as private and what as public and especially at what point we are required to show public restraint out of consideration for the privacy of others, Nagel claims. The manner and attitude that complies with these conventions and establishes the greatest possible degree of liberal personal freedom in social space is termed 'civility'. Nagel understands this sort of liberal culture based on a separation of personal and public attitudes or issues as an 'anti-communitarian vision of civility', since it respects in particular a highly individual way of living one's life and seeks to maintain public social space as neutral as possible.

In Nagel's opinion, the developments regarding the separation between the private and public realms or dimensions of life have come to pose a threat to a liberal culture of this pluralist yet neutral type. It is not merely the scandalmongering concerning the president that fills him with indignation, but also the new orthodoxy of multicultural and feminist 'political correctness' (NB in the 1990s) which – he feels – seeks to control the public realm and can no longer distinguish between what is left to the discretion of each individual and what requires public supervision. Thanks to this new orthodoxy's craving for control, the old days of a 'genuinely neutral way of talking' are over: 'My main point is a conservative one: that we should try to avoid fights over the public space which force into it more than it can contain without the destruction of civility' (Nagel, 2002: 16).

This is arguably one of the lesser articles Thomas Nagel has published – but it defends a myth which is still very much alive in contemporary theories and especially in contemporary public discourse. Nagel, though, is not *entirely* wrong: there are indeed problems that should *not* be discussed in public because they affect people's private lives. But that is what it is all about: where exactly is the boundary between private and public? And to what extent are we dependent on a democratic, a critical public discourse? Let me briefly raise four critical points against Nagel's neutral conception.

1. *Empirically*, the public sphere has never been neutral: there are no good old days we could refer to (see for instance the criticism in Baer, 2019: 140). Especially the feminist critique has shown that public disputes and exchanges of arguments are very much a struggle for democratic power. *What* we debate and *who* is allowed to take part in these debates is nothing neutral, as can be seen, for instance, in the last 30 years in movements such as the LGBTQ and Black Lives Matter: their striving for democratic participation and freedom of oppression and for their concerns to be heard in public in the first place, proves that the public is not a neutral area. The very question of *who* has a voice in public is a question of power (to reference just one among the many feminist critiques, see Fraser, 1990; Habermas, 1990).

2. *Normatively*, the public sphere cannot and should not be 'neutral': if we understand as one of the tasks of the public sphere to debate issues which are of concern to everyone, then neutrality would pretend that people could exclude their different standpoints, interests, beliefs, and aims, as Nagel in fact suggested. Since some of those voices come with more power and, therefore, some of the voices are louder than others, this pretension would only cover up, but not eliminate the power structures. In the age of social media, this has changed slightly, because everyone can raise their voice. But raising the voice and having followers is not immediately the same as having political power (Marwick, 2023).

3. The public sphere can normatively not be neutral, because it is the site of controversies about practical identities, self-understandings, and self-descriptions which are co-constituted through public recognition. When it comes to the – seemingly private – question of what projects I want to pursue in my life, which plans, which options are available to me, I rely upon the – public – provision of meaningful options and of public recognition, without which I would not be able to describe myself as the person I am or want to be, of becoming who I am.

   To see this, we can refer to the centuries of public refusal to recognize homosexuality and queer forms of life. This social and political refusal evidently proved a decisive and restrictive influence upon the public *and private* lives of homosexuals. The private search for a meaningful life is dependent upon publicly possible, socially, and politically recognized life-options.

4. Normatively, the controversy concerns – and this is my last point – not only topics but also people: it concerns the public presence, the representation of agents and their perspectives in public discourses and *therefore the democratic structures of our society*. To represent a perspective has, as we know, a social as well as a semantic side. And here we can even better understand that we are talking about power structures. *Who* is being heard and *how many voices* are taking part in the struggles is of essential relevance when we talk about the *meaning* and the *reach* of concepts. As many have pointed out before, semantic criticism is always social criticism (Luise Pusch (1984) was the first German linguist who pointed this out). As Fraser argues, 'arrangements that accommodate contestation among a plurality of competing publics better promote the ideal of participatory parity than does a single, comprehensive, overarching public'. The overarching – neutral – public sphere, Fraser claims, would 'mask domination by absorbing the less powerful into a false "we" that reflects the more powerful' (Fraser, 1990: 67) and are less egalitarian and democratic than a variety of publics, which she calls 'subaltern counterpublics'.

In raising these criticisms, we conceptualize, following Fraser, the public sphere as the site or the sites where power is exercised in and over language, over social boundaries, and over meaningful options for ethical, practical identities. It is the site where social transformations take place and are being made visible (see Fraser, 1990; Taylor, 1992; Mouffe, 1999; Fricker, 2007; Rosa, 2010). And it is here that we must place and analyse the migration of issues from the private into the public space.

These different sites, as well as this migration, can be explored from different perspectives: the perspective of hermeneutic injustice and the 'way in which relations of power can constrain women's ability to understand their own [only seemingly private] experience' (Fricker, 2007: 47); the perspective of social media and how they have changed our conceptions of private and public in very different and significant ways (for young women, for instance exploring their bodies; or having their bodies shamed; see Roessler, 2021); and the perspective of sexual harassment in all areas and social milieus of our contemporary societies. This is what I want to discuss in my next step.

Me-too, transgender, and (being private in) the public sphere

The MeToo movement is many things, but perhaps most powerfully, it is a frame. It transformed how sexual assault is perceived, not as something to be kept private but something that could be made public. The declarations on Twitter became a source of empowerment and liberation. MeToo reversed the stigma: women need not be ashamed, and could bring shame upon the men who assaulted them. (Cukier et al, 2021: 24)

In a way, I agree with Cukier, Mayer-Schöenberger, and Véricourt although I think they got it the wrong way round: the separation between the private and the public *is the frame* and sexual harassment is *being framed* in a new way. The me-too movement led to a shift in the boundary between the private and the public and this way it became clear that Weinstein was, in fact, not doing something 'private' which no one else needed to be concerned with. Weinstein, of course, is used here as a symbol for the widespread male idea that they are entitled to use women in this way, in the privacy of their hotel room or even office and do here something which is nothing of public concern or business. Actually, Weinstein did not even worry about whether or not his behaviour was private or secret (everyone seemed to know anyway) precisely because of the men's conviction of entitlement to have sex with women who are dependent on them.

Whereas Catharine MacKinnon argued in the 1980s that what for men was sex, for women was the perception that they 'are violated every day by men' (see Srinivasan, 2021: 20), I think Amia Srinivasan is right here in her criticism: sexual harassment and the me-too movement is not about sex having a different meaning for men than for women. If one maintained this difference, one would try to exculpate men to a certain extent ('they think it's only sex, after all'), and I agree with Srinivasan that this is both psychologically wrong (they know what they are doing) and politically wrong (see Srinivasan, 2021: 20, 84). The difference between sex and harassment or rape is, among other things, that sex should be, can be, and usually *is* private whereas rape must be a public matter: it is a criminal act.

Let me remind you of another, shockingly recent example of the shifting of the boundaries between the private and the public: the fact that rape within marriage was only made illegal in the 1990s in many European legislations – before that, marriage and the behaviour of the partners was a private matter. A woman had no possibility to take legal action against her husband when he raped her. Here, as well, it has only been a development of the last 30 or so years, that the separation between private and public domains or dimensions has shifted in fundamental and liberating ways.

So we can see that within the last 30 years or so there have been fundamental changes in the boundary between the private and the public, changes that are both emancipatory and liberating for women. The language as well as the practices have changed, the social and legal practices and structures: it is no longer evident that men have the power to do what they want when it comes to sex with women. Going public, as in me-too, is often a first step towards shifting the balance of power and giving emancipation a nudge.

I therefore want to suggest that the dispute about the presence of transgender people in the public sphere must also be seen in this tradition. Already the development in the terminology – transsexuals, transgender – is and was always associated with struggles for one's own identity, and it is a development of the last decades that trans people are programmatically stepping out into the public eye. Again, the framing is central here: being trans is no longer about private corners of society or about sporadic, isolated people, but being trans must be publicly recognized: again, this is about fundamental equalities and freedoms in liberal democracies.

The reaction of some people – mostly powerful people – in their 'traditional' public sphere was: trans women are not real women. It is impossible to change your sex and therefore there should and can be no public recognition – or institutional recognition – of trans women *as women* (see *Celebrity News* on the Rowling debate (Gardner, 2024)). This essentialist political position was exemplified in the 'bathroom question': no trans women should enter the women's bathroom, because, as former men, 'normal' women could feel intimidated by them. However, this seems to be a particularly weak move, and is rejected, for instance, by Celikates et al:

> The aim [of referring to particular cases] is to spread the fear that violent men will break into women's spaces under the guise of

transsexuality – toilets are often mentioned alongside prisons. But this argument is absurd: nowhere else do we hold an entire group liable to prevent the possibility of a violent attack. Sexualized violence is predominantly perpetrated by men in families and on the street – but men are still allowed to have families and go outside. (Celikates et al, 2021; my translation)

The 'anti-woke' fraction was in fact aiming at pushing trans people back into the private sphere – if they do not strive/struggle for their place in public, the semantic question as well as the social, legal, and material questions vanish.

On the other hand, the liberal-democratic society demands, as is well known, that everyone should be able to live their life in public places with whichever identity they choose.

This new challenge to the boundary between private and public is obviously, among other things, a challenge to power and a struggle for public recognition. Therefore, it is no surprise that people react fearfully, uncomprehendingly, and aggressively. Such border shifts are unfailingly a loss of power over who is allowed to define and determine the meaning of terms and of social practices: this is no different with the affairs of Clinton and Weinstein than with the de-privatization of queer identities. And it is precisely here that the public space and the public sphere are essential, as we have seen, in order to be able to invent and explore one's own identity, how one should live, who one is.

In the debate following J.K. Rowling's tweets, Bonnie Wright, better known as Ginny Weasley, tweeted: 'I do know that my dear transgender friends and colleagues are tired of this constant questioning of their identities, which all too often results in violence and abuse. They simply want to live their lives peacefully, and it's time to let them do so' (Gardner, 2024). Bonnie Wright/Ginny Weasley is, of course, right: critics like Rowling not only do not want to acknowledge that trans women are women, but they also do not want to call them that and they certainly do not want to change their social (or legal) practices. The question of how trans people can live their lives peacefully is, on the one hand, an issue of rights and legal freedoms that are constitutive if one wants to take part in public space. But on the other hand, the issue is about how you live your rights in the public sphere, what is the value or worth (as Rawls put it) of these rights and freedoms.

This brings me to the end: we need privacy, and we need a pluralist, diversified public sphere, each for different reasons. Both sorts of reasons are linked to our freedom to live our own lives. Especially when individual or collective attempts to liberation from patriarchal and sex-essentializing structures, public discourses, and spaces are both difficult to reach *and* crucial for the development of an emancipated identity. And the subtext of the struggles around the meaning of concepts or the possibility of practices ('transgender', or 'trans woman'; or 'my culture', 'your culture') remains: who has the power to define what is private and what is public? Debating concepts, behaviour, or attitudes in public *always* has an emancipatory potential. Who draws the line, therefore, comes down to the question: How can we ensure that the lines can be debated and redrawn in an emancipatory, solidary, egalitarian way?

Acknowledgements

With many thanks to Sille Obelitz Søe and Jens-Erik Mai for inviting me to the original workshop in Copenhagen and for their patience waiting for my final manuscript. I also owe many thanks to Lukas Hjulmann Seidler who helped enormously to finish the manuscript (almost) on time.

References

Baer, U. (2019). *What Snowflakes Get Right: Free Speech, Truth, and Equality on Campus*. New York: Oxford University Press.

Celikates, R., Hoppe, K., Loick, D., Nonhoff, M., von Redecker, E., and Voglemann, F. (2021). Machtverhältnisse statt Mythen. Für ein emanzipatorisches Verständnis von Wissenschaftsfreiheit. *Geschichte der Gegenwart*, 8 December. Available at: https://geschichtedergegenwart.ch/machtverhaeltnisse-statt-mythen-fuer-ein-emanzipatorisches-verstaendnis-von-wissenschaftsfreiheit/ (accessed 12 January 2024).

Cukier, K., Mayer-Schönberger, V., and Véricourt, F. de (2021). *Framers: Human Advantage in an Age of Technology and Turmoil*. Kindle edition. New York: Ebury Publishing.

Dudgeon v United Kingdom (1981). Available at: www.chr.up.ac.za/images/database/sexual_minority_database/cases/SOGIESC-Dudgeon-v.-United-Kingdom-1981.DOC (accessed 28 November 2023).

Fraser, N. (1990). Rethinking the public sphere: a contribution to the critique of actually existing democracy. *Social Text*, (25/26): 56–80.

Fraser, N. (1992). Sex, lies, and the public sphere: some reflections on the confirmation of Clarence Thomas. *Critical Inquiry*, 18(3): 595–612.

Fricker, M. (2007). *Epistemic Injustice: Power and the Ethics of Knowing*. Oxford: Oxford University Press.

Gardner, A. (2024). A complete breakdown of the J.K. Rowling transgender-comments controversy. *Celebrity News*, 11 April. Available at: www.glamour.com/story/a-complete-breakdown-of-the-jk-rowling-transgender-comments-controversy (accessed 15 January 2024).

Habermas, J. (1990). *Strukturwandel der Öffentlichkeit: Untersuchungen zu einer Kategorie der bürgerlichen Gesellschaft*. Frankfurt am Main: Suhrkamp Verlag.

Heinze, E. (1995). *Sexual Orientation: A Human Right. An Essay on International Human Rights Law*. Dordrecht; Boston, MA; London: Martinus Nijhoff Publishers.

Johnson, P. (2010). 'An essentially private manifestation of human personality': constructions of homosexuality in the European Court of Human Rights. *Human Rights Law Review*, 10(1): 67–97.

Marwick, A. E. (2023). *The Private Is Political: Networked Privacy and Social Media*. New Haven, CT: Yale University Press.

Mouffe, C. (1999). Deliberative democracy or agonistic pluralism? *Social Research*, 66(3): 745–758.

Nagel, T. (2002). *Concealment & Exposure and Other Essays*. Oxford; New York: Oxford University Press.

Proust, M. (1993). *The Captive*. Translated by D. J. Enright, T. Kilmartin, and C. K. S. Moncrieff. London, UK: Modern Library.

Pusch, L. F. (1984). *Das Deutsche als Männersprache: Aufsätze und Glossen zur feministischen Linguistik*. Frankfurt am Main: Suhrkamp Verlag.

Roessler, B. (2017). Privacy as a human right. *Proceedings of the Aristotelian Society*, 117(2): 187–206.

Roessler, B. (2021). *Autonomy: An Essay on the Life Well-Lived*. Translated by J. C. Wagner. Cambridge: Polity.

Rosa, H. (2010). *Alienation & Acceleration: Towards a Critical Theory of Late-Modern Temporality*. Malmö: NSU Press.

Srinivasan, A. (2021). *The Right to Sex*. London; New York; New Delhi: Bloomsbury Publishing.

Taylor, C. (1992). *Sources of the Self: The Making of the Modern Identity*. Cambridge: Cambridge University Press.

3

Our Bodies, Our Data, Our Choices: The Value of Privacy for Female★ Self-Determination in a Post-Roe Era

Marjolein Lanzing

Introduction

On 24 June 2022, the US Supreme Court overturned *Roe v Wade*, the 1973 ruling that constitutionally enshrined the right to abortion, in the case *Dobbs v Jackson Women's Health Organization*. *Roe v Wade* had been of historical significance as an important right to self-determination for women★.[1] Importantly and interestingly, this right to self-determination was captured as the right to decisional privacy. By overturning *Roe v Wade*, a case that explicitly formulated the right to make one's own choices without government interference, decisional privacy, as tied to many constitutional freedom rights associated with choosing one's own partnerships, religion, or style of childrearing, disappeared from American jurisdiction (Clark, 2022).

In the wake of this decision, various groups worried about the implications of digital technologies and online surveillance for the autonomy of women★. It is important to realize that the United States' concerns about anti-abortion legislation, access to reproductive data, and menstrual surveillance fit within a wider trend to surveil and control women★'s bodies, decisions, and lives. The European Union, despite its more stringent and explicit data laws, faces similar concerns. Poland, for instance, has recently centralized the storage of pregnancy data after enforcing anti-abortion laws (Posner, 2022). Many emphasized the need for health data privacy to protect women★'s rights. Feminist activists urged users of FemTech, specifically period and fertility trackers, to delete these apps. App-developers such as (Europe-based) Clue and Flo, promised users better protection of their privacy by not complying with any requests for health data by US law enforcement.

Recently, privacy has been criticized for dominating the public and academic debate on the ethics of technology. This chapter aims to point out the importance of privacy as an individual human right while highlighting the limits of conceptualizing privacy as the right to individual (health) data protection using the case of period apps post-Roe. I start by explaining 'FemTech' and its academic critique while *Roe v Wade* was still in effect. Next, I present expert statements from the digital health and digital rights discourse on what they argue to be the main risks concerning period tracking apps post-Roe. For this, I searched specifically for renowned (US) news outlets and medical research report websites that specifically aimed to cover the risks of period tracking apps post-Roe. Moreover, I researched the websites and social media posts of the most popular period tracking apps (Clue, Flo, and Glow) for responses to the Supreme Court's decision to overturn *Roe v Wade*. This limited the search results to articles from *The New York Times*, *The Guardian*, national public radio, STATNews, the *British Medical Journal* and the International Association of Privacy Professionals, as well as social media statements from Clue, Stardust, and Flo.[2] I show that the major risks and solutions that are framed in terms of 'privacy' boil down to 'health data protection'.

After discussing the debate, I introduce the argument that privacy dominates the debate on health tracking apps. I argue that in the case of FemTech this 'privacy hegemony' is justified and shows the need for privacy as an individual human right. However, there are limits to conceptualizing privacy as individual (health) data protection. If we want to understand how new technologies contribute or undermine people's autonomy, we need to acknowledge the social and decisional dimensions of privacy as well as understanding the limits of the concept in matters of social justice. We must avoid privacy becoming synonymous with a quick 'techno-fix': altering the technological design without considering the social and political context of the technology. Encrypting or deleting women★'s health data might be important interventions but should be understood and carried out in a context of recognition of the structural discrimination, repression, and (commercial) exploitation in women★'s health. I conclude that the debate around period apps post-Roe should be informed by a conceptualization of privacy that recognizes its value for our social relationships and the connections between its different dimensions, most notably between its informational and decisional dimensions, and its value for freedom, autonomy, and social justice.

Period apps and academic critique during *Roe v Wade*

FemTech is on the rise. By 2025, the business is predicted to be a 50 billion dollar industry (Frost and Sullivan, 2018). FemTech includes a range of health technologies that, among others, support reproductive health, menstrual health, and sexual health. Fertility and period tracking apps, such as Clue, Flo, and Glow, are among the most well-known examples. They predict when the user is menstruating and when they are (most) fertile. Contraception apps that keep track of one's period and fertility to serve as an algorithmically driven contraception device, such as Natural Cycles, are also increasingly popular. The data that these apps collect are sensitive at the least. Some varieties allow users to log their sexual activities, attempts to conceive, contraception, conception, moods, sex drive, and the colour of vaginal discharge. For the purposes of this chapter, I focus on reproductive and menstrual health apps (fertility and period tracking apps) that I will refer to as 'period apps'.

In academic literature, FemTech apps such as period apps, have been both welcomed and criticized. On the one hand, they are celebrated as empowering, breaking taboos, and levelling the field of health research after neglecting and marginalizing women★'s health issues (Lanzing, 2019; Hendl and Jansky, 2021). FemTech could lead to the much-needed research to close the gap in the field of women★'s health data.

On the other hand, FemTech has been criticized for reproducing stereotypes and social inequalities (Corbin, 2020) and for their lack of informational privacy and the harmful consequences of 'menstrual surveillance' (Jacobs and Evers, 2019; Lanzing, 2019; Mahdawi, 2019). The privacy critique entails the identification of fertility and period apps as new sources for the commercial exploitation of data. In the narrowest sense, the privacy critique is a critique on the lack of data protection, directed against privacy violations by the companies behind period apps that sell and share data collected through these apps. Various period apps, such as Flo, Glow, and Maya, have faced court for selling and sharing data with third parties, such as Meta (Privacy International, 2019).

More broadly, period apps have been criticized for 'menstrual surveillance' and unwanted forms of interference and exclusion enabled by the vulnerabilities created through data collection. For instance, they have been critiqued for the ensuing (commercial) manipulation of (expectant) users, including targeting them with ads for maternity wear and baby products (Tiffany, 2018). And, importantly, for (workplace) discrimination against women★ based on these data (Lanzing, 2019). For instance, companies such as ActivisionBlizzard have been criticized for engaging in 'menstrual surveillance' by encouraging staff to use Ovia health, a set of family planning apps, for $1 a day, prying into private lives and decisions (Mahdawi, 2019).

While Roe was still in effect, most critiques were oriented towards commercial enterprises, such as critique of consumer surveillance, privacy violations of users and employees by corporations and non-inclusive app design of app producers. In the next section, I present expert statements on the main risks of period apps post-Roe. I looked at the solutions proposed in the public debate on period apps in the field of digital health and digital rights as well as by corporations that facilitate period apps.

Public debate on the risks of period apps post-Roe: health and privacy threats

Whereas the risks identified with period apps during Roe were oriented towards commercial enterprises, post-Roe risks involve the interplay between government, law enforcement, and the commercial enterprises that develop and exploit period apps. The first risk identified in the context of period apps post-Roe, is that law enforcement could force providers of technological devices and services to hand over reproductive health data. This includes information that reveals the 'reproductive health status' of users and information about 'reproductive decisions'. Multiple articles interviewed experts on whether HIPAA (the Health Insurance Portability and Accountability Act) of the US could protect people's health data against claims from law enforcement (Aguilar, 2022; Boodman et al, 2022). Since HIPAA *cannot* protect people's reproductive health data against state law enforcement or legal action, the absence of national data protection legislation was explicitly articulated as a threat to 'health' and 'privacy': 'the lack of a national data privacy protection law is hurting everything. It's hurting people's health. It's hurting people's privacy' (Aguilar, 2022).[3]

Second, in the public debate the threat that the government could claim health data is tied to data collection and commodification by commercial enterprises. Companies behind period apps engage in a larger economy of health data that HIPAA cannot control (Aguilar, 2022; Boodman et al, 2022). Period apps are problematized, because they collect enormous amounts of (reproductive) health data, and because they have sold and shared these data in the past: 'Some of these (businesses) have sold or shared information that is fully identified in the past with other companies such as Facebook' (Boodman et al, 2022).[4]

Due to this industrious data collection for commercial purposes and the lack of data protection measures, law enforcement could obtain access to gigantic databases and claim the reproductive health data of millions of users. These data could, for instance, indicate whether someone missed one or more periods, indicating a potential pregnancy. A new period after a sequence of missed periods could indicate a possible abortion (or miscarriage or irregular periods due to (chronic) (hormonal) syndromes or diseases). Of course, many more sensitive insights about reproduction could be derived from the health data on a period tracker. This is merely one example showing how law enforcement could use data to identify women★ who might have had an illegal abortion or who might be likely to plan an abortion (and how this could be inaccurate).

The combination of commercial data collection that could suddenly lead to unintended harmful consequences once in the hands of law enforcement post-Roe has led to a comparison in the public debate with the Cambridge Analytica scandal[5] in terms of (unintended) consequences of health data collection:

> [T]here are analogs in health care to the way Facebook's algorithms prioritized incendiary content that can contain misinformation during the last national elections. ... It's going to lead to unintended secondary consequences. Somebody using the data of a pregnancy app to put a woman in jail. ... Today the issue is reproductive health – but in the future, information seeping out from health apps and services could be used in other discriminatory ways. (Aguilar, 2022)[6]

I return to the issue of discrimination and government interference shortly. For now, it suffices to say that people worry about law enforcement gaining access to databases created by commercial enterprises. Furthermore, the impact of the Supreme Court's decision has been deemed unprecedented in the sphere of health data privacy: 'Health data privacy has never been tied quite so closely, or so publicly, to an event of such widespread consequence' (Aguilar, 2022).

The post-Roe era clearly reveals the legal gaps regarding data protection. Moreover, it shows the fragility of 'freedom from interference' when regimes change. The expert and activist response to the Supreme Court decision to overturn *Roe v Wade*, was to call upon users to immediately delete their fertility apps and period trackers with the intention to delete sensitive information about reproductive choices:

> Right now, and I mean this instant, delete every digital trace of any menstrual tracking. (Neff via Twitter, Kleinman, 2022)[7]

> Fertility and period apps have 'powerful information about reproductive choices that's now a threat'. (Hill, 2022)

The first quote, a (then) Twitter/X post by Gina Neff, a world renowned expert on the politics and economics of self-tracking indicates clearly what is at stake here. Information that is stored on your period tracker reveals your reproductive status and choices.

However, it is not only the health data on your period app that you should worry about (Hill, 2022):

> We think about medical records, but our phones collect an amazing amount of data. It's not a good idea to send texts about your intent to

seek an abortion. It's not a good idea to use an online payment app to buy these services. You might want to leave your phone at home as opposed to taking it to the clinic. You may not even want to search for abortion providers on your phone or computer. (Boodman et al, 2022)[8]

It is not only health data that are informative of our reproductive status and choices. Our geo-locations, our payments, our online buying behaviour and online communication reveal our choices.

Harms: prosecution, discrimination, and social injustice

Experts and activists subsequently elaborated on the harms associated with the access to personal (reproductive) (health) data. They recognized the link between data collection and the extent to which this makes people vulnerable to unwanted interference, such as prosecution and discrimination, both by the government and corporations: 'We're very concerned in a lot of advocacy spaces about what happens when private corporations or the government can gain access to deeply sensitive data about people's lives and activities' (Torchinsky, 2022).[9]

People are concerned that data from FemTech makes women★ vulnerable to criminal prosecution. Or, more explicitly 'somebody using the data from a pregnancy app to put a woman in jail' (Aguilar, 2022). Some point to the harms of discrimination: 'Especially when that data could put people in vulnerable and marginalized communities at risk for actual harm' (Torchinsky, 2022).

While these communities as well as the nature of 'actual harm' were not specified here, Brown likely means that people from 'marginalized populations including Black, indigenous, and people of color; people with disabilities; immigrants; and those living in poverty' are disproportionately affected by lack of access to safe abortions (Human Rights Watch, 2023). A third of all people who receive an abortion in the US are black. The majority of these are low-income. Carrying a pregnancy to term can be life endangering. Apart from threatening women★'s lives and health, it can threaten education, one's career, and financial security. Potential consequences of attempts to terminate the pregnancy, such as prosecution or incarceration, might also then disproportionately affect the black and low-income community (Berger, 2022).

Autonomy, including the right to self-determination regarding reproduction, is inextricably tied to matters of social justice (Berger, 2022). Collecting women★'s reproductive health data in the post-Roe society then is a practice that risks being a gendered, racist, and classist form of surveillance, contributing to the harmful feedback loop of social injustice. Moreover, it has been argued that data of people with less means could be more easily exposed: '"People with less means might be using the free clinic or Planned Parenthood, whereas the wealthy and well-insured are going to the nice medical office building," he said. "The data kind of stands out more. People with less means are more exposed"' (Boodman et al, 2022).[10]

While this quote discusses the data collected by clinics rather than period apps, the argument could hold for technologies that track your data. Most of these technologies are free and easy to download on your phone, which might be an appealing option for people from low-income backgrounds, although it is difficult to find research on the demographics of period app users.

Furthermore, people point to workplace discrimination, arbitrarily depending on the viewpoints your employer happens to have:

> The free-flow of data in health care and the broader economy may also be used to directly discriminate against people based on their use of reproductive health services. If an employer has a certain position on abortion, you may be denied a job if 'they used some predictive algorithm' to examine data available to employers on your medical care. ... Anything you do in health care, in our current state of (regulation), can be used against you. (Boodman et al, 2022)[11]

Data may be used by employers who might exclude you because you might have had an abortion. Obviously, this worry is one side of a double-edged sword because feminists have also worried about the opposite: workplace discrimination based on the desire, likelihood, or decision to in fact become pregnant.

Solutions and reflections

The expert statements on the risks and harms of period apps post-Roe, generate several insights. First, there is a strong focus on informational privacy as individual health data protection. This shows in the way risks are described, such as law enforcement claiming reproductive health data. Second, harmful consequences are mostly described in terms of discrimination and prosecution resulting from a lack of health data protection of one's reproductive status and choices.

This focus on privacy as individual health data protection as the safeguard against these harms is reflected in the solutions proposed in the public debate. The first set of solutions are aimed at health data protection at the legislative level. The most prominent solution is strengthening the laws around health data protection via an update of HIPAA (Aguilar, 2022; Boodman et al, 2022). Second, in the absence of strong (health) data protection regulation, people suggest that companies voluntarily comply with HIPAA (Aguilar, 2022; Ornstein, 2022).[12]

Furthermore, various individual strategies to protect data are proposed: deletion, anonymization, de-identification, and encryption. It has been advised to delete one's period apps (Neff via Twitter, Kleinman, 2022; Aguilar, 2022). Companies such as Natural Cycles, Flo, and Clue offer data deletion upon request (Duball, 2022). In response to Roe and user questions about the security of their menstrual and reproductive health data, companies of period apps promised an 'anonymous mode' to protect user data (Flo, 2022) and de-identification of user data (Clue, 2022). Finally, companies were urged to encrypt their data (Aguilar, 2022).[13] Period app Stardust has started offering end-to-end encryption, advertising it clearly to its users: 'What (encryption) means is that if we get subpoenaed by the government, we will not be able to hand over any of your period tracking data' (Stardust via TikTok, Duball, 2022). This promise led Stardust to soar to the top of the US Apple App Store, as did Clue, being Europe-based and compliant with the GDPR (Clue, 2022). This has not stopped critics from warning users that these period apps are not 'airtight' when it comes to data protection (Privacy International, 2020; Garamvolgyi, 2022; Perez and Whittaker, 2022).

Now, while the focus on health data is important and logical, I think this is too limited, for reasons already identified in the debate. First, not only your health data, but your overall online behaviour are revealing about your most intimate life choices. If we want to protect people from menstrual surveillance, then people should be protected by an overall individual right to data protection, not just health data. Information about one's reproductive status and choices is not protected by deleting one's period app or by advocating for a stronger HIPAA to ensure health data privacy.

Second, by focusing on health data privacy, we focus on 'informational privacy-as-individual-data-protection'. Obviously, this is incredibly important. Data reveal what decisions we make (and how). Rightly, the debate voices the important concern that the data generated by digital technologies make users vulnerable to government interference, to discrimination and prosecution. However, by focusing on data protection, the focus is on protecting individuals with defensive strategies considering the new legislation. Yet, privacy can be conceptualized as a much more powerful ethical value, concept, and legal right to address the heart of the matter: the right to make decisions about one's life without interference from companies or the government (or other inappropriate parties). Especially since the right to decisional privacy was the foundation for the original *Roe v Wade* decision in 1978, it is remarkable that decisional privacy, either as a constitutional right or concept, is not explicitly mentioned in the public debate, let alone recognized for its important relationship with constitutional freedom rights. Rather, the discourse is dominated by health data privacy.

Finally, while some people mention the data economy behind the corporations that produce period apps, they may understate the role these companies play in shaping the technological infrastructures and affordances of period apps. Moreover, I want to argue that the suggested dependency on these corporations to ensure and support data protection is an unwelcome shift that steers us further away from autonomy and, more narrowly, the right to reproductive choice.

In the next sections I build on these insights by exploring the limits of privacy-as-data-protection but the importance of privacy for the debate on period apps post-Roe.

Beyond privacy

Within the context of health apps, an increasing number of philosophers worry about the dominance of privacy in the academic and public debate. Some of them argue that other issues, such as corporate manipulation, are more pressing problems (Sax, 2021). Especially during the COVID-19 pandemic, many suggested that other values that serve the public good, such as the notion of solidarity, should trump individual privacy (Verbeek et al, 2020). Others explicitly state that we should not be blinded by privacy concerns, because it shifts our attention away from infrastructural power, accumulated by technology companies (Sharon, 2020).

As a prominent advocate of this argument, let us zoom in on Sharon's argumentation. Sharon argues that we should look beyond privacy and point our arrows at the digital infrastructure that tech companies are building and on which we are becoming increasingly dependent. Importantly, encryption and data protection are increasingly part of the business model of tech companies. Sharon provides the example of contact-tracing apps. European contact-tracing apps are built on technology from Google and Apple that is well encrypted. On the one hand, this seems to take the wind out of the sails of privacy advocates who want to protect personal data. On the other hand, it seems that even if health apps are secure in terms of encryption and anonymization, there remains a tension with tech giants facilitating crucial digital health infrastructure.

Sharon addresses this tension in terms of sphere transgressions. Big Tech increasingly structures our social spheres, including health and crisis management. Companies such as Google have been investing in the health sector and collecting health data for years. Our main concern, therefore, should be our collective and public dependency on tech monopolists such as Google and Apple to facilitate the technological infrastructures we need for public needs and social services (for example, health, housing, mobility, education, and so on). Ultimately, we should worry about the values that these companies import into these spheres and restructure them rather than be 'blind-sided by privacy' (Sharon, 2020).

Now, to what extent would this view help to address the expert concerns regarding period apps beyond privacy? What insights do we gain if we look beyond privacy-as-data-protection to the corporate digital infrastructures? First, this view is helpful in addressing the underlying concern that corporate entities have increasingly become prominent actors in the field of health. The health sector has become dependent on these enterprises for medical expertise, research data, devices, and health and lifestyle apps. We should not overlook how companies have shaped the (reproductive) health sphere through technology – and the risks this creates in the post-Roe world. The overturn of *Roe v Wade* exposes a change of roles and practices. Patients have become consumers. This resonates with the experience of Olivia Sudjic who was treated as a consumer by the company Natural Cycles after she became pregnant using the contraception app (Sudjic, 2018). The commercialization of period tracking has made people vulnerable to new forms of interference in their lives and decisions. The corporate character of period apps has implications for the protection of data and people. Users are not protected by the laws, norms, and values of the clinic, but instead are dependent on corporations to handle their data responsibly, for instance with encryption. Commercial period apps do not have to comply with strict medical standards or be vetted by the Federal Trade Commission because, in the US, period apps are considered wellness apps. Furthermore, the data obtained by a period app are not considered 'patient data' and therefore are not covered by HIPAA (Haridasani Gupta and Singer, 2021; Ornstein, 2022).

Furthermore, the protection of users is dependent on the beliefs and interests of corporations. Aiding people who seek an abortion is even criminalized in some states and the right to self-determination about reproductive choices is not protected by the constitution. In the expert statements it is suggested that, in the absence of adequate (health) data protection legislation, corporations can voluntarily comply with HIPAA and install privacy measures. Yet do we want to depend on the infrastructure of these companies to guarantee our (privacy) rights? Should they be the bulwark against unwanted government interference?

The important take-away from Sharon is that we should not ignore how corporations shape our different social spheres. It is because of the expansion of corporations, creating an infrastructure across spheres, that government interference is enabled in the health sphere (and many others) (Sharon, 2021). It is because of these expansions that spheres are becoming dependent on and dominated by the logics and values of corporations. On the one hand, women★ might celebrate this role when corporations decide to protect their autonomy by respecting their privacy. On the other, one should also be critical of the dependency on and new discretionary power of corporations to decide what is 'just'.

So, what does this insight mean for the focus on privacy in the debate on period apps post-Roe? While I agree that we should be vigilant to not let privacy be the sole dominant value to monopolize the public debate on technology critique, I want to counter that, in the case of menstrual surveillance post-Roe, it is justified that privacy, *in all its dimensions*, dominates the debate.

Advocates of the 'beyond privacy debate' seem to conceptualize privacy narrowly, as data protection. For instance, they critique the focus on encryption, through anonymization, de-identification, and deletion, as these 'privacy solutions' are often part and parcel of corporate business models. As I argued, data protection is an important aspect of privacy, but the argument for letting privacy dominate the debate becomes increasingly strong when one considers the social and decisional aspects of privacy that go beyond privacy-as-data-protection and will require more ambitious measures. I will discuss these dimensions in the next section. Before I move to the next step, I think it is worth stressing that understanding technological infrastructures is crucial to understand the scope and potential of surveillance practices across social spheres. Yet, this perspective should go hand in hand with advocating privacy as a human right and a constitutional right. Its dominance in the debate, unfortunately, says nothing about the extent to which privacy is maintained and protected as this right is increasingly under duress.

Social and decisional dimensions of privacy

To continue the argument that privacy is a justified focus of this debate I argue that it is important to acknowledge the social and decisional dimensions of privacy if we want to understand how technologies contribute to, or undermine, people's autonomy. To make this argument I want to start with a description of (the interplay between) informational and decisional privacy and their social dimensions.

Informational privacy is generally described in terms of controlled access. This means that people should, reasonably, be able to control who has access to their information and to what extent (Westin, 1967; Roessler, 2005). Moreover, they should be able to form reasonable expectations about this. These expectations are largely based on social norms of privacy. These norms are dynamic and cultural, but nevertheless important because they mediate our social interactions and relationships. What we share with our friends shapes the meaning of our friendship; what information my employer has access to shapes the meaning of our work relationship; what information the state can obtain shapes the meaning of the relationship between citizens and government. A violation of these norms can ruin a friendship, poison a healthy workplace environment, or endanger citizens. Privacy, then, is important because it protects one's ability to present oneself autonomously by engaging in different relationships. It protects the meaningfulness of these social relationships and, with that, the capacity to lead an autonomous life.

While informational privacy is important and widely acknowledged as such, there are several problems with the concept. First, it is often taken to be the only dimension and meaning of 'privacy'. Second, it is often taken to be synonymous with individual data protection. This means that the solution to problems that are perceived to be 'privacy problems' is often formulated in terms of 'deletion', 'encryption', and 'anonymization'. Moreover, the solutions to privacy problems are subsequently often framed in an individualized manner: if you want privacy, then you have to adjust your privacy settings, reject cookies, and encrypt your emails.

However, this approach is dated and based on a misconceptualization of privacy. While the idea that privacy has different dimensions is not new and is reflected in many European constitutions and human rights charters, new technologies make it blatantly clear that privacy is not only about information. Think about domotica such as Alexa or a smart thermostat – technologies that bring out the need to think about privacy and its local dimension of the home (De Conca, 2021); or the manipulative aspects of recommender systems that bring out the decisional dimensions of privacy (Lanzing, 2018). It seems that most problems involve a combination of privacy dimensions (Koops et al, 2017).

Let us zoom in on decisional privacy. This is a particularly interesting notion to consider given the recent revoke of *Roe v Wade*. Decisional privacy in the US 'protects the right to make the decision to have an abortion and informational privacy protects information about that decision from being shared, disclosed or monitored' (Clark, 2022). Decisional privacy as the right to have an abortion stems directly from *Roe v Wade* in which the right to decisional privacy formed the fundament for the freedom to make one's own reproductive and other intimate choices regarding life projects (Allen, 1988: 97). These choices should be 'free from governmental interference'. Other examples include marriage, religion, relationships, child rearing, and political affiliations. In the years after, philosophers broadened this notion. One could also argue that behaviour and lifestyle more generally should be encompassed by decisional privacy (Roessler, 2005: 14–15, 79). Then, decisional privacy could be broadly defined as the right against unwanted access, such as unwanted interference in one's decisions and actions (Allen, 1988: 97; Roessler, 2005: 9). Roughly, 'being interfered with' means that (un)known actors or entities have access to one's behaviour and decisions, which allows them to comment upon, interpret, or change one's behaviour and steer one's decisions, while this access does not fall under the reasonable expectations of the user or subject or was not granted in the first place

(Lanzing, 2018). In other words, the broader account of decisional privacy protects not only against unwanted government interference with one's decisions but also other actors.

Like informational privacy norms, decisional privacy norms are social expectations that shape our social relationships. Instead of information, they regulate who has access to certain decisions and decision-making and to what degree. Access here means forms of commenting, interpreting, objecting but also other more contested forms of interference such as manipulation, nudging, or coercion. To what extent one's decisions can be meddled with depends on whether this is appropriate in each social relationship. For instance, it would be a violation of decisional privacy if one's employer commented on your style of child rearing, but it would be appropriate if your co-parent did so. Of course, the more significant certain behaviour, actions, and choices are in terms of being the author of your life, the more salient the need for calling them 'private'. Some forms of influence might be considered morally wrong as such, like using (personal) data and online profiles for online voter manipulation (Susser et al, 2019). In most of these cases, it is crystal clear that such interference undermines one's autonomy and the relationships that are meaningful for living an autonomous life.

Informational and decisional privacy dimensions are complementary. For instance, one's reproductive status and corresponding choices would be considered 'private' to the extent that both the information and decision-making are not part of the relationship with Meta, one's parents, employer, or government. Rather, this information and choices would be between you, a health professional, your (sexual) partner(s), and/or close friends. However, both dimensions should not be reduced to one another because they address different wrongs. Informational privacy addresses the problem of collecting information, while decisional privacy can address the wrong of using that information to inappropriately interfere with people's decisions and decision-making processes. In the case of period apps post-Roe, both privacies are at play and under threat. Most importantly, the value that they protect is under threat: autonomy.

Autonomy

So far, the discourse on period apps post-Roe has been dominated by health data protection. Yet, as we learned, privacy is more than data protection. If we want to advance female* autonomy, we need to transcend this dominant conceptualization and focus on the value of privacy, in all its dimensions, for living an autonomous life. By the latter I roughly mean a life of one's own choosing filled with actions, choices, and values with which one (by and large) identifies. I take a relational perspective in that I subscribe to the view that such a life should consist of meaningful social relationships

(Christman, 2009). Ideally, these relationships are just and empowering to the benefit of strengthening a person's autonomy, which is something we should strive for in a democratic society.

Surveillance is at tension with such relationships. Women*, especially women* of colour, have historically suffered disproportionately from surveillance and ensuing interference (Browne, 2015; Criado-Perez, 2019; D'Ignazio and Klein, 2020; Allen, 2022). An intersectional lens reveals that women* of colour and women* of lower socio-economic backgrounds suffer differently and disproportionately from the harms of surveillance such as commodification, discrimination, manipulation, and exploitation (Allen, 2022). Moreover, and relatedly, these women have more difficulties appealing to privacy norms and rights (Fraser, 1998; Allen, 2022).

Building on the former section, arguing for the value of privacy for an autonomous life, I think that reducing the issue of the policing of women*'s reproductive data to a data protection issue, means that we individualize the problem rather than putting it in a historical perspective of structural repression and social injustice, considering the specific harms for different women*. To empower women*, autonomy-enhancing interventions should be taken on the institutional, legal, and policy levels, with an eye on their political and social differences (Allen, 2022).

For instance, encryption is a measure to protect certain individual data in certain types of communication on certain types of devices. However, resisting 'surveillance' as a cultural, political, and infrastructural phenomenon and practice requires the acknowledgement of privacy as an important functional value that protects the fundamental value of autonomy. This acknowledgement is best achieved by emphasizing that privacy is a universal human right that protects not only our information, but also our decisions and our bodies, and by enshrining it in our constitutions or federal laws.

Furthermore, solutions such as deletion forgo the relationality of informational privacy as well as the important aspect of 'control' and therefore, the underlying value of autonomy. Deletion is a defensive, limited manifestation of informational privacy with a focus on 'no access'. It lacks the social dimension in which we can decide in which social contexts and relations we do share and in which we do not. Of course, from a defensive angle it seems sensible to argue that within an oppressive system the oppressed are best served by invisibility. If the system oppresses women by surveilling them, it seems prudent to make their health data inaccessible by deleting them. However, invisibility and non-accessibility can also contribute to oppression. The data gap is a good example (Criado-Perez, 2019). In the health sphere, women*'s data, especially women* of colour, have been neglected in favour of a male standard. There are obviously very good reasons for collecting women★'s health data (D'Ignazio and Klein, 2020). For instance, women★ show different signs of heart disease and respond differently to medication. Moreover, menstruation, pregnancy, and menopause are still widely under-researched. This is a systemic injustice that period apps, and FemTech more generally, play into; a gap that corporations promise to bridge in the absence of more structural and systemic research agendas. While this might seem laudable, this development should be approached with caution, especially if these corporations operate in contexts with very weak privacy legislation, but also given, to repeat, the historical and social-political dimensions of surveillance and corresponding vulnerabilities that corporations often tend to exploit in favour of profit rather than aim to remedy (Allen, 2022).

In sum, it seems that post-Roe, privacy, as a defensive strategy, is reduced to its most limited conceptualization, while I think that 'the aim', female★ self-determination post-Roe in the digitalized society, is better served if we understand and value privacy as multidimensional and social. We should demand that informational privacy is conceptualized as the capacity to control the access to information − so that women★ may share their data with clinics, hospitals, and research organizations without the fear that this might contribute to the cycle of systemic gendered surveillance. And importantly, we should insist on the need for decisional privacy, the right to control the access to our most intimate, and some of life's biggest, decisions − the decision to become pregnant or not, to have an abortion or not, to use contraception or not − without the risk of being prosecuted for these decisions. As a prerequisite for autonomous decision-making more broadly, and, more narrowly, for female★ self-determination regarding abortion, decisional privacy played an important role in the history of feminism. It is remarkable that this conceptualization in the debate is moved to the background. As Clark writes:

> With today's decision, the Court has positioned abortion not as a matter of personal decision-making, but as a matter that's best left in the hands of state representatives. It implies, furthermore, that the Constitutional right to privacy is illegitimate, arguing that the existing right has been constructed on shaky grounds. (Clark, 2022)

Moreover, while the individual right to privacy is important − for instance, the individual right to one's reproductive decisions, such as an abortion − there is an important social dimension to decisional privacy as the more general idea, social value (and constitutional right) that we want to live in a society that does not dictate to its citizens who to spend their lives and share their beds with, what religion to believe in, or what political party to vote for. Decisional privacy protects decisions that make us who we are, and should be respected if we want to be respected as autonomous human beings. To protect the right to reproductive choices with a right to health data privacy is an important defence but could be strengthened conceptually by considering the decisional and social dimensions of privacy. Given the fact that decisional privacy was the legal support for the right to an abortion, it is important that this concept is researched further.

By emphasizing privacy as deeply social and as having multiple dimensions beyond the informational dimension, most importantly decisional, we are better able to address the wrongs of digital surveillance post-Roe and what exactly it is that we lose by losing *Roe v Wade*. Moreover, it makes the agenda for solutions more ambitious than corporate (health) data encryption. For women★ to live autonomous lives, they should be able to present themselves as they want across different social contexts, making their own decisions about their lives and bodies. Deletion and encryption should be two among many tools in the toolbox. However, advocating and appealing to the right to privacy as an acknowledged human right intimately connected with freedom and autonomy, and empowering women★ to make this appeal successfully, by recognizing the historical and socio-political harms of surveillance, are important steps towards female★ self-determination post-Roe and social justice more generally.

Conclusion

In this chapter I argued that the discussion on period apps post-Roe could benefit from a multidimensional and social conceptualization of privacy. It has aimed to show the limits of privacy-as-individual-data-protection. This conceptualization invites 'technological solutions' such as deletion, encryption, de-identification, and anonymization. While these solutions are very important, we must avoid privacy becoming synonymous with a quick, defensive 'techno-fix': altering the technological design without considering the social and political context of the technology. Encrypting or deleting women★'s health data in the absence of robust privacy legislation is important. However, we should acknowledge that these interventions are defensive. The discussion around the risks of involving the collection of women★'s (health) data post-Roe should be understood and carried out in a context of recognition of the structural discrimination, repression, and (commercial) exploitation in women★'s health. To advance female★ empowerment and autonomy, it is helpful to comprehend the meaning and importance of decisional privacy rather than (or preferably in combination with) informational privacy. Moreover, we should emphasize and further investigate the relationship between privacy, autonomy, and social justice in the digital society.

Notes

[1] I use the term 'woman' or 'female' as a placeholder while acknowledging that there are many people who suffer the risks and harms discussed in this chapter but who do not belong to or fit this category, hence the asterisk after women*, female*, or woman*.

[2] It is not my intention to present an exhaustive overview of all articles that evaluate the risks of period tracking apps post-Roe, but to give an insight as to how and which risks and harms are identified within the public debate.

[3] Lisa Bari, CEO of Civitas Networks for Health.

[4] Kayte Spector-Bagdady, Professor of Bioethics and Law at the University of Michigan.

[5] The Cambridge Analytica scandal (2018) involves the company Cambridge Analytica that had collected the data of millions of Facebook users. Moreover, this information had been used to steer people's voting behaviour in the 2017 elections, thus influencing political decision-making of individuals.

[6] Christine Lemke, CEO of Evidation Health (consumer health research).

[7] Professor Gina Neff is a sociologist and director of the Minderoo Centre for Technology and Democracy at the University of Cambridge.

[8] Carmel Shachar is the executive director of the Petrie-Flom Center for Health Law Policy, Biotechnology, and Bioethics at Harvard Law School.

[9] Lydia X. Z. Brown: policy counsel with the Privacy and Data Project (Center for Democracy and Technology).

[10] Eric Perakslis: health privacy and cybersecurity expert (Duke University).

[11] Andrea Downing: president and co-founder of The Light Collective (non-profit that advocates health data protection).

[12] Megan Ranney: director at the Brown-Lifespan Center for Digital Health (Brown University).

[13] Kristen Rosati: former president of the American Health Law Association.

References

Allen, A. L. (1988). *Uneasy Access: Privacy for Women in a Free Society*. Totowa, NJ: Rowman and Littlefield.

Allen, A. L. (2022). Dismantling the 'Black Opticon': privacy, race equity, and online data-protection reform (February 20, 2022). *Yale Law Journal Forum*, University of Pennsylvania Law School, Public Law Research Paper No. 22-16. Available at SSRN: https://ssrn.com/abstract=4022653 or http://dx.doi.org/10.2139/ssrn.4022653

Browne, S. (2015). *Dark Matters: On the Surveillance of Blackness*. Durham, NC: Duke University Press.

Christman, J. (2009). *The Politics of Persons: Individual Autonomy and Socio-historical Selves*. New York: Cambridge University Press.

Corbin, B. (2020). Digital micro-aggressions and discrimination: FemTech and the 'othering' of women. *Nova Law Review*, 44(3): 1–28.

Criado-Perez, C. (2019). *Invisible Women: Exposing Data Bias in a World Designed for Men*. New York: Vintage.

De Conca, S. (2021). Smart home for lawyers: IoT in the home and its implications for the GDPR. *Tijdschrift voor Internetrecht*, 2021(6): 231–241.

D'Ignazio, C. and Klein, L. (2020). *Data Feminism*. Cambridge, MA: MIT Press.

Dobbs v. Jackson Women's Health Organization (2022) 597 U.S. 215.

Fraser, N. (1998). Sex, Lies and the Public Sphere: Some Reflections on the Confirmation of Clarence Thomas. In J. Landes (ed) *Feminism, the Public and the Private*, pp 314–337. Oxford: Oxford University Press.

Frost and Sullivan. (2018). Femtech: Digital revolution in women's health, 30 August 2024. Available at: https://ww2.frost.com/files/1015/2043/3691/Frost__Sullivan_Femtech.pdf

Hendl, T. and Jansky, B. (2021). Tales of self-empowerment through digital health technologies: a closer look at 'Femtech'. *Review of Social Economy*, 80: 29–57.

Jacobs, N. and Evers, J. (2019). De Kwetsbaarheid van Femtech. *Podium voor Bio-ethiek*, 26(4): 13–15.

Koops, B.-J., Newell, B. C., Timan, T., Skorvanek, I., Chokrevski, T., and Galič, M. (2017). A typology of privacy. *University of Pennsylvania Journal of International Law*, 38(2): 483–575.

Lanzing, M. (2018). 'Strongly recommended' revisiting decisional privacy to judge hypernudging in self-tracking technologies. *Philosophy & Technology*, 32: 549–568.

Lanzing, M. (2019). *The Transparent Self: A normative investigation of changing selves and relationships in the age of the quantified self*. PhD thesis, Technische Universiteit Eindhoven.

Roe v. Wade (1973). 410 U.S. 113.

Roessler, B. (2005). *The Value of Privacy*. Cambridge: Polity Press.

Sax, M. (2021). *Between Empowerment and Manipulation: The Ethics and Regulation of For-Profit Health Apps* (Information Law Series 47). Alphen aan den Rijn, the Netherlands: Kluwer Law International B. V.

Sharon, T. (2020). Blind-sided by privacy? Digital contact tracing, the Apple/Google API and big tech's newfound role as global health policy makers. *Ethics and Information Technology*. DOI: 10.1007/s10676-020-09547-x

Sharon, T. (2021). From hostile worlds to multiple spheres: towards a normative pragmatics of justice for the Googlization of health. *Medical Health Care and Philosophy*, 24: 315–327.

Sudjic, O. (2018). 'I felt colossally naive': the backlash against the birth control app. *The Guardian*, 21 July. Available at: www.theguardian.com/society/2018/jul/21/colossally-naive-backlash-birth-control-app

Susser, D., Roessler, B., and Nissenbaum, H. F. (2019). Online manipulation: hidden influences in a digital world. *Georgetown Law Technology Review*, 4: 1–45.

Verbeek, P. P. C. C., Brey, P., van Est, R., van Gemert, L., Heldeweg, M., and Moerel, L. (2020). Ethische analyse van de COVID-19 notificatie-app ter aanvulling op bron en contactonderzoek GGD, 30 August. Available at: https://www.tweedekamer.nl/kamerstukken/detail?id=2020D29967&did=2020D29967

Westin, A. F. (1967). *Privacy and Freedom*. New York: Atheneum.

Expert statements

Aguilar, M. (2022). Supreme Court's decision on abortion sparks health tech's Cambridge Analytica moment. *STATnews*, 30 June. Available at: www.statnews.com/2022/06/30/roe-abortion-health-data-privacy-cambridge-analytica/

Berger, M. (2022). Overturning Roe disproportionately burdens marginalized groups. *Penn Today*, 30 June. Available at: https://penntoday.upenn.edu/news/overturning-Roe-abortion-bans-disproportionately-burden-traditionally-marginalized-groups

Boodman, E., Bannow, T., Herman, B., and Ross, C. (2022). HIPAA won't protect you if prosecutors want your reproductive health records. *STATnews*, 24 June. Available at: www.statnews.com/2022/06/24/hipaa-wont-protect-you-if-prosecutors-want-your-reproductive-health-records/

Clark, K. (2022). The repeal of Roe v Wade will impact our privacy landscape at large, experts predict. *The Drum*, 24 June. Available at: www.thedrum.com/news/2022/06/24/the-repeal-roe-v-wade-will-impact-our-privacy-landscape-large-experts-predict

Clue (2022). Clue's response to Roe vs Wade. Clue, 24 June. Available at: https://helloclue.com/articles/abortion/clue-s-response-to-roe-vs-wade

Duball, J. (2022). Roe v Wade reversal sends ripples through privacy world. *IAPP*, 27 June. Available at: https://iapp.org/news/a/roe-v-wade-reversal-sends-ripples-through-privacy-world/

Flo (2022). Announcement of 'Anonymous Mode' in response to Roe v Wade. *X*, 24 June. Available at: https://twitter.com/flotracker/status/1540404337842995200/photo/1

Garamvolgyi, F. (2022). Why US women are deleting their period tracking apps. *The Guardian*, 28 June. Available at: www.theguardian.com/world/2022/jun/28/why-us-woman-are-deleting-their-period-tracking-apps

Haridasani Gupta, A. and Singer, N. (2021). Your app knows you got your period: Guess who it told? *New York Times*, 28 January. Available at: www.nytimes.com/2021/01/28/us/period-apps-health-technology-women-privacy.html

Hill, K. (2022). Deleting your period tracker won't protect you. *New York Times*, 30 June. Available at: www.nytimes.com/2022/06/30/technology/period-tracker-privacy-abortion.html

Human Rights Watch (2023). Human rights crisis: abortion in the United States after Dobbs, 18 April. Available at: www.hrw.org/news/2023/04/18/human-rights-crisis-abortion-united-states-after-dobbs

Kleinman, Z. (2022). The abortion privacy dangers in period trackers and apps. BBC, 28 June 2022. Available at: https://www.bbc.com/news/technology-61952794

Mahdawi, A. (2019). There's a dark side to women's health apps. *The Guardian*, 13 April. Available at: www.theguardian.com/world/2019/apr/13/theres-a-dark-side-to-womens-health-apps-menstrual-surveillance

Ornstein, C. (2022). Federal patient privacy law does not cover most period-tracking apps. *ProPublica*, 5 July. Available at: www.propublica.org/article/period-app-privacy-hipaa

Perez, S. and Whittaker, Z. (2022). Period tracker Stardust surges following Roe reversal, but it's privacy claims aren't airtight. *TechCrunch*, 27 June. Available at: https://techcrunch.com/2022/06/27/stardust-period-tracker-phone-number/?guccounter=1&guce_referrer=aHR0cHM6Ly93d3cuZ29vZ2xlLmNvbS8&guce_referrer_sig=AQAAAEx0OV1pVeoQnX9y2tKKhDoAH93rMbdD5H5Syu3g7XJFLdeiUfobl3l3kdrYJip0AeoSo7lXKlOq6uWYJuob_bp4rzbC5ea5boExDQ6bmw7q3ifCSebSWyy69wyhuQKgEIA3FetD9joNsTIBkQ3U2v2aU-q7Q5h7LaemzsZX7Dpp

Posner, L. (2022). Poland's new 'Pregnancy Registry' raises red flags. *Think Global Health*, 17 October. Available at: www.thinkglobalhealth.org/article/polands-new-pregnancy-registry-raises-red-flags

Privacy International (2019). How menstruation apps are sharing your data. Available at: https://privacyinternational.org/long-read/3196/no-bodys-business-mine-how-menstruations-apps-are-sharing-your-data

Privacy International (2020). We asked five menstruation apps for our data and here is what we found, 4 December. Available at: https://privacyinternational.org/long-read/4316/we-asked-five-menstruation-apps-our-data-and-here-what-we-found

Tiffany, K. (2018). Period-tracking apps are not for women. *Vox*, 16 November. Available at: www.vox.com/thegoods/2018/11/13/18079458/menstrualtrackingsurveillance-glow-clue-apple-health

Torchinsky, R. (2022). How period tracking apps and data privacy fit into a post-Roe v. Wade climate. *NPR*, 24 June. Available at: www.npr.org/2022/05/10/1097482967/roe-v-wade-supreme-court-abortion-period-apps

4

The Right to Silence: Intersections of Privacy and Silence in Networked Media

Taina Bucher

Introduction

Western liberal democracies are founded upon a logocentric order that privileges speech and the voice as the basis for citizens' deliberation and participation in society. A key feature therein, is the idea that people have a duty to express themselves in ways that support the circulation of ideas and the establishment of core societal institutions. To speak one's mind, citizens need to be informed. Together, these ideas – of the informed citizen, freedom (and duty) of expression, participation, and the vocal ideal of democratic citizenship – form the touchstones of modern democratic and political theory. At the centre of these ideas lies a fundamental belief in the power of speech as the modus operandi of democratic life (Gray, 2021). Because the logocentric order of 'Western' liberal democracies puts freedom of speech at the heart of its conception of political participation (Ferguson, 2003), media research has tended to disregard its logical counterpart, the right *not* to speak and the right *not to absorb* or attend to the speech of others. These relatively overlooked aspects of the very definition of freedom of speech and freedom of information, respectively, connect to some core concerns in the privacy literature as well. If, as Westin puts it, information privacy, refers to 'the claim of individuals, groups, or institutions to determine for themselves when, how, and to what extent information about them is communicated to others' (Westin, 1967: 7), this chapter suggests we also need to contend to a much larger degree with the related claim of individuals to determine for themselves when, how, and to what extent information about *others* is communicated to *them* – to the extent that this is possible at all.

To contribute a theorization of the right to silence, this chapter engages with a handful of artworks that offer means to attend more carefully to the management of voice in a networked media environment. I consider the ways in which digital artists critique the social norms that exist around networked hyperconnectivity. Although disparate in purpose and scope, the artworks explore the role of digital media in shaping our understanding of information privacy by mobilizing a politics of withdrawal, concealment, and self-care. While the artworks are not necessarily about silence per se, they are performative of a common concern for managing other people's voices for the sake of self-care and self-preservation. To break down the argument, I will first address how silence has typically been approached in media studies, before expanding on the notion of what I mean by the right to silence in and beyond the context of privacy. To further consolidate the argument, I consider the ways in which artworks such as Sam Lavigne's *Zoom Escaper* (2021) and Lauren McCarthy and Kyle McDonald's *PplKpr* (2016) gesture towards the generative potential of silence by mobilizing a Bartlebyan politics of refusal reminiscent of what the Caribbean philosopher Édouard Glissant (1997) has called the 'right to opacity'.

Beyond and with privacy

In their renowned 1890 article, 'The right to privacy', Samuel Warren and Louis Brandeis defined privacy as the 'right to be let alone', characterized by a person's ability to define the limits of their private life. This notion of freedom from observation has been understood as an individual's right to distance themselves from the prying eyes of others and remain shielded from scrutiny in a private context. At its most basic, privacy can be understood as a form of boundary regulation process, where the boundaries between different spheres of action are continuously being negotiated and regulated (Altman, 1977). Networked media, however, pose challenges to these more conventional notions of privacy. As Wendy Chun (2016) suggests, networks are intentionally 'leaky' structures that cannot confine private information within sealed boundaries. Given that networked media rely on a technical framework driven by the continuous exchange of information, it is more fitting to perceive privacy as inherently *networked* (Marwick, 2023). The networked privacy model assumes that information 'will pass through the network and that privacy can easily be violated by any individual connected to the user' (Marwick and boyd, 2014: 1064). This is not a failure on the part of the network but intentional. In an environment characterized by 'context collapse' and the blurred boundaries, people can no longer determine for themselves *who* can access or *how* a specific piece of information will circulate within the network.

However, the fact that networked notions of privacy move beyond models of individual agency and responsibility, does not mean that negotiating boundaries of information sharing and individual control have become entirely futile. This implies that privacy models that overly rely on a strict division between private and public, openness and secrecy, and individual versus structural aspects should be supplemented or even substituted with more flexible, context-aware, and interrelated interpretations of privacy. Boundaries are still being regulated, just not by individuals alone. Within a networked setting, the boundaries are not merely permeable and susceptible to breaches; they are also subject to influence by major tech corporations and platforms that play an ever-growing role in regulating and shaping these boundaries. In a setting where we have limited control over who sees or hears our communicative actions, we also lack the related ability to select the information that comes our way. It is in this sense that this chapter examines the management of information flows *beyond privacy*. If, for Altman, privacy is the 'selective control of access to the self', an emphasis on the right to silence shifts attention to the selective control of access to *others* (Altman, 1977: 67). While concepts of privacy typically link silence to positive choice in the sense that people choose what to disclose and to whom and what information to keep off-limits, silence, as I see it here, is linked to negative choice. As sociologist Eva Illouz (2019) argues, late modernity is increasingly defined by the freedom to 'unchoose'. The right to silence speaks to this freedom to unchoose by way of disengaging, withdrawing, and dissolving relationships in ways that are not sufficiently encapsulated by existing concepts of privacy.

In a networked media landscape defined by hyperconnectivity, fluid relationships, and ambiguous social boundaries, upholding a concept of privacy as a sheltered sanctuary is at best misleading. In addition to the ability to *partially* control how information about the self flows online, privacy debates should also contend more explicitly with the construction of self-chosen publics. Though these distinctions are matters of degree rather than fundamental differences, a right to silence within the realm of privacy suggests a subtle shift in focus, moving from protection of personal information to the differential protection from other people's voices. Alas, it is less about limiting access to one's own speech and more about restraining access and attention to the speech of others. It also needs emphasizing that in contrast to legal conceptions of privacy, my intention with proposing a right to silence is meant more colloquially. Just as privacy 'is far too heterogeneous to denote a single right' (Roessler, 2017: 188), silence, too, refuses to be a single thing. If the legal concept of privacy entails a freedom from the scrutiny of others (Warren and Brandeis, 1890), a right to silence, seen here as both an extension of and a going beyond privacy, entails in part a freedom from scrutinizing others. The question going forward, then, is what and who should (not) be listened to, and when? How can we contend with the ambiguity of silence in the first place?

The ambiguity of silence

Silence is an inherently ambivalent term, characterized by a multitude of meanings. Nevertheless, in much Western scholarship, silence is regarded as a sign of passivity, weakness, and failure. Because freedom of speech constitutes a core democratic value, silence, often being regarded as its opposite, turns into a democratic threat. If speech signifies freedom, agency, and visibility, not speaking by the same token implies disempowerment, coercion, and invisibility. Such a view is largely predicated on taking silence as the opposite of speech, rather than, for example, a form of speech or expressive of a politics. Indeed, democratic theory to a large extent embraces a voice-focused politics (Vieira, 2020). The vocal ideal of democratic citizenship is thus premised on empowering the voices of citizens in collective decision-making. In this model the news media act as a platform from which a range of different voices can be heard and listened to. Conceptualized as the fourth estate, news media are expected to provide a public forum for debate to articulate public opinion and to force governments to consider the will of the people (Hansen, 2022). Similar expectations are now being levelled at big tech platforms that act as conduits of news and public opinion. When they fail to live up to these standards, platforms, just like news media, are quickly accused of stifling debate and silencing marginalized voices (Couldry, 2010). Extending from this, silence is often construed as coerced in public debates. Elisabeth Noelle-Neumann's 1974 'spiral of silence' theory states that people, fearing social isolation, constantly gauge the prevailing opinions to conform to the majority. If they perceive their stance as marginal, they stay quiet.

In a conventional understanding of silence as an oppressive and passive force, silence is thus seen as something that needs to be broken. It is in these terms that silence has largely been taken up within large strands of Western feminist and liberatory theorizing as something created by patriarchal oppression (Gilligan, 1993). Historically, silence has thus been regarded as a sign of weakness and disempowerment, so that 'feminist heroines who spoke out against male privilege and patriarchy became ideals for younger generations' (Olsen, 1978; Jackson, 2012). Feminist research and social justice scholars have called for the need to regain voice by 'speaking out' against oppression. Although particularly the works of women of colour such as Audre Lorde and bell hooks (hooks, 1989; Lorde, 2012) have added some needed complexity to the overly binary framing of silence/speech, the guiding political imperative of 'breaking the silence' by 'coming to voice' largely remains unchallenged (Ferrari, 2020). What if the things usually coded as passive – the pause, delay, muteness, hesitation, withdrawal, and quietude – offer a catalyst for novel understandings of contemporary media culture?

If sound terminology abounds in how we have come to understand networked media environments, from 'giving voice', to 'amplify' and 'echo chambers', we might also want to think about the silence offered by 'listening' and the quiet as an affective sonic modality of refusal. According to Kanngieser and Beuret (2017), we might think of listening and silence in at least three interrelated ways. First, as the attentiveness to when one is being forced to speak. Second, as a means for knowing when worlds require listening to, and third, as a matter of refusing to be recognized (Kanngieser and Beuret, 2017: 367). Of course, freedom of speech does not mean you *have to* speak, nor does it require us to take other people's statements to heart. Still, democracy is founded upon the idea that speech and voicing one's opinions are not just desirable but expected and that, as listeners, we need to stay attuned and attentive. By the same token, social media have turned this expectation into their business model. While not exactly claiming that we are forced to speak when navigating networked environments, big tech and social media platforms certainly *prefer* us to speak to the extent that digital capitalism is built on monetizing users' communicative traces. In this equation, speech equals participation, which in turn leads to increased visibility and attention. In such a model, silence is punishment for not engaging or speaking one's mind, often confined to evanescent clicks, shares, and likes.

A calculus of uncaring

Digital artists have variously taken up this wrongful equation to engage critically with the ways that digital capitalism is designed to spark participation in the guise of democracy. Finding ways to disrupt what seems like the democratic potential of digital connection, these artists often use tactics of 'destructive creativity' (Hu, 2022), humour and hacktivism to co-opt and turn the logics of hyperconnection on its head. For an example of this mode, take Sam Lavigne's *Zoom Escaper* (2021), an app and art project that offers its users a series of disruptive audio samples to be played during a Zoom call to give an excuse to leave the call. As with the rest of the world during the global COVID-19 pandemic in 2020–21, Lavigne found himself in the presence of never-ending Zoom calls. He was looking for an escape. As with other artworks that he created the same year (for example, *Zoom Deleter*), *Zoom Escaper* embraces silence by means of sonic sabotage. In a world turned too noisy and chaotic, where connection and communication are no longer presented as choices but demands, *Zoom Escaper* exemplifies a subversive attentiveness to when one is being forced to both speak and listen. While it may seem paradoxical to refer to the sound samples of crying babies, weeping men, construction work, echoes, and technical failures as 'silent', that is exactly the point.

This is not the kind of aural or textual silence that we usually associate with the term, but a kind of hushing the sounds of the world that have grown increasingly unbearable. We might thus think of *Zoom Escaper* as a form of what sound scholar Mack Hagood calls 'orphic media', devices that 'promise to help users ... remain unaffected in changeable, stressful, and distracting environments, sonically fabricating microspaces of freedom for the pursuit of happiness' (2019: 3). Taking his cue from Greek mythology's Orpheus, who fought sound with sound to create a safe passage for the Argonauts, Hagood's concept of orphic media usefully describes the sonic power in silencing the Sirens as an affirmative means of choosing 'not to attend to unwanted aspects of self and world' (2019: 4). Self-sabotaging a Zoom call by amplifying the sound of bad connection demonstrates how orphic mediation speaks to the generative potential of silent citizenship. In a world that has grown noisy on multiple accounts (both in acoustic and information terms), turning to an expanded notion of silence can provide a way to move beyond privacy understood as a freedom from *being heard*. If privacy concerns have been accelerated by the ubiquitous nature of digital surveillance, I would argue that the murmurs of digital hyperconnectivity also asks us to make room for an understanding of silence that signifies a freedom from having to hear.

Paradoxically, perhaps, hushing the sounds of an increasingly unbearable world by blocking access to the speech of others is not merely a form of self-care but also of allowing oneself to *not care*. If we take seriously the *Oxford English Dictionary*'s definition of deliberate as both 'well-considered' and 'unhurried', quietude asserts itself back into the equation. A feminist ethics of care (Mol, 2008; Tronto, 2020), reveals how silence might teach us to value waiting and slower ways of living. This does not mean, as de la Bellacasa (2017) suggests, that *to care* should be taken as a moral obligation in all situations. Indeed, as black feminist scholarship (Quashie, 2012; Hartman, 2019) has emphasized, the power of cultivating indifference can also be seen as a form of quiet revolt.

Paying attention to silence instead of voice may help reveal how *not caring* can hold emancipatory power. For cultural theorist Xine Yao (2021), indifference holds generative possibilities as a tactic from below. Rather than measuring humanity based on their emotional capacities – what she refers to as the colonial sentimental model of justice – Yao argues we need to resurrect the negativity of *unfeeling*. Here, a lack of sentiment is not a failure to be fully recognizable as human but a way of exercising disloyalty to oppressive regimes of authority by refusing to care or act within such colonial hierarchies of worth. We can observe this notion of 'unfeeling' paradoxically exemplified in Lauren McCarthy and Kyle McDonald's art piece and application called

PplKpr (2016). This app employs GPS and a heart rate wristband to monitor, assess, and autonomously manage individuals' relationships by utilizing an emotion classification algorithm. As a twist on the concept of quantified living and sentiment analysis, *PplKpr* prompts users to assess their emotional experiences, such as excitement, arousal, anger, fear, anxiety, boredom, or calmness when they engage with others. Over time, the system will create rankings for the user's contacts, taking into account how strongly these contacts evoke specific emotional responses, with the aim of optimizing the user's social life accordingly. The app will provide an analysis of individuals who have the most pronounced influence on the user's emotions and will take actions on the user's behalf. These actions may involve inviting people to spend time together, sending messages, or even blocking and unfriending those who appear to have a negative impact. On the one hand, this automatic and algorithmically assisted people management system does exactly what Yao critiques. By measuring the value of a user's various connections through the standards of sentiment analysis, *PplKpr* establishes a hierarchy of people based on their affectability, as co-opted by the machine. On the other hand, the automatic reduction and blocking of relationships and individuals who do not align with the user's emotional state demonstrates the 'operations of unfeeling as a form of antisocial discontent about, if not outright defiance of, the compulsory norms for expressing feeling along with susceptibility to the feelings of others' (Yao, 2021: 7).

Like the orphic mediation found in *Zoom Escaper*, *PplKpr* alludes to the concept of a right to silence to the extent that it provides a means for knowing when the world requires being listened to and when it does not. Keep the friends who make you feel good and block the ones who make you feel bad. If this sounds a bit tongue-in-cheek and somewhat gimmicky, it is because it is. Using subversive and humorous tactics, *PplKpr* is both disturbing, liberating, and chillingly banal. As Lambert (2016) notes, there is nothing unique about *PplKpr*; there are many similar commercial mood tracking apps on the market. Yet, the artwork usefully demonstrates how our hyperconnectivity also raises the need for breaking away from potentially toxic or emotionally straining conversations. As scholarship on digital disconnection has usefully argued, exercising the right not to engage constitutes a vital form of freedom today (Kaun, 2021). As seen in the antisocial turn in queer theory (Halberstam, 2008) and the sociology of negative relations (Illouz, 2019), acts of opting out are not signs of vulnerability but a form of self-assertion that refuses to conform to prevailing heteronormative societal norms. As pointed out by Illouz (2019), just as we experience wants, desires, and love, we also encounter avoidance, rejection, and the end of love. However, these aspects of what Illouz terms 'unloving' often go unnoticed. While our culture is filled with narratives about the beginnings of relationships, stories about the termination of relationships are far less common. To the extent that *PplKpr* encapsulates unloving – and by extension demonstrates a right to silence – it does so by freeing the user from making a choice altogether. While social media platforms offer plenty of design features to end, take a break from, or reject relationships, the social stigma associated with such undoings still makes negative choice feel like a burden. Rather than having to make an active choice to ignore someone who makes you feel bad, which only risks making you feel even worse, the real contribution of *PplKpr* seems to lie in the automation of the choice to unchoose altogether. To a certain extent, then, what the algorithm offers in the case of *PplKpr* is not just the freedom to ignore but 'a calculus of uncaring' that allows us to take better care of ourselves and others (Yao, 2021: 28) in the long run.

I prefer not to

In the context of a networked media environment, be it on social media platforms or other digital spaces, both freedom of expression and the right to silence are significantly shaped by technical infrastructures. Online, the choice to speak or to remain silent, to engage or disengage, connect or disconnect, is subject to an algorithmic logic. While platforms certainly prefer users to 'speak' by contributing explicit forms of communication, silence speaks too. The demand for ever more speech sits (un)comfortably alongside the potential communicability of all data points on the Web. As the business and machine learning models of digital media platforms make clear, acts of deletion, absence, and silence do not necessarily result in *less* data, but even *more* data points (Bucher, 2020). Remaining silent online cannot simply be dismissed as non-participation, given that behaviours such as listening and lurking are constantly being computed as speech. Instead of seeing participatory culture as something wherein one *must* speak, a renewed understanding of silence implies an 'attentiveness to when one is being forced to speak' as Kanngieser and Beuret put it (2017: 367). Contrasting conventional understandings of freedom of speech, what this comes down to is refusing 'a conception of the world in which it is impossible *not* to communicate' (Guillaume, 2018: 479). This seems particularly important, given digital environments engineered to process nearly every action, even those that may seem silent, such as skipping, scrolling, or reading. Rather than seeing silence as something to be overcome or eradicated for political and social life to flourish, we might think of it as gesture (Agamben, 2000). For Agamben, gesture is not a means to an end, but a carrier of potentiality. As seen in negations of engagement, verbal or otherwise, gestures make means visible as such: Rosa Parks not moving an inch on the bus; Iranian women cutting off their hair in protest, each not just bespeaking a politics but making a statement. This is not to say that Rosa Parks' gesture cannot be considered an active speech act in legal and constitutional terms but that it sits at an uneasy intersection between language and action, the physical and the symbolic. Here, silence is not the opposite of language, but something that sits at the threshold of pure bodily movement and the realm of explicit communication.

Just think of Herman Melville's famous character Bartleby whose gesture of inaction opens a new avenue for thinking about refusal (Melville, 1853/1967). In Melville's story we are introduced to Bartleby, a scrivener whose main activity consists of copying documents until the moment he decides to resist his employer's demands by uttering the subdued 'I'd prefer not to'. Throughout the story, Bartleby maintains this position of preferring not to until his lawyer boss cannot take it anymore and closes the shop to escape an unintelligibility that turned too unbearable. Bartleby's refusal to elaborate when confronted, his inclination of not needing to explain himself, and to seemingly not care, pushes against the expectations of affectability, in a manner similar to Yao's notion of disaffection and unfeeling. As Sianne Ngai suggests, a text like 'Bartleby', 'foregrounds the absence of a strong emotion where we are led to expect one or turn entirely on the interpretive problems posed by an emotional illegibility' (2007: 10). In other words, refusing the colonial sentimental model of justice through various forms of disaffections and unfeeling, Bartleby's refusal to elaborate when asked, demonstrates a right to silence by hushing care.

Interestingly, both 'Bartleby' and the orphic sound samples in the case of *Zoom Escaper* represent ways of harnessing a form of silence that feels unbearable to others. In fact, in all three examples discussed so far, silence foregrounds unfeeling, masked as unbearability. In both the scenarios of 'Bartleby' and *Zoom Escaper*, intolerable circumstances drive other individuals to want to exit, while in the case of *PplKpr* it is the insufferability of certain people that requires algorithmic measures to be silenced. What constitutes silence in each of these cases, however, differs. If Bartleby's silence marks a form of speechlessness, or non-communication, the silence in *Zoom Escaper* is rather loud. To see silence as gesture, as I do here, is to resist conventional understandings of silence as the negation or absence of sound and speech. Silence speaks; it can be loud; silence defies illegibility, and silence waits.

The gesture 'of not being able to figure something out in language' (Agamben, 2000: 59) makes silence resemble what Roland Barthes (2005) called the Neutral. According to Neil Badmington (2020), Barthes observed that when faced with a woman's response that diverged from the anticipated simple yes or no, he considered the Neutral as being 'more nuanced' (2005: 112) than mere silence; her answer was deemed a 'deviation'. While the woman's simple decision to 'reply in a manner that shifts the rules of the game, that keeps the discussion open and ongoing, that fails to close the conversation with a simple "yes" or "no"' is described as more powerful than silence, I see silence as having the same power to exercise derailments and to neutralize or stall the usual order of things. Unlike the appropriation of sentiment analysis used to *avoid* choice, as in the case of *PplKpr*, Bartleby's stubborn non-response seems to exist *beyond* choice. According to Deleuze, with Bartleby we are not confronted with a being who makes a choice, but with indifference, or a 'nothingness of the will' (1998: 73). In a world that tries to pin him down, expects a certain way in response, Bartleby remains unaffected. As such, we might find in Bartleby's relatively silent 'I prefer not to' a response that speaks up against digital capitalism's preference for participatory speech. In a society where we are constantly expected to care and participate, 'trying to find new – and somewhat original – modes of engagement', as Barthes (2015: 116) put it in an interview, is not about resignation or retreating into an inner room as it were, but to remain in 'the hold' (Moten, 2016). Being in the hold is not a stepping away from oppressive power structures, but a way of 'staying with the trouble' (Haraway, 2016) within those very structures.

In being at loss in language, silence is not necessarily a sign of unproductive numbness (although it can certainly be) but carrying the potentials for resisting the urge to add even more speech under libertarian and capitalist systems that demand otherwise. If the business logic of platforms is fundamentally driven by their engagement metrics and algorithmic amplification, then refusing to participate according to the terms given to us, by remaining silent or seemingly passive, may offer a fruitful avenue for resistance. Preferring not to, then, is less a negation and more like a suspense. Bartleby is no revolutionary, no rebel, or as Beverungen and Dunne aptly note, 'he does not recognize these trivial conventionalities' (2007: 178). More fundamentally, and perhaps more radically with regards to the current media age dominated by an industry of so-called influencers, Bartleby has no opinion. In a world that not just valorizes speech, but also hinges on it, and ultimately demands of us to speak, what the gesture of silence makes visible, particularly in the digital context of data accumulation, is not necessarily meaning, but *communicability*. This is where I see the generative potential of silence, not necessarily as the absence of speech, as if these were opposites, but as something that upends our taken-for-granted assumptions about the univocal appeal for speech and communicative affectability. Even if Bartleby's 'I prefer not to' is not representative of an absolute silence, it shares the same enigmatic character. As I will argue in the next and final section of the chapter, Bartleby's non-response exercises the right to silence by means of refusing to be recognized, a right reminiscent of what the Caribbean philosopher Édouard Glissant (1997) has called the 'right to opacity'.

Opacity

In *Poetics of Relation* (1997), Glissant describes the radical potential of opacity as a form of epistemic refusal. For Glissant, the right to opacity signifies the right not to make sense, to exist and resist beyond identificatory transparency

(Sundén, 2023). This is where the concepts of privacy and silence interlink again to the extent that they both gesture towards the question of what and who should (not) be listened to, and when. Due to the networked condition of privacy, listening, too, is partly out of reach and our control. How can we decide who or what (not) to listen to, if this decision is already structured, filtered, and partial to begin with? Who or what serves us these choices, if not merely ourselves? What role do algorithms and networks play in conditioning the right to silence in the first place? In the face of extensive surveillance, Claire Birchall (2016) proposes moving beyond the traditional idea of privacy, asserting that it has lost its relevance in an era saturated with state and consumer data surveillance. Instead, Glissant's concept of opacity serves as a pertinent reminder that the right not to be observed and easily comprehended extends beyond the conventional notion of privacy, which typically involves the right to be left alone. For Glissant, opacity is not the same as obscurity but resistance to rendering the other transparent and legible. At first sight, the conception of privacy as secrecy, understood as the freedom from scrutiny seems not too far removed from Glissant's (1997) notion of a right to opacity. After all, Glissant also advocates for the right to refrain from the scrutiny of others. Yet, more than simply the right to retreat into a private setting, Glissant argues for the right to not be known at all, based on a radical relational account of the self. For Glissant, such a relationality entails the importance of consenting not to be a single being, of remaining irreducible and imperceptible to the Euro-centred view of universal truths.

Given ubiquitous surveillance and algorithmic profiling, practices of opacity have gained common ground as activist and artistic means of digital resistance. 'Going dark' has thus emerged as a major theme in examining algorithmic identity in networked environments. Contemporary digital artists such as Zach Blas, Adam Harvey, and Hito Steyrl are known for their practice of avoiding recognition technology by rendering themselves unidentifiable or unrecognizable by it (de Vries and Schinkel, 2019), while scholars focused on privacy, such as Brunton and Nissenbaum (2015), advocate for tactics of obfuscation. Most recently, a major exhibition titled *Going Dark: The Contemporary Figure at the Edge of Visibility* at the Guggenheim Museum, New York, prominently features such strategies of concealing and obscuring identity markers as a central motif. While such artistic practices of obfuscation hold great merit as critical sites for refusal, they often fall short on their own criticism. To the extent that many of these projects are designed to explicitly critique algorithmic politics of identification, they tend to sidestep the fact that the very same algorithms resist universal truths and singular conceptions of identity in the ways that they operate.

Machine learning algorithms do not really care about a person's coherence, insofar as one's 'algorithmic identity' (Cheney-Lippold, 2017) is in a constant state of modulation based on changing inputs and actions. Instead, predictive algorithms operate on the basis on what John Cheney-Lippold calls 'measurable types', understood as algorithmic interpretation about who we are computationally calculated to be. On the internet, conventional demographics are not so much predefined as they are constructed over time, so a person might be categorized as 79 per cent Hispanic one day and 30 per cent the next, based on their behavioural traces and activities. To a certain extent, then, algorithms paradoxically uphold the right to opacity by enabling a form of profound relationality that is not reliant on sanctioned identities. Algorithms both monitor and simplify, yet they also refrain from reducing a person into universal truths, or so it seems. Given that algorithms support the right not to be a single being, where does it leave privacy and our conceptions of silence as refusing to be recognized? Where does this leave resistance?

The critical impasse of a right to silence: concluding remarks

By way of concluding, one answer can be found in revisiting the notion of disaffection and unfeeling. In a networked environment fuelled by the 'speaking', participatory subject, resistance is perhaps less about covering faces or weaponizing them as per Zach Blas' artworks and more about weaponizing a Bartlebyan politics of having no opinion and nothing to say. For platforms, having no opinion or choosing not to attend to the speech of others, arguably poses a greater threat than concealment or obfuscation as such. As Carina Albrecht and Wendy Chun (2023) have argued, in an environment that hinges on the calculation of interestingness, 'not being interesting or interested in this context means not being registered as a relationship'. Not being registered as a relationship arguably constitutes a more subtle form of going dark than the camouflages in artistic imaginaries of surveillance (de Vries and Schinkel, 2019). It is here that I see the generative potential of a right to silence as manifest in the unfeeling of Bartlebyan politics. While the right to silence is not exactly like the right to opacity in that it does not rely on a radical relationality that insists on an irreducible unknowability of the subject, it shares with Glissant's notion of opacity the right to refrain from the scrutiny of others. That is, in addition to the right not to make sense *to* others – reminiscent of notions of privacy – the right to silence exercises the right not to make sense *of* others or the world as given to us – going beyond notions of privacy. Even if Barthes theorized the Neutral as something more subtle than silence, I see silence as having a similar denaturalizing power in the networked media environment. As a utopian 'opening in the direction of an undefined something else' (Barthes, 2005: 112), silence outplays analysis. In an environment of influencers capitalizing on having an opinion, silence begets an alternative. To return to the question of what and who should (not) be listened to, and when, silence foils any clear answer. Silence may hurt. Silence may haunt. But silence may also liberate and feel like a relief. The kind of inaction that silences seem to represent, are not simply to be read as 'ugly', but also as a freedom to exit something that does *not quite feel right*.

References

Agamben, G. (2000). Notes on Gesture. In *Means Without Ends: Notes on Politics*, pp 49–62. Minneapolis: University of Minnesota Press.

Albrecht, C. and Chun, W. K. H. (2023). *Interest, disaffection, and unfeeling in the age of social media*. Paper presented at the 73rd Annual ICA conference, Toronto, 25–29 May.

Altman, I. (1977). Privacy regulation: culturally universal or culturally specific? *Journal of Social Issues*, 33(3): 66–84.

Badmington, N. (2020). An undefined something else: Barthes, culture, neutral life. *Theory, Culture & Society*, 37(4): 65–76.

Barthes, R. (2005). *The Neutral: Lecture Course at the Collège de France (1977–1978)*. Edited by T. Clerc, translated by R. E. Krauss and D. Hollier. New York: Columbia University Press.

Barthes, R. (2015). *'Simply a Particular Contemporary': Interviews, 1970–79*. Translated by C. Turner. Calcutta: Seagull Books.

Beverungen, A. and Dunne, S. (2007). 'I'd prefer not to': Bartleby and the excesses of interpretation. *Culture and Organization*, 13(2): 171–183.

Birchall, C. (2016). Shareveillance: subjectivity between open and closed data. *Big Data & Society*, 3(2). DOI: 10.1177/2053951716663965

Brunton, F. and Nissenbaum, H. (2015). *Obfuscation: A User's Guide for Privacy and Protest*. Cambridge, MA: MIT Press.

Bucher, T. (2020). Nothing to disconnect from? Being singular plural in an age of machine learning. *Media, Culture & Society*, 42(4): 610–617.

Cheney-Lippold, J. (2017). We Are Data. In *We Are Data: Algorithms and the Making of Our Digital Selves*. New York: New York University Press.

Chun, W. H. K. (2016). *Updating to Remain the Same: Habitual New Media*. Cambridge, MA: MIT Press.

Couldry, N. (2010). *Why Voice Matters: Culture and Politics After Neoliberalism*. London: Sage.

de la Bellacasa, M. P. (2017). *Matters of Care: Speculative Ethics in More Than Human Worlds*. Minneapolis, MN: University of Minnesota Press.

de Vries, P. and Schinkel, W. (2019). Algorithmic anxiety: masks and camouflage in artistic imaginaries of facial recognition algorithms. *Big Data & Society*, 6(1). DOI: 10.1177/2053951719851532

Deleuze, G. (1998). Bartleby; Or, the Formula. In *Essays Critical and Clinical*, pp 68–90. Translated by D. W. Smith. London: Verso.

Ferguson, K. (2003). Silence: a politics. *Contemporary Political Theory*, 2(1): 49–65.

Ferrari, M. (2020). Questions of silence: on the emancipatory limits of voice and the coloniality of silence. *Hypatia*, 35(1): 123–142.

Gilligan, C. (1993). *In a Different Voice: Psychological Theory and Women's Development*. Cambridge, MA: Harvard University Press.

Glissant, É. (1997). *Poetics of Relation*. Ann Arbor, MI: University of Michigan Press.

Gray, S. W. (2021). Towards a democratic theory of silence. *Political Studies*, 71: 815–834.

Guillaume, X. (2018). How to do things with silence: rethinking the centrality of speech to the securitization framework. *Security Dialogue*, 49(6): 476–492.

Hagood, M. (2019). *Hush: Media and Sonic Self-control*. Durham, NC: Duke University Press.

Halberstam, J. (2008). The anti-social turn in queer studies. *Graduate Journal of Social Science*, 5(2): 140–156.

Hansen, E. (2022). The fourth estate operating by means of silencing. *Journalism*, 25: 141–157.

Haraway, D. J. (2016). *Staying With the Trouble: Making Kin in the Chthulucene*. Durham, NC: Duke University Press.

Hartman, S. (2019). *Wayward Lives, Beautiful Experiments: Intimate Histories of Riotous Black Girls, Troublesome Women, and Queer Radicals*. New York: W. W. Norton & Company.

Hu, T.-H. (2022). *Digital Lethargy: Dispatches from an Age of Disconnection*. Cambridge, MA: MIT Press.

Illouz, E. (2019). *The End of Love: A Sociology of Negative Relations*. New York: Oxford University Press.

Jackson, C. (2012). Speech, gender and power: beyond testimony. *Development and Change*, 43(5): 999–1023.

Kanngieser, A. and Beuret, N. (2017). Refusing the world: silence, commoning, and the Anthropocene. *South Atlantic Quarterly*, 116(2): 363–380.

Kaun, A. (2021). Ways of seeing digital disconnection: a negative sociology of digital culture. *Convergence*, 27(6): 1571–1583.

Lambert, A. (2016). Bodies, mood and excess: relationship tracking and the technicity of intimacy. *Digital Culture & Society*, 2(1): 71–88.

Lorde, A. (2012). *Sister Outsider: Essays and Speeches*: Crossing Press.

Marwick, A. E. (2023). *The Private Is Political: Networked Privacy and Social Media*. New Haven, CT: Yale University Press.

Marwick, A. E. and boyd, d. (2014). Networked privacy: how teenagers negotiate context in social media. *New Media & Society*, 16(7): 1051–1067.

Melville, H. (1853/1967). Bartleby the Scrivener. In *Billy Bud, Sailor and Other Stories*. London: Penguin (Classics).

Mol, A. (2008). *The Logic of Care: Health and the Problem of Patient Choice*. London: Routledge.

Moten, F. (2016). *Poetics of the Undercommons*. Brooklyn, NY: Sputnik & Fizzle.

Ngai, S. (2007). *Ugly Feelings*. Cambridge, MA: Harvard University Press.

Noelle-Neumann, E. (1974). The spiral of silence a theory of public opinion. *Journal of Communication*, 24(2): 43–51.

Olsen, T. (1978). *Silences*. New York: Delta/Seymour Lawrence.

Quashie, K. (2012). *The Sovereignty of Quiet: Beyond Resistance in Black Culture*. New Brunswick, NJ: Rutgers University Press.

Roessler, B. (2017). X – privacy as a human right. *Proceedings of the Aristotelian Society*, 117(2): 187–206.

Sundén, J. (2023). Digital kink obscurity: a sexual politics beyond visibility and comprehension. *Sexualities*. DOI: 10.1177/13634607221124401

Tronto, J. C. (2020). *Moral Boundaries: A Political Argument for an Ethic of Care*. New York; London: Routledge.

Vieira, M. B. (2020). Representing silence in politics. *American Political Science Review*, 114(4): 976–988.

Warren, S. D. and Brandeis, L. D. (1890). The right to privacy. *Harvard Law Review*, 4(5): 193–220.

Westin, A. F. (1967). Privacy and freedom. *Washington and Lee Law Review*, 25(1): 166.

Yao, X. (2021). *Disaffected: The Cultural Politics of Unfeeling in Nineteenth-century America*. Durham, NC: Duke University Press.

Practices

5

Atmospheres of Privacy

Karen Louise Grova Søilen

Introduction

The notion of privacy is often described in spatial terms: we speak of privacy as a space of withdrawal; a room of one's own; a threshold, an alcove; as that which happens behind closed curtains or doors; protected by walls, 'an indoor business'; where something may be 'whispered in the closet' (Warren and Brandeis, 1890: np; Duby, 1992: viii; Liu, 2011). Yet in more immaterial ways, too, a sense of spatiality clings to the concept of privacy, as well as to the often-overlapping notions of 'the private' and 'private life'. For example, the 'private' is described as 'a zone of immunity to which we may fall back or retreat' (Duby, 1992: viii) and 'private life' is referred to as 'that zone of space, of time' where one is not an object, but a subject (Barthes, 2000: 15). There is also the notion of a private 'sphere' in which subjects may form their ideas and identities in an environment devoid of (state) interference (Habermas, 1989). By the same token, threats to privacy also tend to be embedded in a spatial discourse, such as when we talk about invasions of privacy, or privacy leaks, in both of which privacy is understood as something (no longer) contained which needs to be protected, sheltered. Indeed, privacy scholar Julie Cohen has proposed that the recurring spatial metaphors, which sticks to the concept of privacy, is an indication that 'something about the experience of privacy, and that of privacy invasion, is fundamentally and irreducibly spatial' (Cohen, cited in Koops, 2018: 619). In a similar vein, privacy suggests an emotional component. As an affective experience, privacy is tied to the individual subject, and often associated with positive connotations. For instance, privacy is frequently linked to a space of comfort, often tied to the home, where one is shielded from the look of the other and free to be *oneself.* Yet both old and new collective feelings of anxiety also stick to the concept. Most notably, fears connected to technological developments have haunted the concept of privacy since its first legal formulations (Warren and Brandeis, 1890). Finally, as emotions and expectations tied to privacy are culturally and historically contingent, they are subject to change (Ariès and Duby, 1992; Weintraub and Kumar, 1997).

This chapter offers a reflection on how privacy can be theorized as a distinct form of sphere, namely an atmosphere (Böhme, 2017; Griffero, 2018; Bruun and Koerner, 2020). Drawing on perspectives from phenomenology and aesthetics, atmospheres are understood as having both a spatial and an emotional component and, as a concept, it speaks of how one *feels* in an environment (Böhme, 2017). By theorizing privacy as an atmosphere, the chapter provides a conceptual framework for exploring the embodied and felt experience of privacy in everyday lived spaces.

While spatial privacy is but one of multiple dimensions of privacy (Koops et al, 2017), and recent focus within the field of privacy studies has tended to centre on informational privacy and data protection, this chapter maintains the importance of understanding privacy as an embodied, spatially situated, and crucially, affective experience. By offering a concept which, borrowing from the French ambiance and urban studies scholar Jean-Paul Thibaud (2021), sharpens our perception to the nuances of experience and guides our attention to the feelings generated by the spaces we inhabit, this chapter aims to extend the discussion of privacy beyond the focus on legal rights and protection of personal data to explore how phenomenological and aesthetic theories on atmosphere provide new perspectives on privacy.

The chapter is organized as follows: first, I further unfold the notion of atmospheres of privacy and argue that it offers a conceptual language adept to expand our understanding of privacy today. In the second part of the chapter, I discuss two cases that bring forth the atmospheric qualities of privacy within the home in various illustrative ways. The first case is the artwork *The Neighbors* (2012) by American photographer Arne Svenson, which consists of a series of fleetingly beautiful, yet deeply voyeuristic images caught by the artist of his neighbours inside their dwellings in a modern glass building in Tribeca, NYC. The artist used a long telephoto lens previously employed for birdwatching to record his neighbours and their everyday behind the glass façade over the course of a year (*The Neighbors* (arnesvenson. com)). Despite the fact that the images were of a clear artistic nature and barely contained any recognizable subjects, they stirred great controversy in the US media at the time of their exhibition in 2013, not least because one of the families among Svenson's neighbours filed a lawsuit for invasion of privacy (Khatchadourian, 2013; Weeks, 2013). A decade later, current exhibitions still cause heated debate (Lubow, 2023).[1] My reading of the images and their aftermath foregrounds how a private atmosphere within the home is extended spatially through the screen of the built environment of floor to ceiling glass windows so characteristic of the 21st century to be surprisingly broken by the affordances of a 500 mm Nikon telephoto lens.

Following this I turn to the second case, and a discussion of how the artificial intelligence (AI)-enabled home surveillance assistant *Lighthouse* (2017–18) affords new forms of remote access to the home and its inhabitants, thereby providing a different example of the changing spatial and affective experience of privacy, this one linked to living in a smart home. Through a close reading of the marketing materials and website of the interactive home surveillance assistant *Lighthouse*, I question how the atmosphere of privacy within the home may change as other members of the household can access the space from afar at any time through an app on their smartphone. I argue that *Lighthouse* foregrounds how the atmosphere in the smart surveillance home is haunted by remote gazes, where the notion of the home as shelter is made vulnerable by the constant access to the home through connected technologies. This case underscores how individual privacy within the household is at stake in new ways, as connected technologies often are installed and maintained by one person on behalf of the entire household (Aagaard, 2023). Taken together, the cases tune into different nuances and tensions of the changing spatial and emotional experiences of privacy within contemporary domestic spaces. In closing, the chapter reflects on how works of art and technologies, each in their own way, may open up new insights and attune us to the presence of the atmospheres of our everyday life.

Atmospheres of privacy

Atmospheres are frequently spoken of as that which 'surround, envelop and influence us' (Thibaud, 2020).[2] They involve sensorial and affective qualities widespread in space and can be understood as a vague power resonating in our lived body (Griffero, 2018). Originally, the term comes from Greek, composed of ἀτμός, 'vapour', and σφαῖρα, 'sphere', and it is first associated with meteorology, where it refers to the gas envelope surrounding a planet (Francesetti and Griffero, 2019). Atmosphere has been used metaphorically for describing moods, feelings, and senses that somehow seem to be 'in the air', in-between the private and the shared, since the late 18th century (Böhme, 2017). From this follows that atmospheres are experienced as intimately connected to the environment, or milieu, of our bodily presence. As a concept, atmosphere first entered academic discourse with the German psychiatrist Hubertus Tellenbach's description of the specific smell of the nest, a certain 'air' that makes us feel at home (Böhme, 2021). This link to the home is important for the purposes of this chapter. The German phenomenologist Gernot Böhme, who has been particularly influential in developing the philosophical concept of atmosphere, argues that atmosphere is what *mediates* and relates between 'objective factors of the environment' and the 'aesthetic feelings' of subjects (Böhme, 2017: 1). Thus, following Böhme, the atmosphere of a certain environment is responsible for the way we feel about ourselves in that environment. Drawing on the idea of the home as a sheltered space, the notion of atmospheres of privacy may immediately resonate with many of us once we think of it. Yet atmospheres are notoriously hard to pinpoint and, as phenomena, they remain vague and elusive, dependent on both the subjects feeling them and the objects and spaces from which they emerge (Böhme, 2017; Søilen, 2020). Thus, they can be described as occupying a peculiar ontological status in-between subject and object, and in-between the intangible and the material, as they 'seem to fill the space with a certain tone of feeling like a haze' (Böhme, 1993: 114). What is more, atmospheres might be intense or barely noticeable, unintentional or instrumentally produced. Notably, Böhme argues that atmospheres can be identified from a double analytical perspective, that is, they can be both *perceived* and *produced*. In the latter case, the art of scenography illustrates the practice of careful staging through the use of lighting, colour, sound, the arrangement of space and objects as 'generators of atmosphere' to create specific desired associations and emotions in an audience (Böhme, 2017: 2, 31–32).

Returning to the home, the Italian phenomenologist Tonino Griffero argues that our desire for 'the right' domestic atmosphere is a search for an atmosphere 'as protective of privacy as it is capable of satisfying the socio-expressional needs of the inhabitants. Atmosphere and domosphere are thus inextricably linked' (Griffero, 2021: np). In this view, privacy is integral to the atmosphere of the home. Indeed, buildings and domestic spaces can be defined by their atmosphere and protective qualities, and the Swiss architect Peter Zumthor describes the specific atmosphere of a building as 'an unbelievable feeling of concentration when we suddenly become aware of being enclosed, of something enveloping us, keeping us together, holding us' (Zumthor, 2016). Thinking along the lines of Zumthor, the desired emotional qualities of dwelling spaces can be understood as a matter of safekeeping and holding, of ensuring a safe space of retreat. Obviously, the opposite qualities also exist; there are buildings that can be characterized by their cold and vast atmospheres, where one is made to feel vulnerable and exposed. Drawing on Böhme's double perspective introduced earlier, atmospheres of privacy may also be (or at least sought to be) actively produced, for example by architects through their work with the arrangement of space and the material structures of residential buildings, by interior designers, and in various ways by the inhabitants of a home. Danish anthropologist Mikkel Bille (2020: 3) has studied the care people take in orchestrating a 'homely' atmosphere through the use of lighting, which he refers to as an 'atmospheric technology', and a similar point can be made in terms of how people seek to orchestrate atmospheres of privacy in their homes through the use of curtains, dimming of the lights when darkness falls, or in other ways making arrangements to ensure the experience of the home as a shelter and controlling the access of others. This chapter contends that the concept of atmosphere provides a productive vocabulary for exploring the nuances of the embodied and affective experience of privacy in the spaces of our everyday lives, exactly because it allows us to tune into the felt qualities of spatial environments. Yet we should also keep in mind that the emergence of privacy as a legal concept at the end of the 19th century coincided with specific bourgeois ideas of homeliness and the private sphere as a space of identity formation, which has contributed to shaping notions of the home as a 'privacy space' which still strongly influence Western cultural imaginaries of the home as a sheltered space today (Koops, 2018).

In fact, the home as a shelter is an idealized and privileged space, and, for example, for women who experience domestic abuse the case is quite the reverse: comfort is replaced by terror and confinement, an important point that has been vital to feminist critique of privacy (Dobash and Dobash, 1979). Thus, it is more precise to describe the home as an ambivalent space (Søilen and Veel, forthcoming). Atmospheres of privacy may also be ambivalent, as well as ambiguous and fleeting. Spatial and emotional notions of domestic privacy are historically and culturally dependent, changing according to time and place. They are continually in transformation. My argument here is that by directing our attention to privacy as an embodied and felt phenomenon, the notion of atmosphere offers a conceptual lens attentive to the subtle nuances of how one feels in an environment, and thus to the various and changing experiences of the home as an intimate privacy space with porous boundaries in the early decades of the 21st century. In the following, I turn to two examples where privacy within the home is at stake in new ways to further explore how privacy can be understood as affective and spatial atmospheres sensed in our surroundings through the body (Böhme, 2017). The home is typically considered a space where one can refuse the access of others (Koops, 2018), and this makes it a prime site for exploring how the spatial and emotional aspects of privacy currently intersect in new ways.

The glass house

In 2012, the American photographer Arne Svenson (b 1952) started photographing his neighbours who lived across the street in The Zinc Building in Tribeca, NYC, a high-end condominium building which features large glass windows. Svenson used a 500 mm Nikon telephoto lens often used for birdwatching but pointed it towards the human habitat of people living behind the glass façades across his studio. This became *The Neighbors* (2012), an artwork which conveys a vulnerable atmosphere of privacy unfolding at the threshold of public space. The first part of the series was shot over the course of a year and is comprised of fleetingly beautiful images which are meticulously composed, leaving little doubt that these are the work of a patient photographer who has spent time and effort crafting his compositions, rather than merely taking quick snapshots. The series of images are framed by the structures of the windows of the building, which allows for symmetrical compositions. The harmonious and deuce colours of the photographs add to their almost painterly qualities, which are further suggested by a sense of thickness resulting from the layers of details and dust on the glass of the windows. The images evoke a sense of private and intimate domestic atmospheres, where the subjects depicted are unaware of being caught on camera while going about their daily lives, oblivious of the photographer's gaze. The photographs include scenes from the breakfast table, people doing household chores, a small dog looking out of the window, someone changing behind a transparent curtain. The way the structures of the windows frame the images explicates the fact that both the photographer and we, as spectators, are looking in from the outside, hence the composition highlights the private nature of the scenes depicted as well as the voyeurism and trespassing of the viewer's gaze.

American philosopher and cultural critic Susan Sontag argues in her seminal work *On Photography* (1977) that 'there is something predatory in the act of taking a picture. To photograph people is to violate them, by seeing them as they never see themselves, by having knowledge of them they can never have; it turns people into objects that can be symbolically possessed' (Sontag, 1977: 14). Indeed, *The Neighbors* may generate feelings of unease in the viewer, as the penetrating gaze from the outside in multiplies via the photographers' lens to the spectators own peering eyes. However, according to the artist, he took great care not to reveal any of the residents' identities.[3] In the images, we see people who are primarily shown from behind or from the side, or with their head left outside of the frame, such as in *Neighbors #01*, where the only thing we see is two pairs of legs underneath a kitchen table. In this way the framing of the images creates a productive tension between revelation and concealment. In general, if faces are shown, it is mostly as fragments. As a result, the images convey a fleeting and transient atmosphere of domestic everyday life in a contemporary urban glass structure, showing intimate moments in the lives of others which nevertheless remain unknown to us.

In the image *Neighbors #11*, we see a man from behind lying on a couch next to the window, caught in an intimate moment of sleep. His T-shirt has slid up, revealing an area of naked skin at his lower back. The composition resembles the trope of the reclining nude, and it is a private, slightly vulnerable scene. Simultaneously we also see a tall toy giraffe looking up from behind the man, adding a bit of surreal humour to the scene.

Another image, *Neighbors #14*, shows a woman sitting at her bed, in the confines of her bedroom, with her hair wrapped in a towel as after having taken a bath. She is concentrated on something she is holding in her hand, perhaps her mobile phone. The image includes a distant view of the right side of her face, and it is dark with only her figure and the bed lit up by her bedside lamp behind her, implying that the image is taken at night, when those inside glass wall apartments are particularly vulnerable to the gaze from the outside unless their curtains are closed. *The Neighbors* speaks of contemporary life in glass houses, where the boundaries of the home are blurred in new ways, allowing for extensive spatial openings into the interior. The work suggests that in these kinds of domestic spaces, the private atmospheres within the home are extended spatially through the screen of the built environment of floor to ceiling glass windows. In this way the work also speaks of the particular tension between vulnerability and exhibitionism in contemporary glass dwellings. Notably, while the view into the windows of neighbours is not a new phenomenon in the metropolis (think of Hitchcock's classic film *Rear Window* from 1954), what is hitherto unprecedented is the scale and the number of people who are living their lives behind glass façades. This architectural tendency, which took on from the 1990s onwards, is designed for a lifestyle with high degrees of transparency and can be situated as part of a larger surveillance culture (Steiner and Veel, 2011). As such, *The Neighbors* can be read as a comment on this trend of exhibiting the private space of the home, and in conjunction with the original exhibition at the Julie Saul Gallery in May 2013, the artist noted that 'For my subjects there is no question of privacy; they are performing behind a transparent scrim on a stage of their own creation with the curtain raised high' (Bacon, 2013).

However, Svenson's neighbours disagreed. In *Neighbors #06* and *Neighbors #12*, fragments of the faces of two children are visible, and for example in the latter image, the right side of the face of a girl is depicted, hanging upside down from the arms of a woman. These images of the children of the Foster family (then aged 2 and 4) which was included in the original exhibit at the Julie Saul Gallery led to a lawsuit against Svenson for the invasion of privacy. The plaintiffs found out about the images through their neighbourhood newspaper and were, according to the charges put against Svenson, 'greatly frightened and angered by defendant's utter disregard for their privacy and the privacy of their children'.[4] Moreover, they now feared that 'they must keep their shades drawn at all hours of the day in order to avoid telephoto photography'. Following this, the reception of the work was characterized by immense media attention, which mainly focused on the invasive and controversial nature of the photographs. Arne Svenson won the first court case in 2013, which ruled that his right to artistic expression was protected under the First amendment, and again the appeal in 2015.

Yet the reactions to *The Neighbors* clearly indicate that despite voluntarily living in a glass house with all the progressive and even exhibitionist connotations this lifestyle might imply, the inhabitants as well as the public had expectations of privacy more in tune with lives behind solid walls. This sentiment was also expressed in relation to the work's exhibition a decade later in the spring of 2023, as already noted in the introduction to this chapter. Moreover, the plaintiff's statement that because of the artwork they now felt that 'they must keep their shades drawn at all hours of the day in order to avoid telephoto photography' reveals both a behavioural modification resulting from being under observation, and the desire to reinstate the emotional and spatial experience of the home as a sheltered space. These reactions attest to the perceived violence in the breaking of the protection, or illusion, of the spatial and felt privacy of the home, even in the case of voluntary transparent lives behind large glass windows. Correspondingly, an atmosphere of privacy comes forth which depends on social norms to serve as a protective shield against the fact that Svenson's neighbours lived in a floor to ceiling glass house, creating an illusion of privacy suddenly broken by the affordances of a 500 mm Nikon telephoto lens. In this way, the atmosphere of privacy calls attention to the underlying dynamics of exposure and shelter, that is, to the liminality of inside and outside implied in the transaction of the social. And finally, by performing the double movement of both evoking and breaking an atmosphere of privacy, *The Neighbors* effectively conveys the tensions at the threshold of the public and the private in contemporary glass houses.

Lighthouse

I now turn to a different type of habitation which is also characteristic of the 21st century, namely the smart home. How are atmospheres of privacy at stake in this kind of domestic setting? To get a sense of the changing spatial and affective experience of privacy in the smart home, the interactive surveillance assistant *Lighthouse* is an illustrative example. This AI-enabled interactive home surveillance system was available on the US market from spring 2017 to December 2018, and was a pioneer in introducing 3D sensors, artificial intelligence, object recognition, and facial recognition technologies into the home.[5] The system featured a smartphone app which alerted users according to their areas of interest, such as 'person or pet detection, facial recognition, children and waving' (Lighthouse AI, Inc, 2018). *Lighthouse* also had a two-way audio with microphone and speaker, and a security siren.[6] Daily recaps of all activity were available in short time-lapse videos, and in the press release launching the technology on the market, users were promised an interactive assistant which 'provides insight to three core things: what has happened, what is happening and what is happening that shouldn't be happening' (Lighthouse AI, Inc, 2017). Bearing in mind that the home may be considered a key space of withdrawal from the gaze of others, how is an atmosphere of privacy within the home affected by the possibility that other members of the household can access the space from afar at any time through an app on their smartphone?

The website and marketing materials of *Lighthouse* provide important insights to this question. First and foremost, the overall sensation evoked by the narrative on the website and in the press release launching *Lighthouse* on the market is that of an omnipresent gaze. Put shortly, the concept of *Lighthouse* centred on 'peace of mind', which is directly linked to total awareness. In an endorsement of *Lighthouse*, one of the then newly established company's major investors highlights how '[once] consumers experience the peace of mind and convenience of having a comprehensive view into what's going on at home, they won't know how they lived without it' (Lighthouse AI, Inc, 2017).

When taking a closer look at the website and narratives describing *Lighthouse*, there is also a promise of entertainment: 'color-coded halos make it easy to follow and sort out activity around adults, children and pets. And they're just so cool.' The tone of this section of the website is light, fun, and alluding to the trivialities of the everyday. The visual design of the website is dominated by light pastel colours of green, yellow, blue, and pink, and *Lighthouse* presents itself as a harmonic place, a utopia of sorts. Yet a strong undercurrent of control is present. What emanates from the text and visual material of the website and press release is the sense that the user's gaze is remote, but ever-present within the home. It is a gaze that desires to see and to know immediately, and the website furthermore evokes strong sentiments of paranoia. For instance, the *search* feature encourages users to search the video feed by voice, simultaneously reassuring them that 'if you're the quiet type, you can instead type a brief search – just like you're Googling your home'. Privacy for other members in the household must yield for the need to know urgent matters such as:

What did the kids do while I was out yesterday?
Has the cat done anything interesting since I left?
Who did you see at the front door on Tuesday between 8 and 10 am?
Did you see Chris with the dog at the front door last week while I was away? (Lighthouse AI, Inc., 2018)

Furthermore, the *Activity* section promised full control at a glance:

What's important, at a glance
Whether it's knowing when family members come and go, or what the dog's up to while you're away, get a quick rundown with the built-in

Events feed. And with rich notifications, you don't even have to open the app to know what's up.

The tone of language and functionalities promised in this section stand in stark contrast to the lightness and entertainment described earlier. The tone and affordances described here seek to normalize behaviours that take control and surveillance within the home to the next level, at the expense of privacy. Under the header 'Children, pets and facial recognition', it is noted that 'while facial recognition should not be used solely for security, it can be used to keep track of both familiar and unfamiliar faces, such as child too young for a cell phone or a teenager's new friend' (Lighthouse AI Inc, 2018). The affects emanating from the text are the pleasures of control and desires for total knowledge, and again a persistent sense of paranoia is haunting the technology. What stands out as the key affordance of *Lighthouse* is the total awareness of everything that goes on in one's home. In other words, it is not just a matter of being notified of the potential trespassing of strangers, rather the promotional materials openly endorse the need for oversight over the actions and comings and goings of the other members of the household. As such, the protective veil of the home is withdrawn, but as opposed to the case of the glass house, this time the transformation of the experience of the home is brought about by the remote gaze of other inhabitants *within* the household, such as a parent or a partner.

Returning to the question of how connected surveillance technologies may transform the spatial and affective experiences of privacy within the home, my argument here is that the case of *Lighthouse* suggests an atmosphere haunted by remote gazes, potentially leading to chilling effects, broadly understood as how the fear or possibility of being watched affects one's behaviour (Stevens et al, 2023). Furthermore, who is the 'you' addressed in these materials? Questions come to mind regarding whom this technology serves and what happens to individual privacy within the household. Importantly, moreover, pressing issues arise with regard to how access to the application is distributed among the members of the household. Recent studies indicate that connected technologies often are installed and maintained by one person on behalf of the entire household, and not seldom this person is male (Strengers et al, 2019; Aagaard, 2023). Furthermore, reports point to how smart home surveillance systems can be used to dissolve peace of mind altogether: smart home technology is increasingly involved in cases of gender-related domestic abuse, employed to intimidate, watch, listen in on, and control current and former partners (Lopez-Neira et al, 2019). Yet it is also worth asking how these technologies open up the home for more mundane practices of control and surveillance which has consequences for the felt experience of privacy within domestic space. Surveillance studies scholar David Lyon argues for the need for paying attention to how participation and the active role played by users in engaging with surveillance have become defining for surveillance today (Lyon, 2018). No longer primarily tied to the state or the organization, 'surveillance is also initiated and engaged by those who have become familiar with and even inured to surveillance' (Lyon, 2018: 2). Indeed, this is most clearly expressed in the proliferation of domestic surveillance systems and appliances with surveillance capabilities, such as the *Ring* doorbell, *Google Nest*, Amazon's *Alexa*, and the like. Connected technologies with surveillance capabilities, including the increasingly commonplace 'smart devices' such as robotic vacuum cleaners, smart thermostats, lights, and so on, contribute to making the home 'leaky'; meaning that the home is now increasingly pervaded by connected devices and sensors that collect, transmit, receive, and share data (Wellendorf et al, 2022). The home leaks beyond its traditional architectural and spatial boundaries and can be accessed remotely through, for instance, the smartphone. Crucially, the leaky and porous spatiality of the home is intimately linked to our sensuous and affective experience of privacy within the home (Søilen and Veel, forthcoming).

In regards to *Lighthouse*, it becomes clear that the boundaries of the home become porous in new ways as the remote gaze through the smartphone can access it at all times. This has consequences for the shielding and protective qualities of the home as well as dominant notions of domestic privacy, as understood through a spatial discourse of solid forms, withdrawal, and protection. A close reading of the website and press release of *Lighthouse* finds that the atmosphere in the smart surveillance home can be described as paranoid and haunted by remote gazes, and that domestic privacy as connected to a sense of withdrawal is yielding its way for desires of total transparency and the felt omnipresent gaze of other members of the household.

Conclusion

In this chapter, I have proposed the concept of 'atmospheres of privacy' as a theoretical framework to better understand the changing spatial and affective experiences of privacy in everyday lived spaces. The notion of atmosphere directs our attention to privacy as a felt phenomenon and contributes with a conceptual lens as to how one *feels* in an environment – such as the home – and thus to the transformation of the experience of the home as a privacy space in the 21st century. The juxtaposition of the cases of the glass house and *Lighthouse* offers important insights into how the spatial boundaries of the home are dissolving in new ways, and how thinking about privacy as an atmosphere sharpens our perception to the nuances of the feelings generated by the spaces we inhabit. Both cases, in various ways, showed a renegotiation of the boundaries of privacy: in the glass house, the trend of living with large openings into the interior puts new pressures on privacy as a social expectation. In *Lighthouse*, privacy within the home is under pressure from other members of the household as the home can be accessed from anywhere at any time through an app on their smartphone. In addition, both cases foreground how privacy as a felt experience is affected by a contemporary participatory surveillance culture. Finally, the chapter has suggested that atmospheres of privacy can be investigated through artworks and the narratives of the marketing materials of smart home surveillance technologies. My argument here is that artworks can make atmospheres available for perceptual experience because they engage us through our bodily sensations. In this way art offers a realm where we may become more attentive to embodied and affective experiences, and art is particularly well suited to articulate the invisible and to defamiliarize the everyday. Moreover, in my view, contemporary art has a unique ability to articulate and identify the collective emotions and atmospheres of our time. In a related manner, as cultural artefacts, technologies and their affordances, as well as the narratives they are wrapped in, simultaneously attest to and direct the cultural imaginaries and fantasies of our time. Artworks and technologies, each in their own way, may speak of emergent atmospheres of privacy.

Notes

[1] In relation to a spring 2023 exhibition in the US at the James Danziger Gallery in Santa Monica, CA, *The New York Times* featured an article on Svenson's work which generated 152 heated comments for or against the work before the 'comments section' was closed. www.nytimes.com/2023/03/03/arts/design/voyeurism-arne-svenson-photographer-danziger.html#commentsContainer (accessed 26 October 2023).

[2] The first part of this section draws on and expands materials from my PhD thesis (Søilen, 2021).

[3] Arne Svenson, artist statement. www.arnesvenson.com (accessed 23 October 2023).

[4] The full complaint can be read here: https://iapps.courts.state.ny.us/fbem/DocumentDisplayServlet?documentId=xfy1AdVZ3RB8DWxeAVDt0g==&system=prod

[5] *Lighthouse* case draws on materials from chapter 3 of my PhD thesis (Søilen, 2021). For an analysis of the link between *Lighthouse* and the military-industrial complex, see Søilen (2022); and for the relationship between smart technologies such as *Lighthouse* and the technological uncanny, see Søilen and Maurer (2023).

[6] All references to the content from the company's website are based on the author's web archive downloaded 18 December 2018.

References

Aagaard, L. K. (2023). When smart technologies enter household practices: the gendered implications of digital housekeeping. *Housing, Theory and Society*, 40(1): 60–77.

Ariès, P. and Duby, G (eds) (1992–1998). *A History of Private Life* (5 vols). Cambridge, MA: Harvard University Press.

Bacon, J. (2013). New Yorkers furious over photos taken through windows. *USA Today*, May 17, 2013. Available at: https://eu.usatoday.com/story/news/nation/2013/05/17/nyers-furious-over-photos-taken-through-wind ows/2193353/ (accessed 23 August 2024).

Barthes, R. (2000) [1980]. *Camera Lucida: Reflections of Photography*. Translated by R. Howard. London: Vintage Books.

Bille, M. (2020). *Homely Atmospheres and Lighting Technologies in Denmark: Living with Light*. London and New York: Routledge.

Böhme, G. (1993). Atmosphere as the fundamental concept of a new aesthetics. *Thesis Eleven*, 36: 113–126.

Böhme, G. (2017). *The Aesthetics of Atmospheres*. London and New York: Routledge.

Böhme, G. (2021). Atmospheres: New Conditions for Design. In K. K. Loenhart (ed) *Breathe! Investigations Into Our Environmentally Entangled Future*, pp 175–184. Basel: Birkhäuser.

Bruun, M. B. and Koerner, N. P. (2020). Visualizing privacy: atmosphere and medium. *Hypotheses*, 10 May [blog entry]. Available at: https://priv acy.hypotheses.org/1133 (accessed 7 February 2023).

Dobash, R. E. and Dobash, R. (1979). *Violence Against Wives: A Case Against the Patriarchy*. New York, NY: Free Press.

Duby, G. (1992). Foreword. In P. Veyne (ed) *A History of Private Life 1: From Pagan Rome to Byzantium*, pp vii–ix. Cambridge, MA; London: Harvard University Press.

Francesetti, G. and Griffero, T. (eds) (2019). *Psychopathology and Atmospheres: Neither Inside nor Outside*. Cambridge: Cambridge Scholars Publishing.

Griffero, T. (2018). Introduction. In T. Griffero and G. Moretti (eds) *Atmosphere/Atmospheres: Testing a New Paradigm*, pp 11–14. Milan: Mimesis International.

Griffero, T. (2021). The atmospheric 'skin' of the city. *Ambiances*. DOI: 10.4000/ambiances.399

Habermas, J. (1989). *The Structural Transformation of the Public Sphere: An Inquiry into a Category of Bourgeois Society*. Cambridge: Polity Press.

Khatchadourian, R. (2013). Stakeout. *The New Yorker*, 20 May 2013. Available at: www.newyorker.com/magazine/2013/05/27/stakeout (accessed 7 February 2023).

Koops, B. (2018). Privacy spaces. *West Virginia Law Review*, 121(2): 611–666.

Koops, B., Newell, B. C., Timan, T., Škorvánek, I., Chokrevski, T., and Galič, M. (2017). A typology of privacy. *University of Pennsylvania Journal of International Law*, 38(2): 483–575.

Lighthouse AI, Inc (2017). Press release. Web archive captured by author 18 December 2018.

Lighthouse AI, Inc (2018). https://web.archive.org/web/20180331035423/https://www.light.house/. Web archive captured by author 18 December 2018.

Liu, C. (2011). The wall, the window and the alcove: visualizing privacy. *Surveillance & Society*, 9(1/2): 203–214.

Lopez-Neira, I., Patel, T., Parkin, S., Danezis, G., and Tanczer, L. (2019). 'Internet of things': how abuse is getting smarter. *Safe – The Domestic Abuse Quarterly*, 63: 22–26.

Lubow, K. (2023). Were these photographs voyeurism, or art? *The New York Times*, 3 March 2023. Available at: www.nytimes.com/2023/03/03/arts/design/voyeurism-arne-svenson-photographer-danziger.html (accessed 1 August 2023).

Lyon, D. (2018). *The Culture of Surveillance: Watching As a Way of Life*. Cambridge: Polity.

Søilen, K. L. G. (2020). Safe is a wonderful feeling: atmospheres of surveillance in contemporary art'. *Surveillance & Society*, 18(2): 170–184.

Søilen, K. L. G. (2021). *Atmospheres of Surveillance*. PhD thesis, University of Copenhagen. Available at: https://research.ku.dk/search/result/?pure=en%2Fpublications%2Fatmospheres-of-surveillance(f189c148-cb5d-43a5-ac75-597d968d1dcf).html

Søilen, K. L. G. (2022). The haunting of the automated gaze. *MAST*, 3(1): 15–40.

Søilen, K. L. G. and Maurer, K. (2023). Ferngesteuertes Wohnen: Die Totalüberwachung des Alltags im Smart Home. In A. Hordych and J. Ungelenk (eds) *Trouble Every Day: Zum Schrecken des Alltäglichen*, pp 55–78. Paderborn: Fink Verlag.

Søilen, K.L.G. and Veel, K. 2024 (forthcoming). The leaky home: conceptualizing the remote control of smart technologies in the domestic sphere. *Theory, Culture & Society*.

Sontag, S. (1977). *On Photography*. London: Penguin Books Ltd.

Steiner, H. and Veel, K. (2011). Living behind glass facades: surveillance culture and new architecture. *Surveillance & Society*, 9(1/2): 215–232.

Stevens, A., Fussey, P., Murray, D., Hove, K., and Saki, O. (2023). 'I started seeing shadows everywhere': the diverse chilling effects of surveillance in Zimbabwe. *Big Data & Society*, 10(1): 1–14.

Strengers, Y., Kennedy, J., Arcari, P., Nicholls, L., and Gregg, M. (2019). Protection, productivity and pleasure in the smart home: emerging expectations and gendered insights from Australian early adopters. *Proceedings of the 2019 CHI Conference on Human Factors in Computing Systems*.

Thibaud, J. (2020). A brief archeology of the notion of ambiance. *Unlikely – Journal for Creative Arts*, 6. Available at: https://unlikely.net.au/issue-06/notion-of-ambiance

Thibaud, J. (2021). The Atmospherization of Everyday Experience. In K. K. Loenhart (ed) *Breathe! Investigations Into Our Environmentally Entangled Future*, pp 163–174. Basel: Birkhäuser.

Warren, S. D. and Brandeis, L. D. (1890). The right to privacy. *Harvard Law Review*, 4(5). DOI: 10.2307/1321160

Weeks, J. (2013). The art of peeping: photography at the limits of privacy. *The Guardian*, 19 August. Available at: www.theguardian.com/artanddes ign/photography-blog/2013/aug/19/art-peeping-photography-privacy-arne-svenson (accessed 7 February 2023).

Weintraub, J. and Kumar, K. (eds) (1997). *Public and Private in Thought and Practice: Perspectives on a Grand Dichotomy*. Chicago, IL: University of Chicago Press.

Wellendorf, K., Søilen, K. L. G., and Veel, K. (2022) Calm surveillance in the leaky home: living with a robot vacuum cleaner. *The Journal of Media Art Study and Theory*, 3(1): 41–62.

Zumthor, P. (2016). *Thinking Architecture*. Basel: Birkhäuser.

6

Lost in Digitalization: The Blurring Boundaries of Public Values and Private Interests

Bjarki Valtysson and Rikke Frank Jørgensen

Introduction

For the past 25 years, the Danish state has formulated digitalization policies and implemented digital services and infrastructures in different layers of society. As digitalization has penetrated society, new relations and forms of cooperation have emerged between the private and the public sector to an extent where scholars speak of a 'paradigm shift' in the provision of public services (Dencik and Kaun, 2020; Andreasen et al, 2021). Private companies are now instrumental in processes of datafication and obtain new powers in relation to services that previously were largely controlled by the state. In Denmark, examples of such public/private cooperation include platforms and devices used in public schools, smart city projects, and predictive policing. The close integration between commercial technology companies, including tech giants, and the state have raised several privacy-related issues. The Danish Data Protection Agency (DPA) has, for instance, ordered public schools in Helsingør municipality to stop using Google Chromebook with its installed Google Workspace due to privacy concerns in relation to student data. Drawing on this case, as well as other examples related to public schools in Denmark, this chapter will discuss the growing reliance on technology companies to provide the underlying infrastructure and services for public schools. We examine the blurring boundaries between public values and private interests as an example of market colonization into a core welfare service and illustrate its implications for students' privacy.

To do this, we apply recent literature on *platforms* and *infrastructures* and how these have been instrumental in shaping the current texture of the *digital welfare state.* We then turn to older and more recent writings of Habermas' conceptualization of system and lifeworld, as this allows us to further account for systemic shifts between the state and the market, and how these are manifested in relation to public schools in Denmark.

The framework

Empirically and methodologically, we use public schools as a case which provides a real-life, contemporary bounded system that allows for extensive data collection (Cresswell and Poth, 2018). Main sources of information are documents, reports, and interviews (Bryman, 2016; Gaskell, 2000) which were conducted with experts, public school teachers, and parents that interact and operate technologies designed for the public school system.

In terms of documents and reports, the public digitalization strategies provide a valuable insight into the dominant rationale of major actors. The six strategies[1] are made commonly in cooperation between the government, municipalities, and regions, and thereby illustrate and amplify how the public sector perceives the importance and function of digitalization, including how these processes are supposed to intervene with the lives of Danish citizens. In its own expression, the Agency for Digital Government refers to Denmark as having an 'international pole position within the digitalization of the public sector' (Agency for Digital Government, n.d.) and these strategies exemplify the sector's main aims and ambitions. The overarching framework put forward in the strategies will serve as an important basis to further inspect two concrete cases in the Danish public school system: The Helsingør/Google case, and the implementation of the communication platform Aula.

We will use document analysis (Bowen, 2009) to account for the main rationale detected in the digitalization strategies, as well as in the documents and decisions provided by the DPA regarding Helsingør municipality's use of Google Chromebooks in public schools. To support the document analysis, we also draw on data that we collected in relation to the platform Aula,[2] which we use as a case that further demonstrates the platformization of the public education system. Excerpts from these data will be used to support the document analysis and provide different perspectives on how experts, teachers, and parents perceive the blurring boundaries between public values and private interests.

Platformized system

Since the mid-1990s, the Danish government has deployed technology to facilitate public administration and public services across a broad range of areas. Alongside the general datafication of society, this digitalization of the public sector has increasingly been supplemented with artificial intelligence in the form of big data analytics, automated decisions, and predictive algorithms. The growing reliance on automated systems is often motivated by goals of efficiency and public savings as well as positive expectations related to welfare services, such as faster and more consistent case-handling. However, as illustrated by the growing body of (critical) literature on the digital welfare state, the increased datafication and digitalization of welfare provisions and services carry implications for citizens' rights and participation in society (Eubanks, 2018; Schou and Hjelholt, 2018; Alston, 2019; Dencik and Kahn, 2020; Andreassen et al, 2021; Jørgensen, 2021; Collington, 2022; Pink et al, 2022; Reutter, 2022). Areas of concern include new means of monitoring, targeting, predicting, and surveilling citizens, not least vulnerable groups; new forms of bias and discrimination in automated systems; new structures of inequality in access to public services; exclusion of the 'digitally challenged' citizens, and so on. These concerns have also been aimed specifically at the education sector as critical studies of digital data and education (Selwyn, 2015; Cone, 2023) ask questions concerning data inequalities, 'dataveillance', reductionism in data-based representation, and managerialist modes of organization and control, within education and platform environments.

Also, specific tensions pertain to the still closer cooperation between private actors guided by market values and public actors guided by public interest (Alston, 2019; Dencik and Kaun, 2020; Andreassen et al, 2021; Collington, 2022; Dencik, 2022). While privatization of specific public services such as health and education has been ongoing in Denmark (and elsewhere) since the 1970s, the intense *datafication* and *platformization* of the public sector implies a new kind of public-private partnership. Datafication refers to platforms' ability to render into data various aspects of the world that were not quantified before (Mayer-Schonberger and Cukier, 2013). Platformization is meant to describe the wider power of platforms as it does not only penetrate infrastructures, economic processes, and governmental frameworks, but reorganizes cultural practices and imaginations (Poell et al, 2019). Platforms are technocultural constructs and socio-economic structures (van Dijck, 2013), and as such, they are decisive in shaping markets, infrastructures, and governance (Poell et al, 2022). This is particularly the case with infrastructural and sectoral platforms (van Dijck et al, 2018) provided by major tech giants such as Alphabet/Google, Meta, Amazon, and the like. Platforms of this sort do not stand alone but are parts of complex ecosystems where data are channelled through different services, and as in the case of Google, guided by the same terms and privacy policy. So, when Helsingør used Google Chromebooks and Google Workspace in public schools, this platform automatically became a part of an ecosystem which also contains other Google platforms and services, such as YouTube, its advertising service program, search engine, pay services, and app store.

These platform ecosystems cement a further integration and validation of the ever-increasing power of major platform providers and how they aggressively overtake critical elements of society, such as communicative infrastructures. Plantin et al (2018) thus refer to platformized infrastructures and infrastructuralized platforms, and in similar vein, Helmond (2015) writes about the platformization of the Web as 'the rise of the platform as the dominant infrastructural and economic model of the social web and the consequences of the expansion of social media platforms into other spaces online' (2015: 5). These 'other spaces' are certainly not limited to commercial spaces, as van Dijck et al formulate it: 'As it stands now, there is no real public "space" inside the corporately run ecosystem' (2018: 16). They shape infrastructures and markets (Srnicek, 2017; Poell et al, 2022), and in wider contexts, they set the terms to situational understanding of values, challenge notions of social responsibility, and make the public sector dependent on specific forms for platform capitalism. Dencik perceives this datafication as *responsibilitization* and *rentierism*, which has the following repercussions: 'When public sector organisations integrate tools and platforms from providers within this economy to administer the welfare state, they implement not only the systems themselves, but also a regime that propels the further datafication of social life' (2022: 159). This has resulted in a digital welfare state that develops and utilizes technical systems and infrastructures that are implemented in close partnerships between public authorities and private companies, or as Habermas would have it, between the *systemic forces* of the state and the market.

The system and the lifeworld are key notions in the manifold modifications which Habermas has made throughout the years on his original thesis on the public sphere. According to him, the system is contained by the state and the market and driven by non-social instrumental actions and social strategic actions. As opposed to this, Habermas defines the lifeworld as being motivated and defined by communicative action driven by cognitive, aesthetic-expressive, and ethical rationalities (Habermas, 1987). The system and the lifeworld influence each other via the mediating space of public spheres, which, according to Splichal (2010: 29), constitutes 'the arena in which civil society informs itself and exchanges ideas and opinions with other social actors "representing" the two remaining realms: those of the state and the economy'. According to Habermas, the strategic rationale of the system is driven by a goal-rational instrumental logic that aims to maximize profits and increase the effectiveness and power of bureaucratic administration. Furthermore, Habermas detects structural violence from the system towards the lifeworld which leads to colonization: 'In the end, systemic mechanisms suppress forms of social integration even in those areas where a consensus-dependent coordination of action cannot be replaced, that is, where the symbolic reproduction of the lifeworld is at stake. In these areas, the *mediatization* of the lifeworld assumes the form of a *colonization*' (Habermas, 1987: 196; italics in original).

Importantly, Habermas' societal modelling is dynamic, as processes of colonization can be met with acts of emancipation. The strength of Habermas' approach in our current context is its focus on the different interests that drive the different rationale of the *state*, the *market*, and the *lifeworld*. This is what McGuigan (2004) refers to as the discursive formations of *stating*, *marketizing*, and *communicating*. He underlines that they have several variants and that they are not internally unified. However, even if they are porous and there exist various interactions between them, they do all the same stand out as discourses which characterize signification and meaning in specific contexts. As Hall (1997), in drawing on Foucault claims, discourses define and produce the object of our knowledge and govern and constitute topics and the way we meaningfully can talk about and reason about given topics. According to McGuigan, *marketizing* is, for instance, a powerful discursive formation which applies market principles to everything, including education and public schools.

Our focus in this chapter is both on the strategic colonization of the system towards the lifeworld, as well as how datafication and platformization have escalated a process in which the logics of the market play an increasingly central role in shaping a core welfare service traditionally carried out by the state.

This regime of major platforms, driven by datafication, platformization, and marketization, colonizes the lifeworld in which the public schools reside, a process which Habermas foresaw when he maintained that there is 'considerable evidence attesting to the ambivalent nature of the democratic potential of a public sphere whose infrastructure is marked by the growing selective constraints imposed by electronic mass communication' (1992: 456–457). In a recent article, Habermas addresses the implication of digitization more directly and specifically refers to the 'platform character of the new media' which is 'taking place in the shadow of a commercial exploitation of the currently unregulated internet communication' (2022: 146). He directly addresses the power of the tech giants in commercializing the use of digital networks and the global range of the neoliberal economic programme:

> The globally expanded zone of free flows of communication, originally made possible by the invention of the technical structure of the 'net', presented itself from the outset as the mirror image of an ideal market. This market did not even need to be deregulated. In the meantime, however, this suggestive image is being disrupted by the algorithmic control of communication flows that is feeding the concentration of market power of the large internet corporations. The skimming and digital processing of customers' personal data, which are more or less

inconspicuously exchanged for the information provided free of charge by search engines, news portals and other services, explains why the EU Competition Commissioner would like to regulate the market. (Habermas, 2022: 167)

As our discussion of recent literature on the digital welfare state indicates, Habermas is not alone in sharing observations that indicate a strategic colonization from platform providers towards the public sector. Yeung (2018) has described this new welfare regime as new public analytics, characterized by increased delegation to – and reliance on – complex algorithmic systems. The algorithmic systems are based on generative rules and represent a more invisible form of power with implications for citizens' agency and their ability to claim rights such as privacy (Jørgensen, 2021). Indeed, when addressing global tech companies and their role in the digital economy, Busemeyer et al (2022: 16) maintain that 'the digital revolution could indeed lead to a significant qualitative change in the relationship between state and business'. When substantial parts of the digital welfare state rely on algorithmic systems and the market that develops them, we need to rethink the relationship between the state and the market, including the means of holding private power accountable when their practices impact on rights such as privacy.

As we already addressed, there are also larger questions to be asked concerning the monopoly power of large platform conglomerates and how data generated via the educational services of a giant like Google are personalized and commodified as a part of its platform ecosystem. Habermas turns to regulation as a possible answer to some of these questions. Platform theorists such as van Dijck et al (2018) are, however, less optimistic as they maintain that platforms gain from their deliberate hybrid status and thereby have succeeded in bypassing regulation and in escaping professional norms in specific sectors, such as education.

As demonstrated in our analysis, areas such as public schooling, which in Denmark lies within the realms of the state and municipalities (depending on levels of education), have clearly been affected by this market power of large internet corporations. We will dive further into the cases of Google and Helsingør, and Aula, but can for now also disclose the fact that all data that are stored through the Aula app are hosted by Amazon (Jørgensen et al, 2023). Habermas refers to regulation as a central instrument to counteract such processes of colonization, and as our analysis displays, there certainly are elements of emancipation when regulation is applied. Helsingør municipality's use of Google Workspace provides us with a case, to further test how regulation works in practice, and whether it can function as a tool of emancipation from the Habermasian perspective. The question remains whether these are merely adjustments to counteract platform power, or whether they represent real shifts capable of sustaining the lifeworld dimension of public schools untainted by marketization.

Digitalization strategies

The digitalization of the public sector in Denmark is anchored in the strategic cooperation of the state, regions, and municipalities, that has been ongoing for the past 25 years. In this chapter, we focus on public schools, but as van Dijck et al (2018) remark, sectoral platforms certainly form the interactions between public authorities and market actors in other fields, such as transportation, health, and welfare. We therefore start our analysis by accounting for the dominant discourses and rationale found in the six digitalization strategies.

The first strategy sets the stage and includes many of the keywords that pertain in the strategies to follow:

> The ambition is to exploit the potentials of a digital society, across state, regions and municipalities, to furnish the public sector more flexible, more efficient and with larger quality for citizens. The core of digital administration is improved and more effective solutions to public administration is implemented with the use of information technologies. (Towards Digital Management, 2002: 4)

From the very start, focus is on *cooperation*, *efficiency*, and *quality*. The strategy iterates that digital administration should prepare citizens and businesses for the network society, the public sector should work and communicate digitally, the public sector's services should be centred on citizens and businesses, and public service tasks should be performed where they are most relevant. Concerning the last point, the strategy emphasizes that digital administration should be decentralized, which means that the strategies set the framework, but the individual institutions are responsible for their own processes of digitalization. This strategy was published in 2002 and, evidently, is referring to a very different communicative environment from the current one. The first strategy refers to 'the network society', and frames digitalization as being equally effective for businesses and citizens.

With the subsequent strategies, it becomes clear that the first strategy was indeed setting an agenda. While the following strategies respond to an ever-evolving communicative environment towards platformization, focus is still on terms like *modernization*, *coherence*, *effectiveness*, better *service*, more *quality*: 'Digitization should contribute to the creation of an effective and coherent public sector with high quality for services, where citizens and businesses are at the centre' (*Strategy for Digital Management 2004–2006* (2004): 4). The third strategy continues this process by introducing three main areas of intervention: better digital *service*, increased *efficiency*, and stronger *cooperation* (*Towards Better Digital Service, Increased Streamlining and Stronger Co-Operation 2007–2010* (2007)). It also brings on new concerns, such as safe and secure processing of data in the public sector, and in terms of stronger cooperation it is specifically stated that, in many cases, this includes private actors.

In the fourth strategy (*The Digital Path to Future Welfare 2011–2015* (2011)), Denmark's leading position within digitalization is repeatedly stated and the term *new digital welfare* is introduced and mentioned in relation to school children, patients, the elderly, the unemployed, and students. The strategy focuses on the use of IT technologies in public schools and applies concepts such as platforms and infrastructure. It also refers to better services and the *sharing of solutions* between the public and private sectors: 'When the solutions (and thereby also the investments) can be shared between the public and the private sector, the citizens will simultaneously get a more coherent user-experience, which stimulates an increase in the application of digital channels' (The Digital Path to Future Welfare 2011–2015 (2011): 36), using NemId (citizen identification) and digital post, as examples.

While the strategies develop their conceptual framework, moving for instance from the network society towards platforms and infrastructures, they also entail a discursive stability around notions of *effectiveness*, *cooperation*, *coherence*, *quality*, and now *digital welfare*. This stability pertains in the two most recent strategies *A stronger and more secure digital society (2016–2020)* and *Digitalization that lifts society (2022–2025)*. Interestingly, while the first strategy focused (also in its title) on effective administration, digitalization now permeates the whole of society. In the strategy for 2016–2020, digitalization is seen as a central part of withholding and developing the welfare society and the cooperation between the public and private sectors is yet again underscored:

> The continued development and testing of digital welfare-solutions and new technology for the public sector will often happen in cooperation with the private business community. This way, the competences and experiences of businesses can be utilised in the public development of services. When digital welfare-solutions will be widespread on a bigger scale in Denmark, these will simultaneously create new business opportunities for corporations and provide them with experiences that can open up for export on the global market. (A Stronger and Safer Digital Society 2016–2020 (2016): 29).

In terms of education, this strategy is focused on the implementation of a common platform to public schools (Aula), and digital technology's potentials to target teaching to each student's individual needs. In terms of morphing the public and the private, the strategy sees great potential in the use of public data, to support the economic growth of the private sector: 'The public sector has great amounts of data, which corporations can exploit to optimize their businesses, and which can create the basis of new business opportunities and innovation. The public sector should therefore increasingly display public data and support the corporations' use of it' (2016: 34). The strategy also mentions the public sector's use of cloud computing as a means to reduce costs, to which we will return later.

The tighter relations between public and private are prominent in the latest strategy from 2022. In line with the previous documents, the strategy articulates new technology in terms of effectiveness. The difference is, however, that now automation, artificial intelligence, and robot technologies are included as means to enhance effectiveness. Also, as a new theme the strategy is preoccupied with climate concerns. In terms of public–private cooperation, it highlights the potentials of data in creating innovative solutions to the challenges of the future and, finally, the strategy stipulates the necessity of clarity regarding legal frameworks and the need for regulation to mirror the digital reality.

What can be learned from tracing the discursive path constituted over more than 20 years by the six digitalization strategies is discursive stability in terms of key concepts and rationale and in the strategic need of increased cooperation between the public and private sectors. In the strategies, the needs of citizens and businesses coincide and so do public values and private interests, all in the name of increased growth, efficiency, and cooperation. Seen with a Habermasian lens, there is no clear distinction between the interest and rationales of public authorities and those of the market. However, the last two strategies put renewed focus on legal frameworks and regulation, which is also a dominant theme in the Helinsgør case. As we will return to later, it is precisely regulation that disrupts the seemingly frictionless cooperation between public authorities and private interest.

The Helsingør case and Aula

In 2019, a Danish citizen in Helsingør municipality complained to the DPA when he discovered that the school had created Google accounts for his then eight-year-old son. The school had created YouTube and Gmail accounts for all students, as part of their usage of Google Chromebooks with its installed Workspace for Education program. Since then, the Danish DPA has issued four decisions related to Helsingør municipality's data processing in primary and lower secondary school. Moreover, they have issued warnings to more than 20 other municipalities using Google Chromebooks in their public schools. In the Helsingør case, the DPA found that the municipality had failed to consider the risks to students' data rights posed by Google's practices and thereby violated several GDPR requirements, as explained in the first decision of September 2021 (DPA, 2020), the second decision of 14 July 2022 (DPA, 2022a) and the third decision of 18 August 2022 (DPA, 2022b). In consequence, the DPA issued a ban against using Google Chromebooks and Workspace for Education in the municipality.

Since then, the municipality has acknowledged that several practices need to be changed. This recognition, and the finding of similar conditions in other municipalities, led the DPA to temporarily suspend its ban, as detailed in the fourth decision of 8 September 2022 that gives the municipality several orders to legalize the data processing:

> When we make the choice to suspend the ban, it is because the municipality has now recognized and described the problems that must be legalized. There has been reasonable clarity about what remains to be done – and therefore we are now giving the municipality two months to manage it together with its suppliers. (Frank, 2022).

The case entails several interesting perspectives concerning public and private cooperation within public schools in Denmark. First, the case can be seen as an illustrative example of how a public welfare provider (the municipality and its public school system) engages with a private service provider (Google) in line with the strategic vision of Denmark. As mentioned above, Denmark's digitalization strategy from 2011–2015, *The Digital Path to Future Welfare*, emphasizes the way digitalization may serve welfare recipients, such as school children. The strategy proposes to advance the use of IT technologies in public schools and to secure investments for public schools' transition into the digital future. This includes the replacement of old learning tools with digital tools, to use digital technologies creatively and critically in the schools, and to secure pupils' access to computers, potentially supplied by the schools. The strategy refers to a well-developed market for digital teaching tools and stresses that the state will support this market by coordinating demands for digital learning tools: 'Government and municipalities will create frameworks which ensure that before the end of 2012, there will be established one or more market-based distribution platforms (for instance some kind of "app stores"), which will make the access to digital learning tools for teachers and pupils easier and more manageable (*The Digital Path to Future Welfare 2011–2015* (2011): 23).

The introduction of Google Chromebooks and Workspace for Education in public schools is thus in line with the strategic direction outlined earlier, and reflects a development by which technology companies are enacted as cooperative partners in the development of the digital public school.

Second, the introduction of Google Chromebooks into public schools is part of a digital trajectory that also includes the nationwide school platform

Aula, which was highlighted specifically in the fifth strategy from 2016, *A Stronger and More Secure Digital Society*. Since 2019, Aula has served as a mandatory platform for teachers, schools, pupils, and parents in lower and secondary primary school. Aula was developed by the association of Danish Municipalities (KL) in cooperation with the municipalities' IT procurement association (KOMBIT) and was deliberately designed to include commercial products. Early in the process, a political decision was made that Aula should neither compete nor interfere with the teaching tools already available on the market but rather interoperate with these by serving as a central hub that linked to products such as class schedules, grading, teaching replacements, and so on (Jørgensen et al, 2023). Effectively, each of the 98 Danish municipalities choose the products they want to have connected to Aula. Moreover, Amazon Website Services serves as cloud partners for storing information shared on Aula, which reflects the most recent digitalization strategy from 2022, *Digitalization That Lifts Society*, which specifically mentions cloud computing as a means to reduce costs when operating IT systems.

The schools also deploy a range of Microsoft products such as OneNote, Teams, and OneDrive that are used for a variety of tasks. The teachers use the products, for example, to facilitate teacher cooperation on courses, to store data related to pupil evaluations, and meeting with parents. As such, the public schools rely on a complex digital infrastructure that teachers (as well as schools, pupils, and parents) navigate. When questioning the teachers about how they navigate these interrelated public and private products, they point to ongoing uncertainty and ambiguity about the flows of personal data. Some maintain that personal data are safely stored on 'local services' such as Aula, while others question the privacy implications of the broader platform ecosystem:

> Alternatively, we store it in Office, which is our file portal. This does not have the same security clearing as Aula, but on the other hand, it gives us the possibility to share files and work together and adjust things in teams synchronously. I might well have them in the Danish subject, but perhaps the teacher that has them in visual arts also needs to make a note, and this is not possible in Aula. (Female school teacher, age 48)

While the teachers believe that Aula is designed to protect pupils' data, they question whether the Microsoft and Google products may lower the level of data protection, and consequently have a negative impact on the pupils' privacy. One teacher, for example, reflects on the use of OneNote and how teachers anonymize the names of pupils: 'We don't, for instance, put the names of pupil in our notes if we are writing about something sensitive, simply because we are not sure whether this is within the framework, whether we are allowed to do this at all. There are uncertainties about these things' (Male school teacher, age 55).

Moreover, it is noted that while the agreement between public schools and Google requires Google to not share personal data beyond Google's Workspace for Education, once the pupils leave the school, they have their data transferred to a Google account, at which stage it becomes part of the broader Google ecosystem. As such, data-related risks arise at various points within the complex ecosystem of public and private systems/products that the teachers navigate. The pupils' personal data reside in a variety of platforms and services, including Aula, OneNote, OneDrive, Google's Workspace for Education platform, and no one seems to fully comprehend how data travel between these different services. As such, Google Chromebook is just one element in a digital infrastructure where boundaries are blurred between a core welfare service (the school) and commercial products (Amazon, Google, Microsoft).

Third, the case highlights that public-private cooperation that involves sharing of personal information is subject to strict regulatory boundaries and conditions and that lack of adherence to these conditions may effectively disrupt the cooperation. When the Danish DPA found that Helsingør municipality had not carried out the required risk assessment in relation to Google's processing of the pupils' personal data and had failed to take appropriate technical and organizational measures to mitigate risks associated with the data processing, they effectively banned the use of Google Chromebooks in the schools. They did this by issuing an injunction against the municipality to bring their processing activities in line with the legal requirements (GDPR). With reference to Habermas, this is an example of how regulation may play a role in countering processes of colonization. The regulatory framework – the GDPR – that informs the DPA decisions arguably provides the public schools (and to some extent the pupils' lifeworld) with measures to push back the market colonization exemplified by Google. However, as illustrated by the most recent DPA decision, the ban they issued on Helsingør municipality in terms of not using Chromebooks in public schools was lifted when the municipality agreed to adjust their practices. As such, the regulation has served to push back on certain practices but has not prevented the continued use of Google products in the public schools. The close imbrication of a tech giant within the Danish public education system thus continues to exist, despite their data-driven business model and the ongoing critique of their privacy practices (Reuters, 2023).

Conclusion

Our case is an example of how private companies are instrumental in processes of public sector digitalization and become key actors in welfare infrastructures. As pointed to by Dencik (2022) and Collington (2022), specific tensions pertain to the still closer cooperation between private actors guided by market values and public actors guided by public interest and an obligation to protect citizens' privacy rights. However, this immanent tension is largely unaddressed in the digitalization strategies. On the contrary, close cooperation between private and public sectors is increasingly emphasized and encouraged in the strategies. The cases that we engage with in this chapter illustrate that the rationale put forward in the strategies has been fulfilled. Indeed, the digital future school in Denmark, which was called for in the strategies, is now embedded in infrastructures which tech conglomerates such as Google, Amazon, and Microsoft own and operate.

As illustrated by our interviews, and previous research on Aula (Jørgensen et al, 2023), the teachers navigate in blurring boundaries between public and private systems/products, which creates uncertainty at several levels. This ecosystem can be seen as a further integration and validation of major platform providers into the public school system. These private providers now play a more prominent role in relation to critical elements of society, such as communicative infrastructures, or what Plantin et al (2018) refer to as platformized infrastructures. With reference to Habermas' (1987) conceptualization of system and lifeworld, the strategies as well as the public school case speak to systemic shifts between the state and the market within public sector digitalization in Denmark, with implications for students' privacy. In the Helsingør case, regulation functions as a tool for temporary disruption between the systemic integration of state and market. The constraints posed by regulation, however, are fixed with adjustments in the contractual basis between the municipality and the companies, that is, by more elaborate risk assessments and revised data processing agreements. As such, the regulation does not alter substantially the integration of tech giants into the provision of public services (public schools), but rather describes some minimum standards for data processing that must be followed. Judging by this case study, the regulation has not emancipated the lifeworld dimension of the school system from marketization – and thereby provided the boundaries that Habermas was hopeful of – but instead specified the terms whereby tech giants may continue to exist as an integral part of Denmark's digital school. As such, the case has confirmed Habermas' older conceptualization, namely market colonization into a core welfare service.

Notes

[1] These are: *Towards Digital Management: Vision and strategy for the public sector* (2002), *Strategy for Digital Management 2004–2006* (2004), *Towards Better Digital Service, Increased Streamlining and Stronger Co-Operation 2007–2010* (2007), *The Digital Path to Future Welfare 2011–2015* (2011), *A Stronger and Safer Digital Society 2016–2020* (2016) and *Digitialisation that Lifts Society 2022–2025* (2022).

2 We conducted nine interviews with teachers in three different public schools in the autumn of 2020, and five interviews with parents of public-school children. Additionally, we conducted five interviews with experts within the fields of privacy, data ethics, and digitalization of the public school system. The experts chosen for interview were: Morten Hass, project manager KOMBIT; Maria Ørskov Akselvoll, PhD in home and school interaction; Jakob Volmer, chief adviser KOMBIT; data ethics adviser Pernille Tranberg; and Stephan Engberg, security and privacy expert.

Acknowledgement

This chapter is written as part of the research project *'Don't Take it Personal': Privacy and Information in an Algorithmic Age* generously funded by Independent Research Fund Denmark (grant number 8018-00041B).

References

A Stronger and Safer Digital Society 2016–2020 (2016). Copenhagen: Agency for Digital Government.

Agency for Digital Government (nd) 25 years of joint digitalisation strategies. Available at: https://digst.dk/strategier/den-faellesoffentlige-digitaliseringss trategi/25-aars-faelles-digitaliseringsstrategier/ (accessed 31 January 2023).

Alston, P. (2019). *Report of the Special Rapporteur on extreme poverty and human rights, Philip Alston (A/74/493)*. 11 October. United Nations, Human Rights Council.

Andreasen, R., Kaun, A., and Nikunen, K. (2021). Fostering the data welfare state: a Nordic perspective on datafication. *Nordicom Review*, 42(2): 207–223.

Bowen, G. A. (2009). Document analysis as a qualitative research method. *Qualitative Research Journal*, 9(2): 27–40.

Bryman, A. (2016). *Social Research Methods*. 5th edition. Oxford: Oxford University Press.

Busemeyer, M. R., Kemmerling, A., Marx, P., and van Kersbergen, K. (2022). Digitalization and the Welfare State: Introduction. In M. R. Busemeyer, A. Kemmerling, P. Marx, and K. van Kersbergen (eds) *Digitalization and the Welfare State*, pp 1–20. Oxford: Oxford University Press.

Collington, R. (2022). Disrupting the welfare state? Digitalisation and the retrenchment of public sector capacity. *New Political Economy*, 27(2): 312–328.

Cone, L. (2023). The platform classroom: troubling student configurations in a Danish primary school. *Learning, Media and Technology*, 48(1): 52–64.

Creswell, J. W. and Poth, C. N. (2018). *Qualitative Inquiry and Research Design: Choosing among Five Approaches*. 4th edition. Thousand Oaks, CA: SAGE Publications, Inc.

Dencik, L. (2022). The datafied welfare state: a perspective from the UK. In A. Hepp, J. Jarke, and L. Kramp (eds) *New Perspectives in Critical Data Studies*, pp 145–165. Cham: Palgrave Macmillan.

Dencik, L. and Kaun, A. (2020). Introduction: datafication and the welfare state. *Global Perspectives*, 1(1). DOI: 10.1525/gp.2020.12912

Digitialisation that Lifts Society 2022–2025 (2022). Copenhagen: Agency for Digital Government.

DPA (2020). First decision [online]. Available at: https://gdprhub.eu/index.php?title=Datatilsynet_(Denmark)_-_2020-431-0061_(Helsingor_decision_no._1)) (accessed 31 January 2023).

DPA (2022a). Second decision [online]. Available at: https://gdprhub.eu/index.php?title=Datatilsynet_(Denmark)_-_2020-431-0061_(Helsingor_decision_no._2) (accessed 31 January 2023).

DPA (2022b). Third decision [online]. Available at: https://gdprhub.eu/index.php?title=Datatilsynet_(Denmark)_-_2020-431-0061_(Helsingor_decision_no._3) (accessed 31 January 2023).

Eubanks, V. (2018). *Automating Inequality: How High-Tech Tools Profile, Police and Punish the Poor*. New York: St Martin's Press.

Frank, A. (2022). Chromebooks: The Danish Data Protection Agency suspends bans and orders legalization. *Datatilsynet*, 8 September 2022. Available at: www.datatilsynet.dk/presse-og-nyheder/nyhedsarkiv/2022/sep/chromebooks-datatilsynet-suspenderer-forbud-og-giver-paabud-om-lovliggoerelse- (accessed 31 July 2023).

Gaskell, G. (2000). Individual and Group Interviewing. In M. W. Bauer and G. Gaskell (eds) *Qualitative Researching with Text, Image and Sound*, pp 38–56. London: SAGE.

Habermas, J. (1987). *The Theory of Communicative Action – Volume 2. Lifeworld and System: A Critique of Functionalist Reason*. Cambridge: Polity Press.

Habermas, J. (1992). Further Reflections on the Public Sphere. In C. Calhoun (ed) *Habermas and the Public Sphere*, pp 421–461. Cambridge and London: The MIT Press.

Habermas, J. (2022). Reflections and hypotheses on a further structural transformation of the political public sphere. *Theory, Culture & Society*, 39(4): 145–171.

Hall, S. (1997). The Work of Representation. In S. Hall (ed) *Representation: Cultural Representations and Signifying Practices*, pp 13–74. London: SAGE.

Helmond, A. (2015). The platformization of the web: making web data platform ready. *Social Media + Society*, 1(2): 1–11.

Jørgensen, R. F. (2021). Data and rights in the digital welfare state of Denmark. *Information, Communication and Society*, 26(4): 1–16.

Jørgensen, R. F., Valtysson, B., and Pagh, J. (2023). Working with Aula: how teachers navigate privacy uncertainties. *The Information Society*, 39(4): 225–235.

Mayer-Schonberger, V. and Cukier, K. (2013). *Big Data: A Revolution that Will Transform How We Live, Work, and Think*. Boston, MA: Houghton Mifflin Harcourt.

McGuigan, J. (2004). *Rethinking Cultural Policy*. Maidenhead: Open University Press.

Pink, S., Berg, M., Lupton, D., and Ruckenstein, M. (eds) (2022). *Everyday Automation: Experiencing and Anticipating Emerging Technologies*. Abingdon: Routledge.

Plantin, J. C., Lagoze, C., Edwards, P. N., and Sandvig, C. (2018). Infrastructure studies meet platform studies in the age of Google and Facebook. *New Media and Society*, 20(1): 293–310.

Poell, T., Nieborg, D., and Duffy, B. E. (2022). *Platforms and Cultural Production*. Cambridge: Polity Press.

Poell, T., Nieborg, D., and van Dijck, J. (2019). Platformisation. *Internet Policy Review: Journal of Internet Regulation*, 8(4): 1–13.

Reuters (2023). US court sanctions Google in privacy case, company's second legal setback in days. Available at: www.reuters.com/legal/us-court-sancti ons-google-privacy-case-companys-second-legal-setback-days-2023-03-30/ (accessed 13 October 2023).

Reutter, L. (2022). Constraining context: situating datafication in public administration. *New Media & Society*, 24(4): 903–921.

Schou, J. and Hjelholt, M. (2018). Digital citizenship and neoliberalization: governing digital citizens in Denmark. *Citizenship Studies*, 22(5): 507–522.

Selwyn, N. (2015). Data entry: towards the critical study of digital data and education. *Learning, Media and Technology*, 40(1): 64–82.

Splichal, S. (2010). Eclipse of 'the Public': From the Public to (Transnational) Public Sphere. Conceptual Shifts in the Twentieth Century. In J. Gripsrud and H. Moe (eds) *The Digital Public Sphere: Challenges for Media Policy*, pp 23–38. Gothenburg: NORDICOM.

Srnicek, N. (2017). *Platform Capitalism*. Cambridge: Polity Press.

Strategy for Digital Management 2004–2006. (2004). Copenhagen: The Digital Taskforce.

The Digital Path to Future Welfare 2011–2015. (2011). Copenhagen: Agency for Public Finance and Management.

Towards Better Digital Service, Increased Streamlining and Stronger Co-Operation 2007–2010. (2007). Copenhagen: The Digital Taskforce.

Towards Digital Management: Vision and Strategy for the Public Sector. (2002). Copenhagen: Project Digital Management. The Digital Taskforce.

van Dijck, J. (2013). *The Culture of Connectivity: A Critical History of Social Media*. Oxford: Oxford University Press.

van Dijck, J., Poell, R., and de Waal, M. (2018). *The Platform Society: Public Values in a Connected World*. Oxford: Oxford University Press.

Yeung, K. (2018). *Algorithmic government: towards a new public analytics?* Paper presented at the Ethical and Social Challenges posed by Artificial Intelligence workshop, Cumberland Lodge, Windsor, 25 June.

7

Accounting for Impersonal Platform Media: A Challenge to Personal Privacy

Greg Elmer

Introduction

Privacy scholars are a frustrated lot. And who can blame them? Rarely does a week pass without a public figure or tech guru pronouncing the death of privacy, again. Yet while some privacy critics have tried to push the concept into the networked age (Marwick and boyd, 2014), others still cling on tightly to the belief that privacy is a deeply personal and proprietorial right. Such frustrations over the loss of personal privacy are often fuelled by an apparent contradiction, a so-called privacy 'paradox' (Solove, 2021). While research and consumer polling has suggested that individuals are concerned about privacy intrusions and transgressions, they are at the same time all too quick to overshare online. Perhaps as a consequence of this paradox, other scholars have begun to articulate and embrace a privacy politics of exhaustion, where individuals treat privacy-related processes with a healthy dose of cynicism. Given the vast scale of privacy intrusions what really can an individual do? (Hoffman et al, 2016). Still other researchers seemingly blame consumers in part for privacy transgressions since they fail to read and heed lengthy privacy policies and terms of service. But how can blaming individuals for 'lying' when asked if they have read the terms and conditions solve privacy harms? (Obar and Oeldorf-Hirsch, 2022).

To be sure, efforts at rethinking theories of privacy have taken on an added sense of urgency in the digital economy, where online platformed life is rife with automated forms of data collection. Platform media are also designed, via the interface and 'backend' algorithms, to encourage and facilitate the sharing of one's personal demographics, habits, likes, dislikes, geographic location, opinions, feelings, and media (audio/video recordings). Not surprisingly, privacy scholars have long raised concerns about a growing list of harms produced by oversharing personal details online, namely doxing, cyberstalking, and other forms of targeted harassment and hate (Zimmer and Hoffman, 2012). As a consequence, while I have reservations about the frustrated accusations of some privacy scholars, it is not my goal here to simply refute or outright reject these personal appeals to – and definitions of – privacy. Targeted harms at individual social media users, particularly youth and racialized communities, continue to plague our societies (boyd et al, 2009; Nakamura et al, 2023). The privacy lens plays an important role in addressing such online harms. The goal of this short chapter is, therefore, to provide another post-privacy ideation, a trajectory that questions how both personal and impersonal transactions on platform media produce individual and social harms.

Herein I propose a speculative framework for understanding privacy frameworks in the context of our current digital media environment. The goal is to ultimately deepen potential solutions to online data harms by – in part – taking into consideration the design of social media platforms and properties, specifically the business models of social media companies, apps, and corporate internet properties. While a more transparent data economy might help to qualify and quantify the scale and scope of privacy harms, questions of accountability remain stubbornly elusive. And it is here that privacy as a form of personalization limits our horizon, for data economies – including personal data economies – *account* for much more than account holders' behaviours, opinions, and histories. We cannot hold social media companies to account for privacy transgressions if we do not recognize what is even accounted for in their data operations. A strict personal approach to media privacy would assume a market of one, where the identity of a single account user is crucial to the functioning of the system. As we shall see, however, such personal information economies are always and already scaled, raising the spectre of an *impersonal* form of privacy, an impersonal media network. Such a trajectory poses a simple question – what else, beyond the individual user is made part of the current personal economy in our networked lives? What needs to be accounted for to drive current social media and platform-based business models (economies of scale)? Furthermore, how can a networked economy of 'scale'[1] reveal, or at least open the door to, impersonal theories of privacy?

Beyond personalization?

It should come as no surprise that personal privacy remains a steady and consistent concept in social media studies, in no small part because of the intense personalization of media interfaces. Indeed, what interfaces are not designed for the individual user/account holder? The *personal* is the principal if not predominant mode of address on media platforms. Personalization is the social/platform media sales pitch, a media technology formatted specifically for *you*.[2] As a consequence, social media interfaces are designed to reflect, amplify, and log personal preferences, behaviours, and communications. Users thus 'gaze out' onto the media universe through personalized screens, through friends, personalized advertisements, and other filtered and profiled content. In a recent article, I refer to this condition as the 'first person perspective', the process by which media properties and platforms seek to personalize content on our screens (Elmer, 2023).

The problem is that *personalization* is not operationalized exclusively through or for an individual user. Or 'behind' the words and online expressions of the user. It is personalization above and beyond the individual person. Personalization, in other words, is not limited to a sole person, or their online inscriptions. Rather, personalization – as a broader algorithmic phenomenon – continuously integrates a user's interactions with a host of other 'data points' – digital objects, users, communities, times, temporalities, and places. As we know, online content is curated and filtered; that is, personalized by algorithms that in part seek to align personal tastes and opinions with like-minded clusters of users, including of course our choice of platform friends and contacts, the digital objects we interact with online (photos, comments, videos, and so on), the hyperlinks we click, files we upload, download, and stream, and the sites we visit. In short, the online person is but a figment of the internet's imagination, the subject of the digital marketer and interface designer to be sure, but also clearly the source of consternation for privacy advocates.

Impersonal, affinity media

Platform media, however, does not just reproduce or curate personal interests. Platform media are not simply personal media. Rather platform media are also affinity media – a medium of the same, the familiar. Personal choices alone do not drive algorithmic platform media. Rather, as many have noted, including platform companies themselves, a key organizing platform actor is decidedly *impersonal*, that is the cluster of users and non-users. The like-minded person. The aggregated person. The affinity person. The clustered person. In short, the *im*personal subject of the platform economy.

While users contribute to aggregate pictures of clusters over time, their identity is not unique or sovereign, in a networked sense. Again, there are no markets of one on Facebook. Put another way, while Facebook and other platform companies closely monitor their userbase, they do not just seek to know the actions and identities of individual users, they look for, encourage, and quantify aggregate activity, how users *engage* with content and other users on the platform. Users might help to refine, update, or challenge their own profiles and clusters, but they are not in and of themselves the subject of the economic model of platforms. Rather, platform engagement – as opposed to individual user activity – is the key metric published by media companies to their investors (Elmer, 2018). This is the reason I refer to contemporary platform media as impersonal media. Platform media desire a certain type of user, a persona, not a person. Engaged users who produce content that can be aggregated to better refine behavioural profiles. That said, *impersonal* media is not a new economic object or concept, it is certainly not unique to contemporary platform media.

In the early years of the internet our online lives were said to be distinct from our 'real' lives, our so-called offline lives. Online life, in other words, was strictly 'virtual', separate from our embodied existence (Rogers, 2009). Early digital media theorist Mark Poster (1990), for example, claimed that we led double or split lives. Dataveillant databases and networked computing produced our 'data doubles', mirrored data-images of ourselves. The concept certainly helped fuel concerns over online privacy, over the loss of personal information. We were being data-cloned, replicated for some unknown yet likely dubious end. For Poster then, online lives were separated from selves, that is to say made impersonal, removed from our control and ownership. Poster's challenge to personal privacy theory thus centred on the displacement of the sovereign individual user and its role in producing other effects, relationships, and potential forms of economic extractivism.

Other scholars, intrigued by questions of anonymity online, also developed impersonal arguments and concepts, for example noting when users started to *impersonate* others online, adopting other characteristics, traits, names, genders, profile images, and so on (Rheingold, 1993). But this is not exactly the impersonal media I would like to develop in this chapter. I introduce these two examples though to highlight long established debates over the sanctity, centrality, or cohesion of the person, the individual platform user, and the process of media impersonalization as a generative dialogue with personal notions of privacy. The online person is, in other words, also a persona, a figure (Lury et al, 2022), or as I suggested in my early work, a profile (Elmer, 2004).

One last point on the person and the private, before moving on to a history of the accountable impersonal subject. Another split in online personhood, on the privacy-seeking, rational person, relates to social media accounts. Platform users, who have their interfaces and content personalized, are not the only persons aggregated by algorithmic clustering – the account holder's affinity to or engagement with non-account holders is a case in point. As Ken Werbin (2012) notes, individuals who sign up for social media accounts immediately receive personalized recommendations, to add friends, colleagues, acquaintances, and like-minded content. But how can this be?

The sovereign user would be in full command of their personalized account. Yet, as we know, a non-account user's behaviours 'elsewhere' throughout the digitized landscape (on other media platforms and properties, and in other digitized social, cultural, and economic spheres), have seemingly *already been accounted for* by social media platforms. In other words, the personal account is not a reflection or anchor of the sovereign subject, the social media user. Consequently, the non-account user is thus always already, at least in part, platform-ready, that is *impersonal*. Such 'non-users' pose a distinct challenge to privacy scholars and advocates who routinely invoke transparent contracts as a solution to privacy transgressions and harms. Media algorithms are not restricted to personal user contracts, they are again scaled impersonal machines. The vertical and horizontal expansion of platform media companies, their purchase of nascent competitors, relationship with data brokers, and contractual data-sharing partnerships with public and private entities seemingly ensure that the ready-made, media platform user is a qualitatively rich object, an algorithmically networked subject, an impersonal subject.

Sombart and the impersonal corporation

Impersonal financial relations have long pre-dated the internet, social media, and the platform economy. My reading and definition of impersonal media, stem in part from financial history, in particular by the early theories of accounting and histories of capitalism articulated by the German scholar Werner Sombart. A controversial Weimar-era economist known for his critique of the craft industry, Sombart (1928) wrote about the transitions between early industrial, entrepreneurial, and finance capitalism. Financial capitalism in England emerged out of the intense capital requirements of large-scale railway construction. Finance capital also worked hand in hand with the expanded role of the London stock exchange and other exchanges in Europe and the United States in the mid-1830s. Given the scale of such projects, railways required complex systems of planning, monitoring of costs at the construction stage, and the separation of capital expenditure from other operation expenses (Edwards, 1989: 12). Sombart, however, largely restricted his analysis of impersonal capital to the corporation as a regulated entity, that is, as a limited liability enterprise, a new corporate form that promised, protected, and distributed large-scale financial risks posed by mega projects such as railways.

Sombart suggested that economic relations and relations of production were forever changed by the introduction of large corporate enterprises, organizations that subsequently introduced a new economic class – namely, managers. Sombart juxtaposed the corporation against the owner-run small or craft business. In the corporation, he argued, the person was separated from capital – that is, they entered an impersonal relationship to capital. The owners of the corporation did not manage or directly control the enterprise, capital, or workers – their proxies did, the company managers and executives. Proxy management was, however, but one important economic shift in the late 19th century for Sombart. The rise of impersonal capital, moreover, also produced the need for *confidence* in corporate managers, confidence in proxy-owners, investors, confidence in those who did not own the operational capital of an enterprise. And perhaps most critically, during the late 1800s, impersonal business enterprises, especially newly incorporated enterprises, required the confidence of government and market regulators, and the so-called public investor, again as a vehicle for distributing potential financial risks.

For Sombart, the emergence of boards of directors and other managerial structures and processes further intensified the process of depersonalizing capital, which he linked to the public corporation and financialized forms of writing. Sombart argued that three factors lead to the growth and independence of public (incorporated) corporations: their legal construction and governance or 'firma', their growth of credit markets or 'ditta', and their overriding imperative of profit or 'ratio' that he located in 'the account' (Most, 1972: 723). Sombart argued that the ratio – 'in particular, double entry book-keeping permitted the full representation of the flow of capital through a business. ... This facilitated concentration on the idea of creating wealth. Furthermore, since the separation of the business from its owners was a necessary feature of the capitalist enterprise, systematic book-keeping gave material aid to the creation of the capitalist enterprise. The business replaced the entrepreneur' (Most, 1972: 724).

For Sombart then, the corporate firma, ditta, and ratio produced the need for a publicly regulated, and independent, impersonal set of economic actors to keep tabs on proxy managers – accountants. Working in conjunction with new corporate legislation that required the public dissemination of transparent financial statements (Britain's Companies Acts), annual reports, and a prospectus for Initial Public Offerings, accountants were tasked with confirming the validity and veracity of a company's economic statements, filings, minutes, and other financial documents. In other words, accountants became mandated, impersonal actors for publicly registered companies. They were tasked with making complex financial transactions more than transparent, they had to be understandable and believable for government and investors. In addition to wholesale changes wrought by industrial capitalism, most historians point to the emergence of limited partnerships, and the need to adjudicate and enumerate assets and liabilities during bankruptcy proceedings as contributing factors to the growth of the accounting profession. In the 1800s, one quarter of all limited liability companies dissolved within three years, thus requiring yet more accounting services (Edwards, 1989: 262). Consequently, by 1831, parliament stepped in to legislate an official role for accountants, passing the Bankruptcy Act, which afforded ' "official assignees", to liquidate estates on behalf of creditors'. Subsequent changes to the legislation in 1869 permitted the direct appointment of accountants – further increasing the amount of bankruptcy work for accountants (Edwards, 1989: 262–263).

19th-century accountants thus set out to enumerate the terms of going public – not just the validity and transparency of assets, liabilities, clients, sales, and company stock – but a new relationship to capital itself. Like Sombart, J. R. Edwards, also returned to industrial capitalism, the precursor to finance capitalism, to trace the growing need to identify and enumerate increasingly complex business enterprises and practices, in an effort to understand the relationship between depreciating assets, fluctuating labour costs, and, most importantly, *profit*. Edwards argued that the significance of such relationships was first highlighted during the close of feudal capitalism. Edwards gave the example of a pottery business in the English town of Stoke (1772) that witnessed a downturn in business. Accountants were subsequently hired to identify the company's costs to determine if the pricing of goods was too high (Edwards, 1989: 280). Thus was born 'cost accounting', a practice enacted today by the likes of KPMG, Deloitte, and PricewaterhouseCoopers – global consulting companies hired to restructure and rationalize business and government practices alike.

While emerging from the same set of factors associated with auditing-focused and externally located or 'independent' accountants,[3] prior to the middle of the 20th century, cost accountants were largely in-house staff – charged with developing and revising forward-looking financial plans and transactions, speculative what-if scenarios of how their company could not only maximize revenues, but also determine what costs or expenses could be cut. Cost accounting, or simply costing, in short opened the corporation and enterprise to a forensics or analytics well beyond the specific purview or capabilities of its managers or other employers. And it is here that we start to see the direct comparison to the contemporary impersonal media subject and platform accounts in the context of privacy debates. All aspects of business were to be accounted for, not just one class of employees or contracts, that is to say not just what was 'on the books', in the accounts, invoices, bills, and ledgers. Rather, *future* economic and financial prospects would be accounted for as well – what *might* or *could* be integrated into the business, or what *might* impact the future financial prospects of the company. Accounting books no longer simply needed to 'balance', justifying all that financially entered or exited the company, accounting or rather cost accounting, became a process of enumeration and valuation, what Mary Poovey (1998) referred to as 'financial writing'.

Again, the valuation and verification of corporate finances needed to be made quantifiable and understandable.

Mary Poovey argued that financial facts were represented through practices and forms of financial writing, the principal mode of which was accounting. Founded in part on the history of accounting books, Poovey (1998) argues that financial writing incorporated not only the formatting of financial documents, books, and balance sheets but also served as a grammar for economic actors, and financial relationships, facticity, and prospects. Thus, financial writing, as a form of accountability and future prospecting, would also serve as a form of economic discrimination, not just a form of translation from numbers to language and narratives. Poovey, in other words, offers a values-based critique of accounting where the objects of analysis, and financial factors, are themselves called into question. She asks: 'Who counted? What did people count? For what social and institutional purposes did people count?' (Poovey, 1998: 5).

Accounting for digital harms

When costing entered into the picture, accounting shifted from an exercise in translating numbers into financial meaning, of tracking objects (orders, purchases, money, employees, customers, and so on) that enter and exit enterprises, to a forward-looking process of valuation. No longer did accountants simply produce reports that laid bare, or made transparent, the financial status and health (or not) of enterprises. Rather, costing involved determining what helped or hurt the goals of a business. Costing was used to plan for the future, to determine potential routes to financial success, including new forms of revenue, customers, staff, or excluding the same. Costing, as enumerated in the financial history of capitalism, integrated an impersonal mode, distinct from sovereign actors – namely, workers and owners. And, moreover, costing no longer simply tracked tangible objects, or currencies. Rather, the process of cost accounting entailed attributing financial value beyond the 'additional' accumulative, or capitalizing. That is to say, it did not simply seek to enumerate profit, assets, or liabilities.

We could draw a parallel between costing and the digital term 'data point', that is, any factor, be it human, non-human, temporal, or environmental could become part of an aggregated form of accounting. In this calculus, data points become costed, or financialized, in the sense that their value is determined in the aggregate. This brings us back to Poovey's questions about what counts, or the discriminatory or harmful consequences of cost accounting. Since cost accounting takes us beyond the tangible, fungible, and traceable, to the imagined, the question of *what counts* is defined through a speculative, relational calculus. This speculative mode of impersonal capital dramatically upends our understanding of not just accounting as a form of transparency (as auditing and publicizing), but also as a means of accounting for tangible decisions, assets, and revenues.

To return to the question of media and privacy from this impersonal costed history of capitalism, we might pose the question, how can we hold social media companies to account? The question assumes that platform media do not begin and end with those that choose to opt in, those that open platform accounts or agree to terms and conditions. It is not simply a question of contractual relationships. Others are also accounted for, or *are discounted*, noted but excluded or dismissed as irrelevant or peripheral to the exigencies of personalized, affinity-based media. Privacy scholars must also account for this discounting, this form of data discrimination, where data points (including groups, clusters, and communities) are deemed to be unhelpful for the future of a business.

Thus, another form of privacy-accountability that a costed, impersonal perspective would suggest, is a temporal one. While overdetermined by personal interfaces and embodied devices that seldom leave personal pockets and hands, media platforms produce future-speculative knowledge for their consumers from impersonal algorithms, from costed logistics, be they forms of engagement or otherwise. It is not exclusively derived from the past history of the user, the objective likes and behaviour of the user, or the so-called rational choices of the user. This 'personalized' media we see on our respective platform media home pages, tickers, and feeds, is rather impersonalized – is juxtaposed against impersonal clusters – effectively profiles of thousands if not millions of individuals. But impersonalized to what end? Clearly, impersonal costing is not merely restricted to a knowing and aggregating past consumer behaviour, it also seeks to understand future prospects, future opportunities culled from myriad data points.

A post-privacy agenda, as envisioned herein through an impersonal lens, mediated through the structure of data economies and business models of contemporary platform companies, would therefore, at the very least, need to account for the integration of non-users, those without formal social media accounts, not just a social form of privacy, or an impersonal one that would suggest a distancing or disconnection, a loss of control or ownership. Rather, a more robust *costed* post-privacy debate would also benefit from a speculative turn toward questions of scale and valuation, of the financialization of not only objects, people, times, and places but the costs of different data points on potential futures, relationships, opportunities, and much more. In this calculus, users or individuals do not simply lose control over 'their' data, they potentially lose the ability to collectively imagine and enact future solutions, plans, and forms of public accountability.

Notes

[1] Perhaps because of the economic imperative for growth, scaling is almost always associated with scaling up, with broadening the possibilities of markets and profits. Yet scaling can also refer to reducing the significance of specific objects, in this case the individual sovereign user. See https://dictionary.cambridge.org/dictionary/english/scaling

[2] In recognition of the social media revolution, *Time* magazine's famous 'Person of the Year' designation for 2006 was 'You'.

[3] Indeed, many cost accounting and consulting firms such as PricewaterhouseCoopers initially began as accounting firms.

References

boyd, d., Marwick, A., Aftab, P., and Koeltl, M. (2009). The conundrum of visibility. *Journal of Children and Media*, 3(4): 410–419.

Edwards, J. R. (1989). *A History of Financial Accounting*. London: Routledge.

Elmer, G. (2004). *Profiling Machines: Mapping the Personal Information Economy*. Cambridge, MA: MIT Press.

Elmer, G. (2018). Prospecting facebook: the limits of the economy of attention. *Media, Culture & Society*, 41(3): 332–346.

Elmer, G. (2023). From the first to the zero personal perspective: neutering the mediated life of affinity. *Computational Culture*, #9.

Hoffmann, C. P., Lutz, C., and Ranzini, G. (2016). Privacy cynicism: a new approach to the privacy paradox. *Cyberpsychology: Journal of Psychosocial Research on Cyberspace*, 10(4). DOI: 10.5817/CP2016-4-7

Lury, C., Viney, W., and Wark, S. (2022). *Figure: Concept and Method*. London: Palgrave MacMillan.

Marwick, A. E. and boyd, d. (2014). Networked privacy: how teenagers negotiate context in social media. *New Media & Society*, 16(7): 1051–1067.

Most, K. S. (1972). Sombart's propositions revisited. *The Accounting Review*, 47(4): 722–734.

Nakamura, L., Stiverson, H., and Lindsey, K. (2023). *Racist Zoombombing*. New York: Routledge.

Obar, J. and Oeldorf-Hirsch, A. (2022). Older adults and 'the biggest lie on the internet': from ignoring social media policies to the privacy paradox. *International Journal of Communication*, 16: 4779–4800.

Poovey, M. (1998). *A History of the Modern Fact: Problems of Knowledge in the Sciences of Wealth and Society*. Chicago, IL: University of Chicago Press.

Poster, M. (1990). *The Mode of Information: Poststructuralism and Social Context*. London: Polity.

Rheingold, H. (1993). *The Virtual Community: Homesteading on the Electronic Frontier*. New York: Perseus.

Rogers, R. (2009). *The End of the Virtual*. Amsterdam: Vossiuspers UvA.

Solove, D. J. (2021). The myth of the privacy paradox. *George Washington Law Review* 1. DOI: 10.2139/ssrn.3536265

Sombart, W. (1928). *Der Moderne Kapitalismus*. Munich: Verlag.

Werbin, K. (2012). Auto-biography: on the immanent commodification of personal information. *International Review of Information Ethics*, 17: 47–53.

Zimmer, M. and Hoffman, A. (2012). Privacy, Context, and Oversharing: Reputational Challenges in a Web 2.0 World. In H. Masum and M. Tovey (eds) *The Reputational Society: How Online Opinions Are Reshaping the Offline World*, pp 175–184. Cambridge, MA: MIT Press.

Politics

8

Beyond Market Fixing: Privacy and the Critique of Political Economy

Paško Bilić

Introduction

Privacy is not (only) an issue of personal data protection. It is a social experience in a digital society shaped by a mode of production driven by surplus value. Understanding privacy, therefore, requires critiquing the underlying political economy in which privacy abuse appears. However, we need more than just dismissing data commodification and profit-seeking motives to understand the nuances of the relationship between social experiences and privately owned technological services. Clarifying this complexity remains challenging despite numerous attempts to make sense of data-dependent platforms in digital capitalism (Rochet and Tirole, 2003; Jin, 2015; Kenney, 2016; Srnicek, 2017; Smyrnaios, 2018; van Dijck et al, 2018; Flew, 2022). Many questions remain difficult to answer: How do you define a product when offered at zero price? How do you determine social and economic harms from zero-price products? How do you trace the exploitation of social experiences for capital accumulation? Are technology users manipulated ideologically?

The underlying problem for data protection and privacy is the production of 'technological forms' instrumentally merged with the social experiences of their users and mediated through aggregated commodified data. While allowing creative expression through user-generated content, the 'technological form' circumscribes the range of experiential possibilities orchestrated by algorithms and conducive to generating surplus value (Bilić et al, 2021; Bilić, 2024). Such an approach sees capitalism as a changing socio-historical mode of production. Social and economic 'forms' (for example, commodities, labour, money, technology) always contain different 'substances' or entanglements of social relations and experiences within a given historical reality. Unlike dogmatic approaches that cling to the original texts written by Marx to legitimize their positions, this approach sees Marxism as an open project in which certain categories must be developed and interpreted anew. The relation between 'form' and 'substance' is argued to be the primary method of Marx's critique.

Using this approach, I will argue that privacy abuse results from the substance of how private entities capture and commodify data through technological forms. New European Union (EU) legislation, such as the Digital Services Act and the Digital Markets Act, does not challenge the underlying premise of social benefits generated from data markets. It aims to fix what the regulators perceive as unfavourable externalities data markets generate. Thus, it has a limited horizon for challenging privacy abuse at source. On the other hand, a critical political economy perspective allows us to consider fragments of capitalist appearance and substance under a single conceptual umbrella. The understanding of privacy in this chapter is close to the proposal by Cohen (2019), who moves beyond the individual autonomy perspective. Instead, she argues for an understanding of a socially shaped experience, which requires new forms of institutional governance. Taking this premise further, I will argue that privacy abuse is also a social relation mediated by digital capitalism's technological and economic forms. To mitigate privacy risks in contemporary capitalism, there needs to be a more substantial investment in public infrastructures where data will not be commodified and enclosed. New regulatory responses are needed, especially at the EU level. They could pursue a variety of directions, such as reducing involuntary data extraction, allowing data portability between private and public infrastructures, strengthening digital rights, or supporting alternative business models.

One of the main concerns in digital privacy discussions is the asymmetry of data control, manipulation, and the loss of individual autonomy (Hacker, 2021). Private entities collect and analyse data to optimize their services, while individuals have limited oversight over their data. Current regulation aims to reconfigure that relationship. However, it primarily targets personal data, remaining 'powerless regarding pseudonyms or aggregated data' (Flew, 2021: 107). A case in point is that once the General Data Protection Regulation was introduced, most websites reduced their connections to technology providers to avoid privacy risks. At the same time, technology services such as Google and Facebook saw increased market share (Peukert et al, 2020; Johnson and Shriver, 2022). The cost of compliance was too high for smaller firms, which created the side effect of strengthening major service providers. On the opposite side of the policy spectrum, restoring competition in data markets is expected to reduce social and economic harm and solve negative externalities such as privacy abuse. The goal is to make data markets more competitive and technology users better informed about involved risks – such an approach risks further legitimizing the *status quo*.

In the first section, I will present theoretical standpoints that see capitalism as a socio-economic form. Contrary to neoclassical economics, which sees markets as natural ways of producing with positive or negative externalities on society, these approaches see the economy as a distorted social form. In the second section, I will discuss the role of social experience in digital capitalism as it becomes the target for abstracting data and profiting from digital services. I will propose the 'technological form' concept to describe this process, the logical consequence of which in capitalism is privacy abuse. The third section moves from the technical abstraction to the economic abstraction. It describes how data become an essential segment in the commodification process of social experience, create competitive advantages in digital capitalism, and exacerbate the privacy problem. The fourth section discusses technological forms outside commodification and the need to disassociate the technical abstraction process from profit-making economic abstractions to establish more democratic management of technological privacy risks.

Social forms of production and digital capitalism

Although the 'market' has multiple competing definitions (see Karppinen and Moe, 2014), influential ideas from mainstream economics hold weight in policy discussions by providing seemingly rational underpinnings to regulating developing and advanced economic exchanges. One such concept is 'market failure' (Bator, 1958) and the associated notions of 'policy failure' and 'market fixing'. Market failure implies that, sometimes, markets are not the most efficient mechanism for allocating resources. Markets can fail to provide so-called positive externalities (public goods). One example is the media, which must provide information for democratic decision-making and inform citizens in the public sphere while maintaining their commercial, profit-oriented goals. Markets can also produce so-called negative externalities such as pollution or privacy abuse. Public intervention is needed in each scenario to support positive, or reduce negative, externalities. The market is seen as a natural production method and a rational allocation mechanism that requires public regulatory intervention to improve efficiency. Policy failure implies that public policy did not fix market failures. However, improving the efficiency of data markets to reduce privacy abuse might not be enough (Stucke, 2022), just as improving competition in the oil industry is not enough to solve pollution problems.

The issue with the market failure approach is that it subtly postulates market supply and demand as having a favourable and privileged position outside society. Markets can have positive or negative effects, and public policy's role is to ensure that markets deliver desired societal goals without too much interference. However, the process of supply and demand is also socially determined, a case that Marx forcefully exposed by looking at industrial capitalism's class relations, exploitation, and alienation. The recent critical theory takes Marx's approach of denaturalizing capitalism one step further and argues that all economic categories (capital, land, labour, and commodity) are social forms that have become fetishized. Economic and societal value is a social relation (see Reichelt, 1982; Reuten, 1988; Heinrich, 2009; Elbe, 2013). In that sense, the critique of political economy is a critique of society (Bonefeld, 2014; Murray, 2018).

Capitalism is a monetary economy of private ownership over the means of production, exploited labour power engaged in commodity production, commodities validated through the exchange, and profit-making. From a cynical perspective, nothing fundamentally changes within digital capitalism and the data-driven economy. From an opposite radical perspective, there is nothing capitalist about digital platforms as they monopolize technology, data, and resources to extract rents (Mazzucato, 2019; Dean, 2020; Varoufakis, 2021). Both options miss that digital capitalism rests on social forms of production in a given historical context. In other words, technology and the digital economy do not exist in a vacuum but are shaped, constructed, constituted, and moulded by changing socio-historical relations. Rent (along with profit and interest) is only a segment of surplus value (Marx, 2010: 819). So, while digital capitalism displays seemingly pre-capitalist characteristics of extracting rents, social relations surrounding digital platforms and capitalism deserve further analytical attention. Platforms afford unique configurations of social relations of production and circulation and, along the way, different forms of domination, profit, rent, and interest-making. To unpack the role of privacy, we need to devise analytical tools for understanding platform technology and data in everyday life. We also need to reconstruct how technical and economic abstractions from everyday life become conducive for commodification, creating privacy problems in contemporary democracy.

Social experience and data aggregation: the 'technological form'

Situating the privacy problem in criticizing capitalism is not a new research endeavour. Among the typical starting points is the critique of surveillance as a business model (Andrejevic, 2002; Pridmore and Zwick, 2011; Allmer, 2012; Zuboff, 2015, 2019) developed by the post-Second World War military-industrial complex and the marketing industry in the USA (Foster and McChesney, 2014). The relationship between surveillance and privacy can best be described as a 'mode of social ordering'. Surveillance is purposeful, routine, systematic, and focused attention, a 'mode of ordering predominantly concerned with producing predictable, rationalised behaviours and information flows. Privacy is a dynamic condition best described as breathing room for socially situated subjects to engage in processes of boundary management' (Cohen, 2019: 12). The social critique of domination and manipulation, once put forward by the traditional Frankfurt School, has once again surfaced in connection to surveillance and the ability of private entities to steer human behaviour. However, as critics of surveillance capitalism have observed, it sometimes fixates on technological threats to our autonomy. It obscures the relationship between technology and the problems of monopoly, inequality, and discriminatory hierarchy that threaten our democracy (Kapczynski, 2020).

To better understand the privacy problem in contemporary society, we need an updated and critical analysis of the Frankfurt School theory to grasp present-day manipulation and domination. Traditionally, the School has been interpreted, from a (postmodern) cultural studies angle, as an elitist and pessimistic account of everyday life. Despite close articulations between the two fields (Kellner, 2002), cultural studies rejected the cultural industry thesis as imposing a mechanical interpretation of human action dominated by commercial interests. Such a position misses a broader understanding of social irrationalities and contradictions in capitalism theorized by prominent members such as Adorno, Horkheimer, or Marcuse. Following the School's argument, the contentious point is to argue that people are ideologically coerced and manipulated while consuming mass media. This position was becoming difficult to sustain in digital communication, where it was claimed that the division between production and consumption was blurred through user-generated content. The digital labour debate reconnected individual, mundane experience with political economy and capital accumulation by conceptualizing user activity as a form of exploited, unpaid labour (Terranova, 2000; Scholz, 2013; Fuchs, 2014; Dyer-Witheford, 2015). However, it did not explain how control of quotidian interactions is enforced in practice. Ultimately, it ended with a similar argument as the traditional Frankfurt School, playing the ideological coercion card.

However, the School also articulated control and dominance over humans and nature (Feenberg, 2014) through technology (Feenberg, 1996, 2017; Marcuse, 1998, 2007; Gandesha, 2018). Technology is not considered a neutral rationality but a constitutive element of how capitalist production structures, organizes, and consolidates human experience. Technology 'was not simply an abstract instrumentality but constituted the principle perceptive structure – the technological *a priori* – through which the world takes shape' (Gandesha, 2018: 657–658). Furthermore, in the context of flexible software systems, algorithms, and artificial intelligence, the connection between experience, technology usage, and production becomes an essential socio-economic dynamic of technological change. The primary goal for owners of technical services is to grow the user base, allowing more adaptation and configuration options for their 'technological form'. Once more users interact with the system and the user base increases, the volume and granularity of collected data increase. As the volume of collected data and the number of users reach a tipping point, it is tough for competing firms to provide services with comparable scale and scope. Monopoly and technological dominance become entrenched (Bilić et al, 2021).

Technical services such as digital platforms can be used creatively for many purposes not directly determined by capital. Moreover, citizens continue using digital services despite increasing awareness and action to protect their online privacy (Acquisti et al, 2020). The 'technological form' allows complex experiences. Usage fills the technological form with the substance of daily life. The power of the technological form lies in the fact that we cannot reprogramme the technical system supporting online communication and socialization or disassociate our experiences recorded in data from it. Hence, it is not just ideology that can determine the boundaries and directions of human behaviour. It is a technical service with its affordances. Platforms reconfigure social relations by allowing multiple actors to interact. The monetization process and economic form determination can take a variety of flexible and configurable appearances. Technical data abstraction is not a part of capitalism until it becomes commodified or enclosed by property relations in multiple ways. Users can pay for platform access through subscriptions and paywalls for particular services or accessibility options. Aggregate data allow the platform to configure the user experience and tailor content exposure according to previous preferences. Users can sometimes access certain services without a charge, while monetization occurs only for business options and commercial use. Aggregate data are used to fine-tune the service. Finally, services can be funded through targeted advertising or retail, in which case a percentage of the exchange on the platform (consumer purchases, attention sold to advertisers) funds the platform. Aggregate data become more closely associated with commodification through surveillance and targeted advertising.

From the 'technological form' to the commodity form

Having defined 'technological form' as social interaction between experience and technology mediated by digital data, the practical question is, what is a commodity that allows capital to reproduce on digital platforms such as those funded by advertising? There have been many competing answers, putting explanatory weight on user labour and audience commodity (Fuchs, 2015), technology as an information commodity (Rigi and Prey, 2015), and data collection and aggregation in the surveillance economy (Andrejevic, 2002, 2004). One of the reasons for the lack of a unified answer is that some digital services in question are offered at no exchange value, an essential characteristic of a commodity in capitalism. This poses a theoretical and regulatory challenge, since social and economic harms in monopoly conditions are usually expected to increase consumer item prices (Baran and Sweezy, 1968) rather than reduce them to zero. For example, services offered by Alphabet Inc. and Meta Platforms Inc. went through long periods of low profitability and losses before a sufficient scale and scope of collected data were reached to provide unique industry services in the form of targeted advertising.

Alphabet Inc. and Meta Platforms Inc. services are funded by advertising, made possible by aggregated experiential data that enable the production of adverts as 'intermediate commodities' that secure profitability. Intermediate commodities speed up the circulation of capital and enable sales of all commodities in the global economy. They allow the excessive production capacity in various industries to find an easier path to potential consumers and markets. This allows advertising-funded digital platforms to govern their technological forms free of charge, loosening the direct association between the technological and commodity forms. However, while the technological form is free of charge, it is instrumentally and indirectly linked to data commodification and the social experience of its users. Profitability drives corporate decision-making and shareholder value creation in financial markets. Regulation and democratic governance become a nuisance and a business risk (Bilić and Prug, 2021). Privacy abuse becomes a side effect and negative externality of data commodification.

Regardless of the commodification and privatization process' actual form, critical theory's role is to 'demystify this appearance' and situate technological rationality within the political 'where its consequences are a challenge to human responsibility' (Feenberg, 2014: 120). The capitalist mode of production determines the social form of technology through a two-sided technical and economic abstraction process. Privacy abuse from aggregate data becomes a negative externality of the dynamic exchange between personal data and accessible technology use in competitive and non-competitive (monopoly) markets. Just as technology attains a fetish-like, neutral appearance disconnected from the social conditions and mode of production that gives it existence, so do commodities gain a similar fetish-like character. The Frankfurt School criticized society and culture as being dominated by commodity exchange. The advertising industry and private interests have come to define mass culture by flooding the media with desires and wants. The School's theoretical departure from traditional Marxian concerns of labour, value, and capital opened the space for a critique of society and the effect of commercialization on culture and communication.

Recent interpreters of Marx argue that the entire method of Marx's finished and unfinished work was to denaturalize economic categories of classical economists, such as capital, land, and labour, and present them as socially and historically determined (Murray, 2002; Heinrich, 2012; Elbe, 2013; Bonefeld, 2014). In other words, classical and neoclassical economists create 'the illusion of the economic' as if there is only one general way of producing (Murray, 2002: 13). On the contrary, capitalism is to be understood as a historically specific social form of production resulting in contradictions, inequalities, and exploitation. This reverses the trend of the social critique initiated by the Frankfurt School and postulates that interaction between social and economic forms always determines the political economy. Social relations are not just a consequence of capitalism but also a starting point, which opens space for sociological analysis of political economy (Prug, 2022). A commodity has a 'natural form' such as a chair, but it also has a 'social form' when it becomes a commodity in a capitalist society (Heinrich, 2012). It is produced with means of production and labour power and, finally, socially validated as a commodity once it is exchanged for money in the market. On digital platforms, the commodification process can occur at any point of the social interaction process that platform infrastructures enable: at the level of users, advertisers, businesses, commodity producers, intellectual property owners, and others. In each case, aggregated data allow competitive advantages and infrastructures for managing these social relations.

Technological forms outside commodification

Platforms configure social relations by allowing flexible economic forms to emerge and acting as multi-sided markets that allow producers, consumers, and distributors to interact. Any part of the interaction can be monetized and turned into an economic form: consumers as targets for advertising, producers by sharing their revenues with the platform, or distributors which can provide access for free, under a subscription, or for a one-off payment. Purely economic reasoning cannot explain the influence of social experience and social relations on the development of targeted advertising and personal data commodification. Economic reasoning in policy debates does not conceptualize privacy as 'boundary management' (Cohen, 2019) that could inform institutional and regulatory responses. It looks at data markets from a naturalized perspective in which supply and demand provide the most efficient mechanism for allocating commodities. However, privacy abuse is not just an externality that can be resolved through legal action that protects individual internet users in cases where privacy is breached. The range of experiential options is subject to constant change and is not fixed. The expectation that legal action can list all these cases will likely fail. Informing citizens through increased transparency does not solve the problem either, as it puts the responsibility of accountable behaviour on the shoulders of individual citizens who must inform themselves before engaging with digital services. A critical political economy perspective moves the problem towards economic processes that instrumentally commodify the technological form to dominate the lifeworld and social experience.

The typical social cost of this association is privacy abuse, and data protection becomes an issue of disentanglement of experience from the commodity form. The question is, can current regulatory measures do anything to renegotiate this coupling? Can we define socially desirable goals without the mediation of experience through commodified technological forms? Judging from current measures in the EU, the answer would be a definitive no, since improved market competition is expected to solve social harms such as privacy abuse (Stucke, 2022). However, this does not mean there is no escaping commodification and capital. When capital goals are rigidly enforced, 'people regularly feel that something has gone wrong, even if they lack the conceptual framework to articulate exactly what has gone wrong and why' (Smith, 2018: 351). All social movements start from lived experience with the capacity for agency beyond capital's imperatives (Smith, 2018).

Big tech companies are usually celebrated as frontrunners of the current stage of capitalism, pushing innovation forward, which is expected to provide societal benefits down the line. However, they all build wealth on top of public investments in early networking technology (Abbate, 1999), free software communities (Birkinbine, 2015; Lund and Zukerfeld, 2020), and data freely harvested from citizens. In light of mounting evidence of the failure of digital (and other) markets to deliver fair, transparent, non-discriminatory services, there is renewed academic interest in what constitutes value in the economy (Mazzucato, 2018; Pitts, 2021), along with the role of new market creation (Mazzucato, 2016) and the public sector (Dencik and Kaun, 2020; Huws, 2020). The technological form embedded in dominant tech's mode of production cannot simply be reformed by listing specific situations where red privacy lines are crossed. 'The mode of production, which produces technological forms, shapes the range of experiential possibilities of the technological form' (Bilić et al, 2021: 46). A political response to the privacy problem is to reconsider data commodification as the best way forward for innovation and the general population's welfare.

Conclusion

Trade and competition law are usually discussed separately from human rights law. However, both share some of the basic premises of the liberal order in which human rights and property rights serve as foundations for the moral justification of capitalism (Whyte, 2019). In this chapter, I used new directions in critical political economy to untangle the privacy issue from its embeddedness in the capitalist mode of production. The 'technological form' concept can be utilized to theorize any entanglement between social experience and technology, whether we talk about work, leisure, political mobilization, or new and future technical systems dependent on data collection and machine learning. As data become commodified, they create numerous contradictions, such as privacy abuse, hate speech, and disinformation. The new politics of digital technology should focus on claiming ownership over citizens' data and using it to reduce involuntary data extraction, allow data portability between private and public infrastructures, strengthen digital rights, or support alternative business models. This would release the social experience of the technology from privatization, monetization, and commodification. Technological forms in different modes of production already exist, as evident in free software and commons projects. However, the role of the state and transnational processes is essential to provide structural changes beyond such fragmented initiatives of social movements.

As currently discussed in EU regulation, privacy legislation should settle the relationship between two private entities: corporations and technology users. However, the set of rights and the asymmetry of power is such that it seems unrealistic to expect legal intervention to resolve potential privacy disputes between these two parties. Individual autonomy notions of privacy legitimize data markets rather than solve the privacy issue. They construct internet users as individuals who should own their digital data and, through contractual engagements such as terms and conditions of use, deliver data in exchange for the benefits of using digital platforms. Market-fixing efforts have the same effect. They legitimize data capture and commodification, smoothing out the functioning of data markets by reducing negative externalities and implicitly positioning 'the market' as the most efficient and rational institution for allocating and utilizing personal data. However, the political question of who reaps the benefits of technological innovation rarely enters the public debate. Suppose we only have individuals and corporations who exchange services for data in the digital society. In that case, we fully delegate the possibility of reaping comprehensive societal benefits from technology to data markets and private entities. Privacy should be envisioned as a social relation in which experience is detached from the commodity form. Only then can we search for political actions that can salvage social experience from economic abstractions conducive to privacy abuse. We are not there yet.

References

Abbate, J. (1999). *Inventing the Internet*. Cambridge, MA: MIT Press.

Acquisti, A., Brandimarte, L., and Loewenstein, G. (2020). Secrets and likes: the drive for privacy and the difficulty of achieving it in the digital age. *Journal of Consumer Psychology*, 30(4): 736–758.

Allmer, T. (2012). *Towards a Critical Theory of Surveillance in Informational Capitalism*. Frankfurt am Main: Peter Lang.

Andrejevic, M. (2002). The work of being watched: interactive media and the exploitation of self-disclosure. *Critical Studies in Media Communication*, 19(2): 230–248.

Andrejevic, M. (2004). The work of watching one another: lateral surveillance, risk, and governance. *Surveillance & Society*, 2(4). DOI: 10.24908/ss.v2i4.3359

Baran, P. and Sweezy, P. (1968). *Monopoly Capital: An Essay on the American Economic and Social Order*. New York: Modern Reader Paperbacks.

Bator, F. M. (1958). The anatomy of market failure. *The Quarterly Journal of Economics*, 72(3): 351–379.

Bilić, P. (2024). Frankfurt School legacy and the critical sociology of digital media and communication. *Critical Sociology*, 5(4–5): 615–628.

Bilić, P. and Prug, T. (2021). Google's post-IPO development: risks, rewards, and shareholder value. *Internet Histories*, 5(2): 171–189.

Bilić, P., Prug, T., and Žitko, M. (2021). *The Political Economy of Digital Monopolies: Contradictions and Alternatives to Data Commodification*. Bristol: Bristol University Press.

Birkinbine, B. J. (2015). Conflict in the commons: towards a political economy of corporate involvement in free and open source software. *The Political Economy of Communication*, 2(2): 3–19.

Bonefeld, W. (2014). *Critical Theory and the Critique of Political Economy: On Subversion and Negative Reason*. New York, London: Bloomsbury.

Cohen, J. E. (2019). Turning privacy inside out. *Theoretical Inquiries in Law*, 20(1): 1–31.

Dean, J. (2020). Communism or neo-feudalism? *New Political Science*, 42(1): 1–17.

Dencik, L. and Kaun, A. (2020). Datafication and the welfare state. *Global Perspectives*, 1(1). DOI: 10.1525/gp.2020.12912

Dyer-Witheford, N. (2015). *Cyber-proletariat: Global Labour in the Digital Vortex*. London: Pluto Press.

Elbe, I. (2013). Between Marx, Marxism, and Marxisms: ways of reading Marx's theory. *Viewpoint Magazine*, 21 October. Available at: https://viewpointmag.com/2013/10/21/between-marx-marxism-and-marxisms-ways-of-reading-marxs-theory/

Feenberg, A. (1996). Marcuse or Habermas: two critiques of technology. *Inquiry*, *39*(1): 45–70.

Feenberg, A. (2014). *The Philosophy of Praxis: Marx, Lukács and the Frankfurt School*. Revised edition. London: Verso.

Feenberg, A. (2017). *Technosystem: The Social Life of Reason*. Cambridge, MA: Harvard University Press.

Flew, T. (2021). *Regulating Platforms*. 1st edition. Cambridge: Polity.

Flew, T. (2022). *Digital Platform Regulation: Global Perspectives on Internet Governance*. Cham: Springer Nature.

Foster, J. B. and McChesney, R. W. (2014). Surveillance capitalism: monopoly-finance capital, the military-industrial complex, and the digital age. *Monthly Review*, 1 July. Available at: https://monthlyreview.org/2014/07/01/surveillance-capitalism/

Fuchs, C. (2014). *Digital Labour and Karl Marx*. New York: Routledge.

Fuchs, C. (2015). Dallas Smythe Today – The Audience Commodity, the Digital Labour Debate, Marxist Political Economy and Critical Theory. Prolegomena to a Digital Labour Theory of Value. In C. Fuchs and V. Mosco (eds) *Marx and the Political Economy of the Media*, pp 522–599. Leiden; Boston, MA: Brill.

Gandesha, S. (2018). Totality and Technological Form. In B. Best, W. Bonefeld, and C. O'Kane (eds) *The SAGE Handbook of Frankfurt School Critical Theory: Volume 2*, pp 642–660. London: SAGE Publications.

Hacker, P. (2021). Manipulation by algorithms: exploring the triangle of unfair commercial practice, data protection, and privacy law. *European Law Journal*. DOI: 10.1111/eulj.12389

Heinrich, M. (2009). Reconstruction or Deconstruction? Methodological Controversies about Value and Capital, and New Insights from the Critical Edition. In R. Bellofiore and R. Fineschi (eds) *Re-reading Marx: New Perspectives after the Critical Edition*, pp 72–98. London: Palgrave Macmillan.

Heinrich, M. (2012). *An Introduction to the Three Volumes of Karl Marx's Capital*. Translated by A. Locascio. New York: Monthly Review Press.

Huws, U. (2020). *Reinventing the Welfare State: Digital Platforms and Public Policies*. London: Pluto Press.

Jin, D. Y. (2015). *Digital Platforms, Imperialism, and Political Culture*. New York: Routledge.

Johnson, G. and Shriver, S. (2022). Privacy & market concentration: intended & unintended consequences of the GDPR. *SSRN Electronic Journal*. DOI: 10.2139/ssrn.3477686

Kapczynski, A. (2020). The law of informational capitalism. *Yale Law Journal*, 129(5): 1460–1515.

Karppinen, K. and Moe, H. (2014). What we talk about when we talk about 'the market': conceptual contestation in contemporary media policy research. *Journal of Information Policy*, 4: 327–341.

Kellner, D. (2002). The Frankfurt School and British Cultural Studies: The Missed Articulation. In J. T. Nealon and C. Irr (eds) *Rethinking the Frankfurt School: Alternative Legacies of Cultural Critique*, pp 31–58. New York: State University of New York Press.

Kenney, M. (2016). The rise of the platform economy. *Issues in Science and Technology*, 32(3): 61–69.

Lund, A. and Zukerfeld, M. (2020). *Corporate Capitalism's Use of Openness: Profit for Free?* Cham: Springer International Publishing.

Marcuse, H. (1998). *Technology, War, and Fascism: Collected Papers of Herbert Marcuse, Volume 1*. Edited by D. Kellner. London; New York: Routledge.

Marcuse, H. (2007). *One-dimensional Man: Studies in the Ideology of Advanced Industrial Society*. Reprint. London and New York: Routledge.

Marx, K. (2010). *Capital: Volume 3*. London: Lawrence & Wishart.

Mazzucato, M. (2016). From market fixing to market-creating: a new framework for innovation policy. *Industry and Innovation*, 23(2): 140–156.

Mazzucato, M. (2018). *The Value of Everything: Making and Taking in the Global Economy*. London: Allen Lane.

Mazzucato, M. (2019). *Preventing digital feudalism*. Project Syndicate, 2 October. Available at: www.project-syndicate.org/commentary/platform-economy-digital-feudalism-by-mariana-mazzucato-2019-10

Murray, P. (2002). The Illusion of the Economic: The Trinity Formula and the 'Religion of Everyday Life'. In M. Campbell and G. Reuten (eds) *The Culmination of Capital: Essays on Volume Three of Marx's Capital*, pp 246–272. Basingstoke: Palgrave.

Murray, P. (2018). Critical Theory and the Critique of Political Economy: From Critical Political Economy to the Critique of Political Economy. In B. Best, W. Bonefeld, and C. O'Kane (eds) *The SAGE Handbook of Frankfurt School Critical Theory: Volume 2*, pp 764–782. London: SAGE Publications.

Peukert, C., Bechtold, S., Batikas, M., and Kretschmer, T. (2020). *European privacy law and global markets for data*. ETH Zurich Research Collection: Center for Law & Economics Working Paper Series. DOI: 10.3929/ETHZ-B-000406601

Pitts, F. H. (2021). *Value*. 1st edition. Cambridge: Polity.

Pridmore, J. and Zwick, D. (2011). Editorial: marketing and the rise of commercial consumer surveillance. *Surveillance & Society*, 8(3): 269–277.

Prug, T. (2022). Marxova analiza društvenih oblika i ekonomska sociologija. *Revija za sociologiju*, 52(1): 87–113.

Reichelt, H. (1982). From the Frankfurt School to value-form analysis. *Thesis Eleven*, 4(1): 166–169.

Reuten, G. (1988). Value as Social Form. In M. Williams (ed) *Value, Social Form and the State*, pp 42–61. London: Palgrave Macmillan.

Rigi, J. and Prey, R. (2015). Value, rent, and the political economy of social media. *The Information Society*, 31(5): 392–406.

Rochet, J.-C. and Tirole, J. (2003). Platform competition in two-sided markets. *Journal of the European Economic Association*, 1(4): 990–1029.

Scholz, T. (ed). (2013). *Digital Labour: The Internet as Playground and Factory*. New York: Routledge.

Smith, T. (2018). *Beyond Liberal Egalitarianism: Marx and Normative Social Theory in the Twenty-First Century*. Chicago: Haymarket Books.

Smyrnaios, N. (2018). *Internet Oligopoly: The Corporate Takeover of Our Digital World*. Bingley: Emerald Publishing.

Srnicek, N. (2017). *Platform Capitalism*. Cambridge: Polity Press.

Stucke, M. E. (2022). *Breaking Away: How to Regain Control Over Our Data, Privacy, and Autonomy*. Oxford: Oxford University Press.

Terranova, T. (2000). Free labor: producing culture for the digital economy. *Social Text*, 18(2): 33–58.

van Dijck, J., de Waal, M., and Poell, T. (2018). *The Platform Society: Public Values in a Connective World*. Oxford: Oxford University Press.

Varoufakis, Y. (2021). Techno-feudalism is taking over. *Project Syndicate*, 28 June. Available at: www.project-syndicate.org/commentary/techno-feudalism-replacing-market-capitalism-by-yanis-varoufakis-2021-06

Whyte, J. (2019). *The Morals of the Market: Human Rights and the Rise of Neoliberalism*. London: Verso.

Zuboff, S. (2015). Big other: surveillance capitalism and the prospects of an information civilization. *Journal of Information Technology*, 30(1): 75–89.

Zuboff, S. (2019). *The Age of Surveillance Capitalism: The Fight for a Human Future at the New Frontier of Power*. 1st edition. New York: PublicAffairs.

9

Synthetic Data: Servicing Privacy

Johan Lau Munkholm and Tanja Wiehn

Introduction

Originating in experiments with computer vision in the 1960s (Nikolenko, 2021), synthetic data have recently gained traction in the data industries. The reasons for the growing interest in synthetic data lie at the heart of well-known issues with data from real-world systems: gender and racial bias in data sets, collection and processing costs, and notably new policy requirements concerning the use of personal information. Unlike organic data, synthetic data are generated in algorithmic models. They are presented as an alternative to manually collected and processed data. Synthetic data can thus be created as novel output by systems of artificial intelligence (AI), such as General Adversarial Networks or generated in fully simulated digital environments (Nikolenko, 2021; Steinhoff, 2022).

Often referred to as generative AI, synthetic data rose to infamy in the forms of deep fakes, photorealistic imagery, and videos (Meikle, 2022). This seemed to prove AI's capability of realistically simulating aspects of the real world. For this contribution to the anthology, we will home in on a specific aspect of the promotion and value of synthetic data. That is, the marketing of synthetic data as a new privacy-compliant technology that resolves political tensions related to the collection and processing of personal information. Intensifying political determination to reel in the power of the corporate data industries or 'big tech', now widely understood to be the purveyor of so-called 'surveillance capitalism', has not only introduced new regulatory measures, most notably the General Data Protection Regulation (GDPR), but also spurred innovation meant to reconcile political and popular disquiet (Zuboff, 2019). The emerging interest in synthetic data, whether touted as panacea or corporate hype, signifies the scope of political discourse and governance in regard to data and their utility.

In this chapter, we contextualize the emergence of synthetic data within a wider socio-political discourse concerning privacy infringements, anxieties about surveillance, and liberal data rights. We argue that to understand the burgeoning market for synthetic data solutions and its pull, it is crucial to understand the form of the socio-political environment in which such commodified solutions are ascribed value. In this environment, synthetic data are symptomatic of a specific political and regulatory concern which references, both directly and indirectly, privacy as a fundamental value. For commercial promoters and academic commentators alike, synthetic data signal a possible rupture between human and data without a loss of quality. This responds positively to the requirements of the predominant regulatory schemes such as the GDPR. Through our analysis we show how the data industries market synthetic data as a solution to persisting problems with personal data use, and how this is stimulated by existing regulatory frameworks of individual privacy rights. Focusing on the GDPR as an incentivizing mechanism, we highlight the implicit direction of data politics when placing privacy and the protection of personal information as a core objective of regulatory intervention illustrating ongoing developments in the politics of data and privacy. By exploring the epistemological presuppositions of the concept of privacy and where it leads politically, we indicate what lies outside the Overton Window of contemporary data politics: a democratic right to model data and produce insights for the benefit of social needs.

Towards the end of the chapter, we build on the analysis of the productive reciprocity between general social concerns, legal requirements, and technological developments to emphasize the limitations of privacy as a political concept that informs regulatory interventions in the world of tech. We do this by highlighting the tendency of the privacy discourse to overestimate the representational aspect of data rather than their productive capacities. Problems of data are often reduced to the issue of an indexical relationship between data and their human source. Among regulators and academics, this understanding informs the assumption that privacy infringement is a central problem of a contemporary information society that should guide regulatory interventions. Stressing this overriding problem consistently works to push questions of valid use and ownership of data and data infrastructures to the side while encouraging private solutions that only entrench existing power structures.[1]

The chapter draws on empirical data collection, combining ethnographic fieldwork (Flick, 2018; Knoblauch and Vollmer, 2019; Bauer and Gaskell, 2000) at data industry conferences and webinars with the collection of documents such as white papers and blog posts (Rapley and Rees, 2018) by major synthetic data companies. We also rely on expert knowledge on synthetic data from two data scientists, one of whom we interviewed for this chapter. To date, there is a limited amount of research on synthetic data in the social sciences and the humanities (Steinhoff, 2022; Jacobsen, 2023). The novelty of synthetic data presents a challenge for understanding their potential political and social impact: most research on synthetic data derives from the field of computer science (Nikolenko, 2021) which creates certain barriers of dissemination in the humanities due to constrained readability and intelligibility of computer science (Amoore et al, 2023). However, this also points to the relevance of qualitative research being conducted on the topics related to computer science (Tracy, 2010). Our empirical work aims to substantiate an analysis on the impact and logic of the data industries' adaptation of synthetic data, with a special emphasis on privacy.

Synthetic data

What are synthetic data? To create a common framework of synthetic data, we first lay out some definitional characteristics of the technology deriving from the field of computer science and the rather limited theoretical voices from the humanities and social sciences. Even though the origin of synthetic data lies in early experiments in computer vision many decades ago (Nikolenko, 2021), a clear-cut definition proves to be difficult to this day.

The Alan Turing Institute and the Royal Society recently published a report to capture the fast developing field of synthetic data. In the report, the authors do not offer a simple definition of the phenomenon, but define it broadly as data generated by a pre-built model or algorithms for a specific purpose (Jordon et al, 2022), pointing to the technologically manufactured origin of synthetic data. The authors outline the technological capabilities of synthetic data as a promising technology to advance data science projects. However, the report also underscores that currently 'systematic frameworks that would enable the deployment of this technology safely and responsibly are still missing' (Jordon et al, 2022: 4).

In a more theoretical vein, which we will return to in more detail, James Steinhoff defines synthetic data by stressing the potential disconnection of data from the real world:

> data which is not a trace, copy or recording, but the product of a computational process. Synthetic data thus purports to attenuate the connection between data and people by synthesising data. ... While all data are to some degree synthetic, ... the contemporary phenomenon of synthetic data is differentiated by its disconnection from the so-called real world. (Steinhoff, 2022: 5)

Here, synthetic data act as a technical innovation that addresses concerns evolving in a regulatory environment where a focus on privacy and legitimate utilization of personal information is prominent. In this environment, severing the supposed ties between the information of real people and the algorithmic models generated by such information without loss of efficiency or precision is a potentially valuable endeavour. The GDPR is symptomatic of this environment and has been a driving regulatory mechanism in incentivizing a new market for privacy service solutions. The regulatory scrutiny born out of a growing political awareness of the value and utility of data has made access to and use of data an increasingly complicated legal affair, which only adds to the processing costs of collecting and storing data. *Syntheticus*, a company offering 'privacy-preserving synthetic data solutions', recommends synthetic data because they eliminate the need for expensive software and hardware while minimizing privacy risks.[2] The economic logic stitching together solutions for privacy and cheaper data processing is prevalent in the promotion of synthetic data. In a blog post published by Mostly AI, synthetic data's simultaneous constitution of utility and privacy is spelled out: 'AI-generated synthetic data is THE way forward to preserve the utility of data while protecting the privacy of every data subject' (Tabakovic, 2020). Similarly, in a workshop organized by the EU's Internet Privacy Engineering Network (IPEN), Stephen Bamford of Janssen Pharmaceuticals called synthetic data 'one of the most cost-effective privacy-enhancing technologies that is available' (IPEN, 2021).[3]

Framed by data companies, the definition of synthetic data therefore revolves around its technical functionality and the legal practicality it affords. Take for instance the Israeli company Datagen. Datagen (2022) frames synthetic data as a convenient alternative to ordinary data, relying on technological understandings:

> Researchers at MIT cleverly drew parallels between diet coke and synthetic data. To be effective, each of them needs to bear a strong resemblance to the 'real thing'. Diet coke needs to taste like real coke; synthetic data needs to have the mathematical and statistical properties of the real-world dataset. Much like diet coke advocates celebrate the removal of calories from their favorite drinks, synthetic data supporters rejoice in the removal of thorny issues surrounding collection, cleaning, and annotation of real-world data.[4]

At the core of many use cases for synthetic data lies the promise of them as a privacy-securing technology and their potential to cost-effectively generate or enhance data sets. However, there are variations in the corporate promotions of synthetic data as inherently privacy preserving. In bridging the commercial incentives and technological understandings of synthetic data, Irish privacy company Truata complicates the branding of synthetic data as a holy grail for data privacy in a white paper called 'Not all synthetic data is created equal' (Fenton et al, 2022):

> Where privacy-enhancing technologies (PETs) are concerned, privacy and utility are generally opposing objectives and synthetic data is no different. That is, if some processing or transformation of a dataset optimizes privacy, its analytic utility will be affected and vice versa. This makes intuitive sense, since most privacy-enhancing technologies operate by adding noise, changing values to be less distinguishable or otherwise altering the dataset's contents so as to be unrecognisable to the original.[5]

Along with growing interest and hype, the market for synthetic data solutions is expected to expand, but the corporate interest and investment in privacy are not new. The flourishing market of synthetic data is closely tethered to the advertising of privacy as a service product available for purchase via technological mediation. Among the largest platforms globally, Apple has taken the driver's seat in marketing its products as inherently privacy-protecting with the release of iOS 14.5 in 2021. With this, Apple staked a claim to the meaning and function of privacy. The operating system gave users the ability to effortlessly choose whether to be tracked by third-party apps or not while causing a push away from unique identifiers towards anonymized advertisement and aggregate solutions (McGee, 2021). The changes to Apple's operating system were accompanied by a wider advertisement and privacy campaign in which Apple marketed itself as a protector of the fundamental human right of privacy in a move to differentiate itself from its competitors. This furthered Apple's reputation as a de facto privacy protector and regulator already established during the COVID-19 pandemic where Apple provided decentralized contact tracing software largely lauded by European regulators (Sharon, 2021). This illustrates a wider industry turn to not merely comply with a demand for privacy imposed by policy makers but to actively shape the functional meaning of it within the digital jurisdictions of private platforms. Synthetic data are another example of the tech sector actively partaking in the development of privacy-protecting technology to satisfy regulatory requirements and the needs of consumers and private clients. However, the corporate embrace of privacy contains other significant implications for the critique and problematization of the corporate control of data and their uses. Developments in synthetic data reveal the limited critical potential of privacy as a political precept as well as its untimely epistemological emphasis. We will develop this point towards the end of the chapter, but first we will qualify the connection between privacy regulation and synthetic data while elaborating on the wider corporate interest in synthetic data.

Beyond privacy

In an article from 2020, Katja de Vries frames the potential use cases for synthetic data. De Vries points to the issue of privacy that synthetic data seemingly solve: 'Creating synthetic data sets that have the same utility and informativeness as the original while escaping GDPR issues because there is no tie to real people: that is a holy grail that could have major impact on any research dealing with personal data' (2020: 2116).

Avoiding GDPR-related issues and policies is explicitly used as a marketing strategy for the promotion of synthetic data by synthetic data companies, especially European-based ones. Put briefly, for synthetic data to successfully avoid the scope of application of the GDPR, the 'data subject' must not be identifiable by any means. If it is proven that synthetic data cannot effectively anonymize data sources, then they become subject to regulation under the GDPR. It remains uncertain whether this is at all possible without a critical loss of utility. Along with several data scientists (Stadler et al, 2020), Kelsey Finch, Senior Counsel at the Future of Privacy Forum, has expressed scepticism as to the promise of synthetic data threading the needle between privacy and utility:

> In many cases, it's likely not a silver bullet solution to this desire to share and use data in new ways. It doesn't automatically resolve that tension between the analytic utility of the data set and the amount of privacy protection that it gives. There is always the chance for small bugs to make their way into the process or for synthetic data to be used in unexpected ways.[6]

Nonetheless, synthetic data are advertised as cost-effective and nearly indistinguishable from organic data while promising to make data sets independent of private information while being equally efficient. This is particularly beneficial for industries that require access to data, which are legally defined as 'sensitive' personal data such as the health sector or in the insurance business. The potential value of synthetic data for private businesses is thus two-pronged. First, they reduce costs. The utilization of data across industries for purposes of learning, optimization, automatization, and modelling is a key concern for any contemporary corporation committed to continuous relevancy and growth. More than just the raw material for the production of personalized advertising in the online sphere, data and machine learning underpin the optimization of, for instance, global supply chains, genomic sequencing, warehouse management, and financial trading. Any private corporation faced with the competitive pressures of the global capitalist economy is increasingly required to invest in the capacity to access and exploit data from commercial processes to improve its position.

However, data that fuel machine learning algorithms do not come pre-packaged. For learning to unfold and effective AI to emerge, algorithms must be taught what to look for to improve existing practices. Traditionally, machine learning algorithms have been trained on data sets annotated by human workers that identify and click on stop signs, various human features, tumours, and everything else that may teach a machine learning algorithm to perceive and discriminate autonomously. Inevitably, there are costs associated with the development of data sets however insignificant wages, or rather micropayments, for labour may be (Jones, 2021). Synthetic data hold the promise of producing more accurate data at a much lower cost. Unquestionably, the decisive calculus underpinning possible investment in synthetically generated data for private businesses is economic in nature.

Second, synthetic data also figure as a solution to the perceived problem of a generalized loss of individual privacy, a public concern strongly connected to the rise of the business of data. Intimately related to a liberal legal tradition, a mainstay of privacy protection and the related discourse is an individualistic bias (Warren and Brandeis, 1890; Westin, 1967; Fried, 1968; Gavison, 1984; Froomkin, 2000). While there has been a concerted effort to disassociate privacy from overly individualistic meanings in contemporary privacy research (Becker, 2019), stressing instead its importance for maintaining boundaries that guarantee unencumbered social interaction, the first principle of privacy-centred analysis remains the individual (Regan, 1995; Solove, 2008; Nissenbaum, 2010; Cohen, 2013). The primary analytical focus on the individual is key to understanding the implicit political function of privacy which informs the promotional drive of synthetic data. Synthetic data are perceived to be a solution to 'privacy'.

Considered from a prominent privacy-centric perspective, the commercial collection of personal information for the possible improvement of predictive algorithms in distinct contexts is problematic, as it make individuals 'legible' and curtails free interactions between two or more autonomous individuals from where sociality and innovation emerge (Cohen, 2013, 2019). In contemporary privacy literature emphasizing the social value of privacy, privacy acts as a shorthand for an enumeration of a host of problems related to data collection and use. It is not a concept imbued with singular definitive meaning. All problems captured as matters of privacy begin with the individual and are ultimately meant to find their solution in a liberal juridical regulation; as Daniel Solove writes, 'the focal point for a theory of privacy should be the problems we want the law to address' (Solove, 2008: 57). Though unsatisfying to Solove (2022), the GDPR is one such legal addressing mechanism which both creates legal demands for proper use of personal information for corporations operating in the EU, and incentivizes the development of privacy-enhancing technology such as synthetic data. The focus on protection of personal data and privacy as a matter of course by prominent legal scholars and the highest supranational institutions circulates a political emphasis on privacy in society. In an interview with the *Financial Times*, Shoshana Zuboff has deemed privacy not just 'extinguished' but a 'zombie category' as a result of the ubiquity of big tech in everyday life (Mance, 2023). Though Zuboff supplies no definition of privacy with which to effectively evaluate its existence, only a deeply selective reading befitting Zuboff's own project allows one to deem privacy a zombie category. The heydays of privacy and regulation of personal information are upon us. In fact, the rise and growing investment in synthetic data technologies correlates directly with the implementation of the GDPR (Fenton et al, 2022) while improvements in machine learning methods for creating synthetic data have evolved rapidly in recent years. The introduction of data protection policies is fuelling the market for privacy-compliant solutions for data heavy industries in Europe, creating new investment opportunities (Anant et al, 2020; Cisco Secure, 2023). Whereas legal concerns were not the only, or even primary, reason for the emergence of synthetic data, synthetic data companies offer privacy-safe data sets as a service to data-reliant businesses forced to comply with the regulatory precepts of the GDPR.

Whether the synthetic data can live up to the task is, as already indicated, uncertain. In EU's IPEN workshop (IPEN, 2021), which has been a substantial part of our fieldwork, legal scholar Dara Hallinan specifies how the use of synthetic data opens up new questions for the GDPR and other similar regulations:

> Synthetic data created from an original set of statistical properties, however, is not necessarily a clear relationship between any data record in the synthetic set and a specific identifiable person. And this raises the relatively novel question, for data protection lawyers at least, as to whether data synthesis technologies then facilitate the possibility to create a legitimately anonymous data set, potentially many legitimately anonymous data sets, whilst also retaining the originally identifiable data.

In the current moment, synthetic data operate in a legal grey zone where the standards of legitimate generation and implementation of synthetic solutions are not entirely clear. This is not necessarily halting the advertising of and investment in synthetic data which opens up to further legal wrangling. As one expert noted in an interview, a common framing of synthetic data as *fake* introduces new problems, such as when synthetic data no longer need to undergo a specific set of scrutiny:

> [S]ome of the bigger vendors have really hung their hat on that message. But the big problem is that the more sophisticated the technique, the

more it has learned about the original and therefore the closer to the original it's synthesising. ... The real danger comes if a regulator or standardisation body comes out and says all synthetic data is safe.[7]

The value of 'fake data' is exactly that they purport to disconnect from identifiable data sources, thus preserving privacy. Synthetic data is a technology formed and promoted in the slipstream of a privacy-centric political discourse native to ongoing debates about the danger of digital platforms. The privacy discourse centres on individual rights of data protection. In this sense, synthetic data conform to an existing course of techno-political development aligned with liberal data politics. If it is not the case that synthetic data necessarily signify a radical new departure in data production, what does the corporate and regulatory investment in the technology suggest about tendencies in contemporary data industries and societies? What are the hidden political implications of synthetic data, and can a critical emphasis on privacy help shed light on them? We will explore these questions in the following. We will approach them by engaging with and questioning certain notions in the existing critical literature on synthetic data that explore the possibility and implications of decoupling people from data.

Contextualizing the development and promises of synthetic data

As mentioned, critical and speculative investigations of synthetic data in the social sciences and humanities are still limited. Articles by Steinhoff (2022) and Jacobsen (2023) are worth mentioning. These both purport to open and think through some of the implications for our understanding of machine learning algorithms and their possible socio-economic effects when their training data become synthetic.

Ben Jacobsen argues that the core feature of synthetic data lies in the ways in which they promise to place algorithms beyond the realm of risk. According to Jacobsen, this is promised by providing data variability to algorithms. When training an algorithm on data sets that derive from the 'real' world labelled by humans, the algorithm adapts to a norm from which it makes recommendations based on the data available for its training. In such cases, 'prediction depends on classification, and classification itself presumes the existence of classes, and attributes that define membership of classes' (Mackenzie, 2015: 433). Continuous change undermines the potential effectiveness of machine learning as Adrian Mackenzie points out (Mackenzie, 2015). Without exposure to data of relatively rare events or unusual patterns of behaviour, the algorithm's capacity to adapt to and respond to volatility is hampered which increases the risk of neglecting important trends or occurrences that may cause further disruptions or breakdowns. Unmoored from the normality of empirical events reflected in real-world data sets, according to Jacobsen private businesses look to synthetic data to infuse more variability and diversity into data sets whereby machine learning algorithms become better equipped to recognize the otherwise unusual and prescribe new modes of action. Synthetic data thus promise to reduce volatility and reconstitute society 'beyond the realm of risk' (Jacobsen, 2023: 6). Part of the appeal of synthetic data and their value, in other words, is that they are proximate to real data though not actually real and therefore do not hold a bias towards the 'normal' distribution of events of behaviours. Instead, algorithms can be tuned to the abnormal and the risks that abnormality carries exactly by escaping the confines of the real via synthetic data. In fact, what this also suggests is that synthetic data enable companies to avoid a potentially fraught relationship to actual individuals, which is typically characterized as a relationship defined by surveillance. If the infringement of individual privacy derives from the collection of a critical amount of data on a person, then synthetic data enable disentanglement between the technical system and the juridical individual according to boosters of synthetic data. Importantly, this is achieved without a necessary loss of value, quite the opposite – the data sets are purported to be better primed for volatility and risk management. Yet, as indicated by Mackenzie, without a continuous capacity to capture and calibrate to complex patterns of real-world data, data generation may provide predictions but that does not necessarily imply that they are applicable to real events and conditions which are themselves in a state of flux. This flux must continuously be accounted for. Yet again, we arrive at the problem of squaring utility with privacy requirements.

The potential decoupling of information and human and what it implies is more explicitly a theme in Steinhoff (2022). For Steinhoff, synthetic data signify a move beyond business models precipitated on the surveillance of actual people and the 'mining of subjectivity' that underpin the sale and distribution of advertisement. The data surveillance business, or surveillance capitalism as Zuboff calls it, has received substantial attention from critical data theory for its efforts to achieve 'the automation of subjectivity' (Steinhoff, 2022: 2). Steinhoff does not reject the saliency of the surveillance capitalism narrative despite its shortcomings (Lucas, 2019; Slobodian, 2019; Kapczynski, 2020), but explains how the commercialization of synthetic data, emerging in response to a general shortage of data, 'aims at the generation of data without the transcendent element of the human subject, substituting embodied, social human actions for simulated objects and environments, the creation and population of which are already partially automated' (Steinhoff, 2022: 11).

Steinhoff considers synthetic data a significant change in the structure and logic of surveillance capitalism away from a necessary monitoring of human individuals towards an autonomous process wherein human inputs are redundant for the continued circuit of data production. This is key because it implies that there is a before and after synthetic data in the data industries, signifying a critical moment of autonomization for data-intensive capital according to Steinhoff. As already covered, this is likely overstating the capabilities of synthetic data. But while it is unlikely that data sets can remain utilizable if completely autonomous from the vicissitudes of the real and its features, the commercial turn to synthetic data does highlight that reliance on aggregated individual data flows, from the point of view of businesses, is not an end in itself but a means to produce predictions about a range of future outcomes that may or may not affect the individuals from whence data came. As we will argue in the following, rather than signifying a radically new development in data and network analysis, synthetic data illustrate how an emphasis on privacy opens specific vistas of technological development and intervention, generally concerned with individual rights, while leaving unaddressed the right to model and exploit data in the first place. With this we highlight the inherent political project of privacy, its limitations and what an overemphasis on the individual as a principle of analysis gets wrong.

Escaping the individual

Synthetic data do not imply a decisive change in the underlying logic and interests of commercial data businesses. Rather, synthetic data are an appropriate technical innovation for elucidating an already existing condition, namely that digital platforms, data brokers, advertisers, and so on do not primarily invest in data for their representational content or their proximity to actual individuals that they desire to monitor. Escaping the legal individual and their government-sanctioned claims to privacy are, for a number of businesses, a reason to invest in synthetic data. Their central interest has long been the production of insights generated from the combination of a multitude of data that do not trace back to any single individual's desires or inner beliefs. In the relationship between an information source and a machine learning algorithm there is always a gap, but its most significant moment comes at the point of production or output which is a function of analysis and the performativity of networks (Healy, 2015).

Abstracted from individual processes of action, data points are not inherently evidential or indexical (Goriunova, 2019). Instead, they are used for creating aggregate products or derivatives that are, as Olga Goriunova writes, 'values, dynamically re-instantiated correlations, rules, and models, shreds of actions, identities, interest, engagements, which are put into relation with each other, disaggregated, categorised, classified, clustered, modelled, projected onto, speculated upon and made predictions about' (Goriunova, 2019: 133). Insights produced from data are not constructed to draw a holistic picture of an individual person. Creating patterns, learning from them, and making predictions or recommendations are created from the combination of many data points synthesized to create a single output that creates a difference in the world (Amoore, 2020). In other words, data production is always synthetic – the key question is what productive difference a data output makes and who gets to make it. This is a question that opens up not just to the specific modes of data collection but to the very economic, juridical, and technological structures of contemporary capitalism. Tethered fundamentally to the individual, privacy is an unsustainable concept for understanding the effects and implications of algorithmically governed businesses and societies, even before the arrival of synthetic data technology as it orients attention towards discrete individuals and their rights. The emphasis on privacy protection as a central problem of contemporary information society implies a political focus on the interface between individuals and commercial computational networks. The excitement around synthetic data is indicative of a regulatory and innovative climate where individual rights and protection of personal information remain a, if not the, central political concern. The strong emphasis on the political problem of relying on large data sets derived from aggregates of individuals and their actions encourages private investment and promotion of synthetic data as a solution reached via technological innovation. While locking in a specific regulatory and innovative trajectory, this also obstructs from a more fundamental discussion about existing ownership models of digital infrastructures, who they benefit, and what insights data modelling are meant to achieve. This focus is part and parcel of a privacy-centric focus on protection of personal data which posits that individuals under surveillance are algorithmically reproduced and represented as discrete profiles or 'data doubles' (Matzner, 2016). Synthetic data are a means to avoid a reliance on individual surveillance, signalling that an innate interest in singular individuals from the point of commercial interest was always overstated. In fact, it may be questioned whether individual surveillance was ever a constitutive practice of correlative network analysis rather than a political framing propagated by a focus on privacy indicative of the continued predominance of the liberalist framework in policy and legal regulation (Benthall and Goldenfein, 2020). As Wendy Chun writes, 'Networks preempt and predict by correlating singular actions to larger collective habitual patterns' which are in many cases created and characterized by an assumption of *homophily*: 'the mechanism by which individuals are "stuck together" so that an affectively intense "we" can emerge' (Chun, 2021: 97). Due to its individualist bias, privacy is maladjusted to conceptualize the implications of the data industries, even as privacy continues to figure prominently in popular and academic discourse on the problems of contemporary information society (Viljoen, 2021).

As an innovation directly addressed as a solution to privacy concerns, synthetic data are characteristic of the kind of incentivizing which privacy regulations, such as the GDPR, and more general anxieties about privacy, motivate. This accentuates the specific course of technological and political development that a specific set of rules induces for private businesses and related political stakeholders. As Randy Martin writes, 'At their most general expression, rules mark the scene of conflict or contestation. They are the material residue of a dispute that, in turn, shapes terms of opposition, conditions of resolution, and strategies of benefits' (Martin, 2015: 55). For companies promoting synthetic data, the GDPR frames the terms of opposition or conflict as well as how resolution can be reached via investment and innovation, showing ultimately how the GDPR can be leveraged for strategic benefits. As legal guidelines for the use of synthetic data mature, synthetic data markets will change accordingly. The emerging market for privacy-as-a-service and the corporate investment in privacy, discursively and technologically, indicate that privacy protection is integral to corporate strategies and technological development. As long as data companies have the power to construct solutions to privacy demands and to stake a claim to the meaning of privacy, privacy does not imply a threatening injunction. Privacy signifies, instead, the path of least resistance towards maintaining the existing balance of power.

Conclusion

As private digital infrastructures become increasingly embedded in the fabric of our social relations, the need for regulatory interventions is widely asserted. Problems concerning personal data flows and their relationship to the status and integrity of the human individual signify central fixpoints in the resulting policy debates and regulations. Such problems, generally related to individual harms caused by surveillance, are frequently articulated as matters of privacy. Though claims to the contrary have been raised, privacy is an inherently political concept with roots firmly planted in the liberal ideological tradition (Bennett, 2011). The foundational focus on the relative protection of individuals in digital environments underpins a specific regulatory inflection which can be traced in the regulatory approach of the EU which accedes to the existing state of networked society where the market determines the best use of digital technology. This conforms to the EU's role as rule-maker and guarantor of the internal market as well as the capitalist status quo.

Privacy concerns stimulate not just policy formations but also market-based solutions to new regulatory requirements in addition to individual demands. To exemplify this, we have suggested that the promotion of, and investment in, synthetic data is symptomatic of a particular political and discursive environment where privacy protection garners significant attention. Simply put, it is somewhat predictable that synthetic data, which purport to decisively rupture the relation between sensitive or personal data inputs and the insights generated from data analysis, are advertised as a solution to privacy transgressions. The corporate enthusiasm around synthetic data highlights that most private corporations do not have an intrinsic interest in personal information for what it says about discrete individuals. The predictive capacities that data may hold are formed by correlating variables in vast sets of data that provide suggestions or recommendations about future events in terms of probabilities. Predictions are *produced* by relating and synthesizing data from different sources. The main value of data is their capacity to infer something about the future rather than giving insights into past events or individual persons. Tellingly, synthetic data are promoted as a way to avoid the contentious problem of relying on data that can be related back to a discrete progenitor. Though it is unlikely that data without some features from the real world can generate usable insights, this should not cause us to assume that there is not a genuine interest in autonomizing data processes and leaving the realm of personal information behind. Not only will this make compliance with privacy regulations easier, it will also reduce costs associated with the procurement of data and their processing. Such steps towards technologically mediated solutions to privacy protection may satisfy GDPR requirements and thus be seen as a boon to individual media users. Yet, here the path of constructing the infrastructural foundation of a present and future information society is traversed in lockstep with private platform providers and data businesses that welcome solutions to privacy concerns as long as their power to intermediate and profit from an expanding range of social relations remains uncontested. Here, the opening to a democratically coordinated information society remains shut: in practice *and* in thought. Rather than dwelling excessively on the promises of individual privacy that synthetic data may or may not guarantee, future research on synthetic data would benefit from asking whether the introduction of synthetic data meaningfully challenges the expanding power of private data corporations and infrastructures and whether it helps undermine discriminatory practices in policing, insurance, banking, healthcare, and so on. If not, synthetic data are technological business as usual.

Notes

[1] While we indicate throughout the chapter that a regulatory focus on privacy works to marginalise a critical analysis of how private digital infrastructures in contemporary capitalism perpetuate existing power asymmetries and injustices, describing how historical inequalities and undemocratic structures are maintained in digitised capitalism lie outside the scope of this chapter (see instead for instance, Srnicek, 2017; Montalban et al, 2019; Jones, 2021; Chun, 2021; Gilbert and Williams, 2022).

[2] Syntheticus AI Blogpost (2023). 'The Benefits and Limitations of Generating Synthetic Data,' https://syntheticus.ai/blog/the-benefits-and-limitations-of-generating-synthetic-data [retrieved 31 July 2023].

[3] Stephen Bamford at IPEN workshop (2021). 'Experiences Implementing Data Synthesis in a Global Life Sciences Company,' https://edps.europa.eu/press-publications/press-news/videos/ipen-2021-synthetic-data-stephen-bamford_en [retrieved 31 July 2023].

[4] Datagen eBook (2022). https://datagen.tech/ai/the-power-of-synthetic-data-ebook/ [retrieved 8 February 2023].

[5] White Paper Truata: 'Not All Synthetic Data is Created Equal' (2022). https://content.truata.com/en/synthetic-data-white-paper

[6] Kelsey Finch at IPEN workshop panel (2021). 'Synthetic data as a privacy enhancing technology and the GDPR', https://edps.europa.eu/press-publications/press-news/videos/ipen-2021-synthetic-data-dara-hallinan-and-kelsey-finch_en [retrieved 31 July 2023].

[7] Excerpt from expert interview with a data scientist, conducted in person in November 2022.

Acknowledgement

This chapter is written as part of the research project *'Don't Take it Personal'*: *Privacy and Information in an Algorithmic Age* generously funded by Independent Research Fund Denmark (grant number 8018-00041B).

References

Amoore, L. (2020). *Cloud Ethics: Algorithms and the Attributes of Ourselves and Others*. Durham, NC: Duke University Press.

Amoore, L., Campolo, A., Jacobsen, B., and Rella, L. (2023). Machine learning, meaning making: on reading computer science texts. *Big Data & Society*, 10(1). DOI: 10.1177/20539517231166887

Anant, V., Donchak, L., Kaplan, J., and Soller, H. (2020). The consumer-data opportunity and the privacy imperative. *McKinsey & Company*, 27 April. Available at: https://tinyurl.com/3fth6432

Apple Privacy (2023). Available at: www.apple.com/privacy/ (accessed 27 January 2023).

Bauer, M. W. and Gaskell, G. (eds) (2000). *Qualitative Researching with Text, Image and Sound*. London: SAGE Publications Ltd.

Becker, M. (2019). Privacy in the digital age: comparing and contrasting individual versus social approaches towards privacy. *Ethics and Information Technology*, 21: 307–317.

Bennett, C. J. (2011). In defence of privacy: the concept and the regime. *Surveillance & Society*, 8(4): 485–496.

Benthall, S. and Goldenfein, J. (2020). *Data Science and the Decline of Liberal Law and Ethics* (unpublished manuscript). Available at: https://ssrn.com/abstract=3632577

Chun, W. H. K. (2021). *Discriminating Data: Correlation, Neighborhoods, and the New Politics of Recognition*. Cambridge, MA and London: The MIT Press.

Cisco Secure (2023). *Privacy's Growing Importance and Impact: Cisco 2023 Data Privacy Benchmark Study*. Available at: https://tinyurl.com/nwr7ap37

Cohen, J. E. (2013). What privacy is for. *Harvard Law Review*, 126(7): 1904–1933.

Cohen, J. E. (2019). *Between Truth and Power: The Legal Constructions of Informational Capitalism*. Oxford and New York: Oxford University Press.

Datagen (2022). *The Power of Synthetic Data* (eBook). Available at: https://datagen.tech/ai/the-power-of-synthetic-data-ebook/

de Vries, K. (2020). You never fake alone: creative AI in action. *Information, Communication & Society*, 23(14): 2110–2127.

Fenton, M., Khan, I., Coyle, M., and Sexton, A. (2022). White paper: not all synthetic data is created equal. *Truata*. Available at: https://content.truata.com/en/synthetic-data-white-paper

Flick, U. (ed) (2018). *The Sage Handbook of Qualitative Data Collection*. London: SAGE Publications Ltd.

Fried, C. (1968). Privacy. *Yale Law Journal*, 77(3): 475–493.

Froomkin, A. M. (2000). The death of privacy. *Stanford Law Review*, 52: 1461–1543.

Gavison, R. (1984). Privacy and the limits of law. In F. A. Schoemann (ed) *Philosophical Dimensions of Privacy: An Anthology*, pp 347–402. Cambridge: Cambridge University Press.

Gilbert, J. and Williams, A. (2022). *Hegemony Now: How Big Tech and Wall Street Won the World (and How We Win It Back)*. London: Verso Books.

Goriunova, O. (2019). The digital subject: people as data as persons. *Theory, Culture & Society*, 36(6): 125–145.

Healy, K. (2015). The performativity of networks. *European Journal of Sociology*, 56(2): 175–205.

IPEN (Internet Privacy Engineering Network) (2021). Synthetic data: what use cases as a privacy enhancing technology? Webinar. Available at: https://edps.europa.eu/data-protection/our-work/ipen/ipen-webinar-2021-synthetic-data-what-use-cases-privacy-enhancing_en

Jacobsen, B. N. (2023). Machine learning and the politics of synthetic data. *Big Data & Society*, 10(1). DOI: 10.1177/20539517221145372

Jones, P. (2021). *Work Without the Worker: Labour in the Age of Platform Capitalism*. London: Verso Books.

Jordon, J., Szpruch, L., Houssiau, F., Bottarelli, M., Cherubin, G., Maple, C., Cohen, S. N., and Weller, A. (2022). Synthetic Data – What, why and how? ArXiv. http://arxiv.org/abs/2205.03257

Kapczynski, A. (2020). The law of informational capitalism. *The Yale Law Review*, 129(5): 1460–1515.

Knoblauch, H. and Vollmer, T. (2019). Ethnographie. In *Handbuch Methoden der empirischen Sozialforschung*, pp 599–617. Wiesbaden: Springer Fachmedien.

Lucas, R. (2019). The surveillance business. *New Left Review*, 121 (Jan/Feb): 132–141.

Mackenzie, A. (2015). The production of prediction: what does machine learning want? *European Journal of Cultural Studies*, 18(4–5): 429–445.

Mance, H. (2023). Shoshana Zuboff: 'Privacy has been extinguished. It is now a zombie. *Financial Times*, January. Available at: www.ft.com/content/0cca6054-6fc9-4a94-b2e2-890c50d956d5

Martin, R. (2015). *Knowledge LTD: Toward a Social Logic of the Derivative*. Philadelphia, PA: Temple University Press.

Matzner, T. (2016). Beyond data as representation: the performativity of big data in surveillance. *Surveillance & Society*, 14(2): 197–210.

McGee, P. (2021). Apple's privacy changes creates windfall for its own advertising business. *Financial Times*, 17 October. Available at: www.ft.com/content/074b881f-a931-4986-888e-2ac53e286b9d

Meikle, G. (2022). *Deepfakes*. Cambridge: Polity Press.

Montalban, M., Frigant, V., and Jullien, B. (2019). Platform economy as a new form of capitalism: a regulationist research programme. *Cambridge Journal of Economics*, 43(4): 805–824.

Nikolenko, S. (2021). *Synthetic Data for Deep Learning*. Cham: Springer Nature.

Nissenbaum, H. (2010). *Privacy in Context: Technology, Policy, and the Integrity of Social Life*. Stanford, CA: Stanford University Press.

Rapley, T. and Rees, G. (2018). Collecting Documents as Data. In U. Flick (ed) *The SAGE Handbook of Qualitative Data Collection*, pp 378–391. London: SAGE Publications Ltd.

Regan, P. M. (1995). *Legislating Privacy: Technology, Social Values, and Public Policy*. Chapel Hill, NC: University of North Carolina Press.

Sharon, T. (2021). Blind-sided by privacy? Digital contact tracing, the Apple/Google API and big tech's newfound role as global health policy makers. *Ethics and Information Technology*, 23: 45–57.

Slobodian, Q. (2019). The false promise of enlightenment. *Boston Review*, 29 May. Available at: www.bostonreview.net/articles/quinn-slobodian-drain-darkness

Solove, D. J. (2008). *Understanding Privacy*. Cambridge, MA: Harvard University Press.

Solove, D. J. (2022). The limitations of privacy rights. *GW Law Faculty Publications & Other Works*: 2–50. DOI: 10.2139/ssrn.4024790

Srnicek, N. (2017). *Platform Capitalism*. Cambridge: Polity Press.

Stadler, T., Oprisanu, B., and Troncoso, C. (2020). Synthetic data: anonymisation groundhog day. *ArXiv*. https://arxiv.org/abs/2011.07018

Steinhoff, J. (2022). Toward a political economy of synthetic data: a data-intensive capitalism that is not a surveillance capitalism? *New Media & Society*, 0(0). DOI: 10.1177/14614448221099217

Tabakovic, A. (2020). Rolling the dice with privacy?! *Mostly AI*, 24 January. Available at: https://tinyurl.com/4czs6epz

Tracy, S. J. (2010). Qualitative quality: eight 'big-tent' criteria for excellent qualitative research. *Qualitative Inquiry*, 16(10): 837–851.

Viljoen, S. (2021). A relational theory of data governance. *The Yale Law Journal*, 31(2): 573–654.

Warren, S. D. and Brandeis, L. D. (1890). The right to privacy. *Harvard Law Review*, 4(5): 193–220.

Westin, A. (1967). *Privacy and Freedom*. New York: Atheneum.

Zuboff, S. (2019). *The Age of Surveillance Capitalism: The Fight for a Human Future at the New Frontier of Power*. London: Profile Books.

10

Can Androids Dream of Electronic Surveillance Targets? Artificial Intelligence and the USSID-18 Defence

Simon Willmetts

Introduction

In March 2013, in a now infamous testimony before the Senate Select Committee on Intelligence, former National Security Agency (NSA) Director James Clapper was asked by Democratic Senator Ron Wyden whether the NSA collects 'any type of data at all on millions or hundreds of millions of Americans?' 'No sir', replied the spy chief, 'not wittingly' (Clapper, 2013). A few months later, an NSA contractor named Edward Snowden leaked hundreds of thousands of internal NSA documents revealing that the NSA had, in fact, been collecting vast amounts of data on American citizens. Snowden himself cited Clapper's response to Wyden's question as one of the key reasons he chose to come forward (Snowden, 2019: 351–352). In stating that the NSA did not 'wittingly' collect data on millions of Americans, Clapper, he believed, had lied to Congress, and to the American people. And so, Snowden took matters into his own hands.

For the NSA, however, Clapper's remark was not as deceptive as it seemed to Snowden. In the weeks and months that followed the Snowden revelations it would become clear that the NSA had a very different operative definition of surveillance to Snowden, Senator Wyden, and much of the general public, especially the portion of the public who supported Snowden, and believed that the NSA were practising mass surveillance. Clapper's choice of words – 'not wittingly' – provides an important clue to the NSA's very different conception of surveillance. What does it mean to collect data on millions of Americans 'wittingly' or 'unwittingly'? Is it even possible to 'unwittingly' collect data on millions of Americans? The NSA believed so.

The NSA's definition of intelligence *collection* can be found in a document known as USSID-18, which sets out safeguards and procedures for minimizing the collection of intelligence on citizens of the United States (US) to comply with US law and ensure the protection of the latter's constitutional rights. Key to the NSA's definition of surveillance is *when* it believes the *collection* of intelligence has taken place. In that document, the NSA defines intelligence collection as the: '*intentional* tasking or *SELECTION* of identified non-public communications for subsequent processing aimed at reporting or retention as a file record' (NSA, 2011, italicization added, capitalization in the original).

According to this rather narrow and somewhat counter-intuitive definition, 'intelligence collection' does not occur at the moment at which information is first, well, collected. Rather, collection only takes place once the data have been intentionally *selected* by a human operator. Human *intention*, 'witting intention', to borrow Clapper's language, is key to the NSA's own definition of surveillance.

This quite particular definition, which enables the US intelligence community to collect vast amounts of metadata from the electronic communications of US citizens *prior* to the *intentional* targeting of a particular person of interest, contradicts most people's everyday conception of intelligence collection and surveillance. Many privacy advocates, including Snowden, have ridiculed the NSA's definition, pointing out that most people are intrinsically uncomfortable with the idea of entities holding vast amounts of information on them, whether or not that entity chooses to do anything with those data (Cohn and Timm, 2013; Miles, 2014; Rusbridger and MacAskill, 2014). Jennifer Granick has argued that the US intelligence community's esoteric definition of certain terms is deliberately disingenuous, designed to obfuscate the reality of their surveillance practices, and divert public attention away from the potential controversies that these practices may inspire. 'American spies have evolved a coded vocabulary', she writes,

> that deflects any nonexpert and sometimes experts as well, from learning the truth. Words like 'collect', 'target', 'in bulk', and 'surveillance' all have concocted meanings in the intelligence gathering context. If you rely on your common understanding of the words as they are generally used, you will not understand what in fact happens in the surveillance world. (Granick, 2017: 27)

Rather than highlighting the US intelligence community's Orwellian use of language in reference to its own surveillance practices, this chapter instead seeks to interrogate the NSA's definition of surveillance *on its own terms*. So much of the ensuing post-Snowden debate between privacy advocates and intelligence practitioners has involved two positions talking past one another, largely as a result of these very different conceptions of 'surveillance' and 'mass surveillance' that each side has adopted. If Granick is to be believed, then this speaking into air may well be the US intelligence community's intended outcome, allowing them to avoid difficult questions by redefining the very terms of the debate. But even if we are to take the US intelligence community's definition of intelligence collection at face value, and accept that 'intentional tasking' and the conscious 'selection' of data is the threshold for surveillance, the reality of many intelligence collection practices today quickly problematizes this definition. In particular, the increasing automation of intelligence practices, including collection, analysis, and tasking, raises the question of what, exactly, constitutes *intent*? Notably, the USSID-18 definition of intelligence collection does not stress *human* intention. It does define 'Selection' as the 'intentional insertion' of things such as telephone numbers and emails into a computer database to retrieve data identified by such selection terms (NSA, 2011: 24). This tends to suggest a human act of typing selection terms into a database, but automated intelligence platforms today are more than capable of querying databases with their own prompts or 'selection terms'. In an intelligence community increasingly driven by automation and artificial intelligence (AI), selection and targeting need not necessarily be human.

This chapter has four parts. The first documents the US intelligence community's (IC) increasing turn to AI, and in particular machine learning. It identifies 'infoglut', or the challenge the IC faces in sifting through the ever-increasing enormity of data that they collect, as the main driver of this trend. The second section explores the impact of this trend upon what is traditionally known as the intelligence cycle: the process via which raw information is targeted, collected, processed, analysed, and disseminated by intelligence agencies. In doing so it aims to show that targeting and the 'intentional selection' of particular datasets are increasingly driven by automated algorithms. It is no longer just humans that decide who the IC should be watching. These two sections are supported by a number of case studies and examples of specific applications of machine learning technologies by the IC. There is a surprising amount of publicly available information on a number of these applications, in part because many of these technologies are developed by the private sector, or through joint public-private partnerships that often involve an open or semi-open bidding process. Various US intelligence agencies, as well as affiliated research institutes such as the Intelligence Advanced Research Projects Activity (IARPA), publish white papers, reports, research calls, and even more granular information about various AI projects and partnerships. Unauthorized leaks, including the Snowden leaks, also provide a wealth of examples of AI and other forms of automation deployed by the IC. These documents provide, if not a comprehensive picture of US IC AI applications, then at least a far more detailed insight than we are conditioned to expect from secretive intelligence agencies.

Having established that the IC is increasingly reliant upon AI algorithms for intelligence collection, processing, analysis, and even the selection of targets, the third section asks whether such automated systems are capable *in themselves* of violating our privacy. Is *intention*, to borrow the language of USSID-18, a necessary precondition for surveillance to have taken place? And if it is, must that *intent* be human? Can androids dream of electronic surveillance targets? Or are they simply inert processing machines, no more aware of the private lives bound up in the data they collect than an automated traffic enforcement camera, identifying 'targets' for speeding tickets, but with little ability to draw inferences about the targets other than how fast they were driving? Under the NSA's definition of 'intelligence collection', the speeding camera was not conducting surveillance. For most drivers who slow down on the motorway to avoid a speeding ticket, it was. The final section asks what it means both for citizens' individual privacy, and for the IC, if machines now meet the NSA's definition of surveillance in USSID-18. If 'intentional tasking or SELECTION' is to remain central to that definition, then the IC must ask itself whether the increasingly common reliance upon artificially intelligent algorithms for the collection, processing, analysis, and even tasking of intelligence, are capable of intent. To ignore this question would not only mask the reality of their surveillance practices via the insincere use of language, as Granick and others have argued, but also entirely ignore a vast and growing area of state surveillance praxis from its own legal compliance regime. For we may have already reached the stage where the notion of surveillance as a human-directed activity is an anachronism for all but a tiny portion of state surveillance practices today.

The problem of infoglut and the solution of AI for the intelligence community

Despite the hyperbole that has often accompanied breakthroughs in AI, there are firm reasons why intelligence agencies in particular stand to benefit significantly from AI-driven technologies (Wooldridge, 2020: 81–82). As the UK Government Office for Science put it: 'Artificial intelligence is particularly useful for sorting data, finding patterns and making predictions' (UK Government Office for Science, 2015). These are precisely the tasks that are at the core of what intelligence agencies do. The need to automate these tasks has become particularly acute in the digital age, where 'infoglut' or information overload has meant that intelligence agencies are now confronted with almost unimaginable volumes of data (Andrejevic, 2013). The US IC's enormous data centre in Bluffdale, Arizona, for example, had an estimated data storage capacity at the time of the centre's completion in May 2014 of somewhere between three and 12 exabytes (Hill, 2013). A mere 400 terabytes (1 exabyte = 1,000,000 terabytes) is required to store all the books ever written in every language (Cisco, 2023). The enormous growth in the volumes of data that intelligence agencies collect presupposes the increasing reliance upon automation. As Mark Andrejevic has argued, digitization and automation go hand-in-hand: 'the advent of digitization made the data searchable and sortable using automated systems. Not only the sorting of data could be automated, but in many cases the collection could be as well' (Andrejevic, 2013: 61). The digital revolution simultaneously entailed both the explosion of data and the possibility of automating its collection and analysis.

For the IC, this conjunction of digitization and automation has spurred significant investment in AI. As Robert Cardillo, the Director of the National Geospatial-Intelligence Agency, put it, without the use of AI, the exponential increase in the volume of images that the Agency processes would require more than 8 million human analysts to pore over the data (Cardillo, 2017). In 2019, the Office of the Director of National Intelligence (ODNI) announced its IC-wide Augmenting Intelligence Using Machines (AIM) Initiative. Tellingly, the AIM report identified the exponential growth in data that the IC collects as the key rationale for adopting AI-driven technologies (ODNI, 2019). In response to this challenge of information overload, the ODNI recommended an aggressive investment strategy into AI-enabled technologies, supplemented by partnerships with the private sector, the Department of Defense, and their Five Eyes partners.

Exact figures for the US IC's investment in AI are hard to come by as the breakdown of the US intelligence budget remains classified. In 2022, the Department of Defense (DoD), which houses a number of major US intelligence agencies, including the NSA, requested $874million for AI development (United States Government Accountability Office, 2022). This figure, however, does not reflect the DoD's total spend on AI. In 2017, for example, it was estimated that the DoD spends a total of $7.4 billion on AI and its related technologies, including big data and cloud computing (Johnson, 2017). AI spending by US civilian intelligence agencies is even harder to specify. It is safe to say, however, that AI represents for them a major and growing area of technological investment and development. In 2018, for example, the CIA's Director for Science and Technology, Dawn Meyerriecks, revealed that the CIA had 137 ongoing AI projects, and two years later she announced the creation of CIA Labs, an office tasked with bringing together industry, academia, and the intelligence community to develop new technologies, including AI-driven technologies, that support the work of the IC. In the late 1990s, the CIA created its own venture capital firm, In-Q-Tel, which invested approximately $120million per year in tech start-ups, including a significant number of companies developing AI technologies (Paletta, 2016). At the time of researching this chapter, 302 companies were listed on In-Q-Tel's website as their investment portfolio,

60 of which were developing AI-enabled applications, a further 64 were working on AI-enabling platforms, while nine more were automation and robotics companies (In-Q-Tel, 2023). Specific companies include Palantir, a well-known AI-driven data analytics firm founded by tech billionaire and political activist Peter Thiel, and cloud security firm Sysdig. Alongside In-Q-Tel's investment of public funds into private sector projects that might benefit the IC, in 2006 the ODNI created the IARPA, a research and development agency intended as the IC's answer to the Defense Advanced Research Projects Agency (DARPA, originally ARPA), which has driven investment in defence technologies since the late 1950s. AI-driven projects funded by IARPA include the somewhat creepy Hidden Activity Signal and Trajectory Anomaly Characterization (HAYSTAC) project, which processes and analyses Smart City data on 'human movement across times' in order to determine 'normal' and 'anomalous' movements, presumably to help target 'suspicious movement' across space and time (IARPA, 2023a). Taken together, these investments, programmes, and initiatives reveal an IC that is increasingly reliant upon AI-driven technologies.

Automating the intelligence cycle

Although the language of the ODNI's AIM initiative suggests that AI-driven technologies will 'augment' current intelligence practices, they may well fundamentally revolutionize them (Moran et al, 2023). Traditionally, the core practices of intelligence have been defined according to a model known as the intelligence cycle. The cycle begins with policy makers *tasking* their intelligence services with areas and issues to focus upon. Once tasked, intelligence agencies must then *collect* information relevant to that tasking. Once collected, the information is *processed*. It is then *analysed*. Finally, this analysis must be *disseminated* back, in the form of reports or briefings, to policy makers, who then adjust their *tasking* requirements according to this disseminated intelligence, and the process begins again. In practice, of course, as a number of scholars and intelligence professionals have pointed out, this neat sequential process often comes undone. Elements of the cycle occur simultaneously, or can be bypassed altogether, for example when policy makers 'cherry pick' raw intelligence that has not gone through the full process of analysis and dissemination (Hulnick, 2006). Despite these perhaps inevitable gaps between theory and practice, the intelligence cycle remains an important model for understanding intelligence, because it identifies, in an ideal world, the different processes, authorities, and expertise required to transform raw information into actionable intelligence.

Implicit within this process, and indeed central to the governance and oversight of intelligence agencies, is the idea that each stage of the cycle involves conscious human decision-making and direction. It is human policy makers who task intelligence agencies with what they should look at. It is human analysts who *select* which information should be analysed. It is human analysts who, despite the use of sophisticated software and data mining techniques, ultimately craft the analysis of that collected information, and it is human officers who brief policy makers upon their core analytic conclusions. There is, in theory, intent, witting intent, behind each of these decisions. AI, however, significantly problematizes this, because it automates many of these previously human choices, and has the ability to collect, analyse, and task almost simultaneously. As the IC itself recognizes, it might well do away with the intelligence cycle altogether.

One area of AI-driven technologies that is already beginning to supplant the human choices made at the various stages of the intelligence cycle is 'sensemaking'. Indeed, the AIM initiative identifies sensemaking technologies as a particular area of focus for long-term investments. This is a class of technologies that utilizes AI to help inform and guide situational analysis and decision-making. It also uses AI to better understand human decision-making and predict where human biases and analytic mistakes are made. For example, the ICArUS programme, also funded by IARPA, was commissioned in 2010 to develop 'neuroscience-based cognitive models of sensemaking' based upon the functional architecture of the human brain. It aimed to help analysts unpack their mistakes, but also, crucially, to 'lay the groundwork for the development of a new generation of automated analysis tools that replicate the unique strengths of human sensemaking' (IARPA, 2023b). Machine-augmented, or machine-led decisions about intelligence targeting and selection will be an increasing by-product of these kinds of sensemaking technologies that the US IC is investing heavily in.

Another AI-driven sensemaking project that the IC explicitly acknowledges will upend the traditional intelligence cycle is the NRO's Sentient programme. As a declassified NRO white paper describes it, Sentient is a programme of Research and Development at the National Reconnaissance Office (NRO) which aims to 'revolutionize' the traditional intelligence cycle by automating both the tasking and the collection of intelligence around a problem-centric Multi-Int approach (NRO, 2012). A multi-int approach combines the various intelligence collection methodologies utilized by the IC, from human intelligence (HUMANINT) to signals intelligence (SIGINT) that includes the collection of our digital data trails. One of the core objectives of Sentient is to '[d]emonstrate [an] automatic tasking and collection capability' (NRO, undated). Here then, USSID-18's focus upon 'intentional tasking or SELECTION' begins to fall apart. Rather than human analysts entering *selectors* or search terms to pull up information from the vast trove of data that the US IC collects (or not, according to them at least),

Sentient will utilize machine learning to detect patterns and draw inferences from large datasets that will, in turn, *automatically* determine which data are 'selected'. Sentient therefore aims, to a certain extent, to take human intention out of the equation, and rely instead upon machine learning to draw inferences from available data to provide dynamic tasking and collection. According to another NRO document, Sentient is also designed to be 'self-aware of available system assets and status, system performance, and capabilities', as well as 'mission-aware with the ability to apply priorities, historical knowledge, signatures, and patterns' (NRO, undated). The focus upon intentional (presumably human) tasking and selection in the USSID-18 definition of intelligence collection is called into question when tasking itself is increasingly automated, when artificially intelligent algorithms are developed to do away with traditional selectors in favour of a more fluid system of extracting automated inferences from large datasets in an iterative process, and where automation is collapsing the boundaries between tasking, collection, and analysis. With a system like Sentient, tasking, collection, and analysis occur almost simultaneously, with new information yielding near-instantaneous automated analysis that could produce new leads that automatically and dynamically task machine learning algorithms with new collection and analysis priorities.

The Snowden leaks also contained evidence that contradicted the NSA's definition of 'intelligence collection' as the intentional, presumably human, tasking and selection of intelligence requirements – a definition that they used to deny that the Snowden leaks provided evidence of mass surveillance. In a leaked 2008 PowerPoint presentation explaining one of NSA and GCHQ's most powerful surveillance tools, XKEYSCORE, one of the slides explains that 'strong selection itself gives us only a very limited capability', in part because a large amount of activity on the internet is performed anonymously. Therefore, the slide explains, XKEYSCORE can enable internet traffic analysis 'to detect anomalies which can lead to intelligence by itself, or strong selectors for traditional tasking' (The Guardian, 2013). Moreover, XKEYSCORE is itself fed by digital tools that automatically collect intelligence. Turbine, for example, was revealed by Snowden as a powerful hacking system that 'allows the [NSA] to scale up the number of networks it has access to from hundreds to potentially millions'. This is achieved by taking humans out of the loop so that the system can perform what is known as 'dynamic tasking', otherwise known as automated tasking (Gallagher, 2014). Through these and other examples from the Snowden leaks it appears that the NSA's USSID-18 definition of intelligence collection was already anachronistic at the time of the Snowden leaks, describing a world of human analysts poring over data and directing intelligence targeting that was already fast fading a decade ago.

Human, all too human

The increasing role of automation and AI in the state surveillance practices described earlier provokes an important question: can my privacy be violated by a machine? As Matthew Reuben and William Smart (2016) put it: 'One could object that privacy is fundamentally a problem between humans. Animals, much less inanimate objects, do not invade upon our privacy ... do they?' Although the IC's definition of intelligence collection in USSID-18 does not specify that 'intentional tasking or SELECTION' must be *human*, it implies that the vast amounts of data already copied and recorded automatically by machines prior to intentional tasking and selection, do not violate the individual's right to privacy. They are supported in this conclusion by Judge Richard Posner, who argued that '[c]omputer searches do not invade privacy because search programmes are not sentient beings. Only the human search should raise constitutional or other legal issues' (Posner, 2008). A number of other legal experts support Posner's conclusion (Tokson, 2009; Boyden, 2012).

Posner's reasoning, however, goes further, by suggesting that the automated sifting of data actually protects privacy, by siphoning off information that is useless to the IC and thereby significantly limiting the number of communications looked at by human analysts. Kevin Macnish supports this idea, arguing that automated surveillance 'brings with it a degree of anonymity and privacy' that human surveillance does not (Macnish, 2012). He gives the example of a person being picked up on CCTV cameras entering a sex shop. If a human operator was behind the camera the person might be much more sensitive to the idea of being watched, particularly if they know the human operator performing the surveillance. But if the images are picked up incidentally by an automatic system, and then stored for a while, there is still a chance they could be looked at by a human, but this is much less likely, and the person being watched is likely to feel less concerned about the camera (Macnish, 2012). Moreover, Macnish argues that the real dangers of surveillance often lie with human operators who select targets according to subjective biases and are likely to target individuals in a much more intrusive way than the kinds of incidental surveillance often performed by automated systems (Macnish, 2012: 157).

Posner, Macnish, and others agree that automated surveillance does not infringe privacy because machines, even very sophisticated AI-driven machines, are not 'sentient'. This is not, as Macnish writes, 'because they are not human ... but because they are incapable of semantic understanding' (Macnish, 2020: 17). Lynne Rudder Baker concurs that machines are simply incapable of sentience, or acting with the *intentionality* required to meet USSID-18's definition of intelligence collection. For Baker, machines cannot act with intent because an irreducible first-person perspective is a prerequisite of intention. A first-person perspective, she argues, cannot be programmed into a computer because 'no amount of third-person information about oneself ever compels a shift to first person knowledge' (Baker, 1981: 160). At best, according to this perspective, machines are capable of *derived intentionality*, that is, intention derived from their programmers.

There are two major refutations of this line of reasoning. The first takes issue with the idea that human or sentient observation is a fundamental prerequisite for the violation of privacy. Kevin Bankston and Amie Stepanovich (2014) examine US case law and identify a number of important court rulings that have confirmed that surveillance, or 'search and seizure' under the US constitution, takes place at the moment a device redirects, copies, or records a communication, regardless of whether and when a human looks at or listens to that copy or recording. As the court put it in the landmark case of *United States v Turk*: 'In a forest devoid of living listeners, a tree falls? Is there a sound? The answer is yes, if an active tape recorder is present, and the sound might be thought of as "aurally acquired". ... The recorder can be the agent of the ear' (*United States v Turk*, 1975).

The NSA, Bankston and Stepanovich point out, install 'splitter cabinets' at key telecoms hubs across the US, and beyond. These splitter cabinets create complete digital copies of the communications passing through these telecoms hubs. This, they argue, in line with the US case law they examine, constitutes surveillance and the infringement of privacy at the very moment the data are copied, whether or not a human analyst later examines them (Bankston and Stepanovich, 2014).

The second critique of Posner et al, is that while even the most sophisticated machine learning software is not 'sentient', at least in the science fiction sense of 'general AI', it is nevertheless capable of relatively complex cognition, up to and including the formation of beliefs and ideas about individuals and their data, and can also take decisions based upon those ideas and beliefs. Indeed, Ian Kerr argues that the focus upon 'sentience' distracts us with fantasies of 'general AI' when the very real 'narrow AI' applications in use today are already capable of significantly infringing our privacy (Kerr, 2019). 'For a couple of decades now,' Kerr writes, 'we have been building robots with sophisticated sensors, powerful processors, and effective actuators' (Kerr, 2019: 148). While Kerr concedes that this stops short of fully fledged sentience, it nevertheless meets the necessary epistemological threshold for the impingement of privacy. 'Sophisticated AI and robotic technologies can sense, process, and act upon the world with increasing agency', he writes (Kerr, 2019: 135). Instead of identifying *human* observation as the common denominator for privacy infringement, Kerr instead adopts the concept of 'epistemic privacy' – 'a theory that understands a subject's state of privacy as a function of another's state of cognizance regarding the subject's personal facts' (Kerr, 2019: 128). Central to most theories of epistemic privacy, is a 'duty of ignorance' towards a data subject. In Kerr's account, sophisticated machines are perfectly capable of contravening that duty via a degree of awareness about the data they process and analyse, and the ability to act upon those data in ways that violate privacy. Others agree. Mireille Hildebrandt, for example, argues that machines are capable of 'data-driven agency' via their sophisticated ability to analyse data and predict human behaviours in ways that might impact human lives. She argues for a conception of agency that is divorced from 'mindness', or having a mind, in favour of recognizing that today sophisticated machines are capable of both perceiving their environment, and acting upon that perception, without the need for human intervention (Hildebrandt, 2015: 37). With a lower threshold for *intention*, one that severs the link between human minds and intent, it is possible that machine learning technologies could meet USSID-18's definition of intelligence collection.

Machine agents: the consequences of non-human intentionality for the intelligence community's understanding of privacy

What are the implications of recognizing that machines are capable of intentional action for our conception of privacy, and for our understanding of contemporary IC surveillance practices that make use of AI? Will this increasing turn to AI necessarily lead to greater privacy violations? Like Richard Posner's claim that algorithms actually protect privacy by filtering out data that are useless for the IC, it could be argued that the increasing sophistication of machine learning data analytics will actually improve privacy. As computers get better at sensemaking and other types of data analysis, their accuracy and precision in identifying real threats to national security will, presumably, improve. It has already been demonstrated that machines are far more reliable than human analysts when performing certain tasks, especially repetitive tasks such as identifying and classifying individuals and objects in a large database of images (Maslej et al, 2023: 72–104). Feasibly, then, a machine could be far more accurate at, for example, separating out terrorists from civilians in large quantities of drone surveillance feeds. Despite the fears around automated killing, a machine might reduce civilian casualties.

In these limited examples there is certainly truth to the claim that machines improve the accuracy of intelligence analysis, and therefore minimize the likelihood of false positives. However, these specific examples tend to overlook the operative logics of machine learning. Such systems mine vast troves of data to make statistical inferences about particular data points or a particular combination of data points. It is never possible for such systems to be 100 per cent accurate in their conclusions because they are *inferring* statistical conclusions from a base rate. It may be that a high percentage of bomb makers working for terrorist organizations purchase particular chemicals and materials in a particular way, but not all people who purchase those things are bomb makers. It is, therefore, close to impossible for machine learning algorithms to entirely eliminate false positives, although admittedly their false positive rate can often be significantly lower than those of humans examining the same data.

One of the major differences between machine learning and those human analysts, however, is that AI is capable of processing enormous quantities of data. This raises a common statistical problem known as the paradox of false positives, a type of base rate fallacy that occurs when attempting to identify very low-incidence events out of a very large pool of data. Intelligence services, almost by their nature, are interested in low-incidence events: terrorists attacks are extremely rare, as are most kinds of national security threat when examined against the normal patterns of behaviour of a general populace. So, for example, machine learning software designed to identify terrorist suspects from a wider population might have a very high rate of accuracy, say 99 per cent. This means that for every 100 people examined by the software there might be one false positive. However, if the software examines the data of 1 million people, there will be 10,000 false positives. Suddenly, the IC is involved in a potentially massive violation of civil rights.

One company concerned with this issue is the Dutch startup Oddity. AI. They have developed an algorithm that can detect violent incidents from large quantities of video footage, presumably a technology that might interest intelligence and security services, and have received funding from TIIN Capital, a Dutch Security tech fund with close links to the Dutch government (Hague Security Delta, 2020). Perhaps their company name is a nod to the infrequency with which violent incidents occur in CCTV footage. For as they reflect in one of their own corporate blogs:

> The False Positive Paradox occurs when the incidence of a specific case within a large body of data is particularly low. In the case of violence recognition, this paradox is omnipresent. This is due to the fact that violence, especially in the case of video surveillance, is actually extremely rare. This is especially true from the perspective of a computer system. (Oddity.AI, 2023)

As they acknowledge, their algorithm, with 0 per cent false negatives can help save human analysts considerable time by filtering out the many thousands of hours of video footage that do not feature violent incidents. But despite their very high levels of accuracy, they can never entirely rule out false positives. Therefore, human oversight remains vital. But while human oversight in combination with machine learning might be able to reduce false positives to a very small percentage, if algorithms are capable of violating privacy without human intervention, and even possibly act upon their conclusions, such as automatically watchlisting a potential terrorist suspect, then innocent people will undoubtably be subject to very powerful and sophisticated forms of dataveillance by machine learning algorithms operated by the IC.

The other important operative logic of machine learning that has the potential to increase privacy violations by the IC, is that such systems require a vast amount of data in order to operate. To be able to distinguish a missile silo from an office block in satellite images a machine learning algorithm must first be *trained* with millions of images of office blocks and missile silos to *learn* how to accurately identify each of them. To identify anomalies that indicate behaviour that might possibly threaten national security, they need to analyse a vast amount of data about people who do not. If these same algorithms meet the epistemic threshold required to violate our privacy, then the vast troves of data that the IC wishes to portray as inert because it has not been selected by a human analyst, is suddenly animate. As much of those data are about us, the claims by the likes of Snowden and other privacy activists that the IC is performing mass surveillance, become increasingly credible.

If increasingly sophisticated algorithms with sufficient epistemic awareness to infringe upon privacy are analysing more and more of our data, even if only to better perfect their analytic capabilities, then the implications are potentially far-reaching. Contra the arguments of Posner and Macnish, that automated surveillance actually protects privacy, Bankston and Stepanovich argue that not only does the automatic collection of data constitute surveillance, but also that it has potentially far worse privacy implications than human surveillance because of the scale, speed, and accuracy with which algorithmic surveillance can take place. As Supreme Court Justice Samuel Alito pointed out in a landmark ruling on the use of GPS trackers for police surveillance, 'in the pre-computer age the greatest protections of privacy were neither constitutional nor statutory, but practical. Traditional surveillance for any extended period of time was difficult and costly, and therefore rarely undertaken'. But computerized devices such as GPS trackers make 'long-term monitoring relatively easy and cheap' (*United States v Jones*, 2012: 963). Up until recently, Bankston and Stepanovich argue:

> society's expectation has been that intelligence agencies would not – and indeed, simply could not – monitor the content of every email of every person who communicates internationally, an effort that would be impossible absent an impossibly large and costly army of humans. But now, the NSA has a robot army to accomplish the impossible. (Bankston and Stepanovich, 2014: 36)

Conclusion

Understanding the increasingly sophisticated machine learning algorithms being deployed by the IC as being capable of intentional surveillance shifts the parameters of the debate concerning the ethics of the IC's bulk data collection. In the aftermath of the Snowden revelations, many privacy activists, including Snowden himself, challenged the NSA's USSID-18 defence by pointing to the *latent* threats inherent to the IC's bulk data collection programmes. It may well be that human analysts today are not interested in your data, they pointed out, but in the future governments, laws and safeguards might change, and with so much data at their disposal, 'turnkey authoritarianism' would be possible. All that an anti-democratic regime would need to do is retrieve the data on its opponents, and on other activists and critics that it deemed seditious, and suddenly the passive data stored in the IC's Bluffdale Data Center would become a powerful instrument of authoritarianism. This remains a legitimate concern. However, this chapter has attempted to demonstrate that the masses of data stored by the IC, though not 'collected' according to its own definition, is not as 'dormant' or 'latent' as the foregoing argument suggests. Increasingly, sophisticated algorithms with the ability to understand and contextualize our data, and act upon them, are making use of the enormous stores of information that the IC still maintains it has not 'collected'. Humans may not be looking at our data, but machines are. They are aggregating it to detect patterns and anomalies. They are training their neural networks on it to boost the speed and efficiency of their analysis. They are filtering it, to attempt to sort targets or communications of interest from all the online chatter, and the more of our data they consume the more incidents of false positives are made possible. Understanding these machines as active and agential rather than passive and inert, should be cause for concern for privacy activists not because of what intelligence services might *one day do,* but for what their machines are doing now. As the sophistication of machine learning continues to develop, these questions will become more acute.

References

Andrejevic, A. (2013). *Infoglut: How Too Much Information Is Changing the Way We Think and Know.* Abingdon: Routledge.

Baker, L. R. (1981). Why computers can't act. *American Philosophical Quarterly*, 18: 157–163.

Bankston, K. S. and Stepanovich, A. (2014). *When robot eyes are watching you: the law and policy of automated communications surveillance.* Paper presented at We Robot 2014: The Third Annual Conference on Legal and Policy Issues Relation to Robotics. Available at: http://perma.cc/V5CK-MB4B

Boyden, B. E. (2012). Can a computer intercept your email? *Cardozo Law Review*, 34: 669–720.

Cardillo, R. (2017). Small satellites – big data: transcript of remarks by Director of National Geo-Spatial-Intelligence Agency, 7 August. Available at: www.nga.mil/news/Small_Satellites_-_Big_Data.html

Cisco (2023). Visual Networking Index IP Traffic Chart. Available at: www.cisco.com/cdc_content_elements/networking_solutions/service_provider/visual_networking_ip_traffic_chart.html

Clapper, J. (2013). Testimony before the United States Senate Select Committee, 12 March. Available at: www.c-span.org/video/?311436-1/senate-intelligence-cmte-hearing-worldwide-threats-us

Cohn, C. and Timm, T. (2013). Busting eight common excuses for NSA mass surveillance. *Electronic Frontier Foundation Webpage*, 25 November [online]. Available at: www.eff.org/deeplinks/2013/11/busting-eight-common-excuses-nsa-surveillance

Gallagher, S. (2014). NSA's automated hacking engine offers hands-free pwning of the world: with turbine no humans are required to exploit phones, PCs, routers, VPNs. *Ars Technica*, 3 December. Available at: https://arstechnica.com/information-technology/2014/03/nsas-automated-hacking-engine-offers-hands-free-pwning-of-the-world/

Granick, J. S. (2017). *American Spies: Modern Surveillance, Why You Should Care, and What to Do About It.* Cambridge: Cambridge University Press.

Hague Security Delta (2020). Dutch security tech fund invests in Oddity.AI. HSD Foundation, 26 March. Available at: https://securitydelta.nl/news/overview/dutch-security-techfund-invests-in-oddity-ai

Hildebrandt, M. (2015). *Smart Technologies and the End(s) of Law: Novel Entanglements of Law and Technology.* Cheltenham: Edward Elgar Publishing.

Hill, K. (2013). Blueprints of NSA's ridiculously expensive data center in Utah holds less info than thought. *Forbes*, 24 July [online]. Available at: www.forbes.com/sites/kashmirhill/2013/07/24/blueprints-of-nsa-data-center-in-utah-suggest-its-storage-capacity-is-less-impressive-than-thought/?sh=28c9256b7457

Hulnick, A. S. (2006). What's wrong with the intelligence cycle. *Intelligence and National Security*, 21(6): 959–979.

IARPA (Intelligence Advanced Research Projects Agency) (2023a). Hidden Activity Signal and Trajectory Anomaly Characterization (HAYSTAC). Available at: www.iarpa.gov/research-programs/haystac

IARPA (Intelligence Advanced Research Projects Agency) (2023b). Integrated Cognitive-Neuroscience Architecture for Understanding Sensemaking. Available at: www.iarpa.gov/research-programs/icarus

In-Q-Tel (2023). Investment portfolio. Available at: www.iqt.org/portfolio/?taxonomy=tech_areas&tax_id=272

Johnson, D. (2017). The Department of Defense spent $7.4 billion in fiscal year 2017 on cloud computing, big data and artificial intelligence technologies, according to a recent Giovani report. *NextGov/FCW*, 4 December [online]. Available at: www.nextgov.com/digital-government/2017/12/pentagon-boosts-emerging-tech-spend/228398/

Kerr, I. (2019). Schrödinger's robot: privacy in uncertain states. *Theoretical Enquiries in Law*, 20(1): 123–154.

Macnish, K. (2012). The unblinking eye: the ethics of automating surveillance. *Ethics and Information Technology*, 14(2): 151–167.

Macnish, K. (2020). Mass surveillance: A private affair?. *Moral Philosophy and Politics*, 7(1): 9–27.

Maslej, N., Fattorini, L., Brynjolfsson, E., Etchemendy, J., Ligett, K., Lyons, T., et al (2023). The AI Index 2023 Annual Report. AI Index Steering Committee, Institute for Human-Centered AI. Stanford, CA: Stanford University.

Miles, K. (2014). Glenn Greenwald on why privacy is vital, even if you have 'nothing to hide', *Huffington Post*, 20 June [online]. Available at: www.huffpost.com/entry/glenn-greenwald-privacy_n_5509704

Moran, C., Burton, J., and Christou, G. (2023). The U.S. intelligence community, global security and AI: from secret intelligence to smart spying. *Journal of Global Security Studies*, 8(2). DOI: 10.1093/jogss/ogad005

National Security Agency (2011). United States signals intelligence directive (USSID) SP0018: legal compliance and U.S. persons minimizations procedures. Available at: www.dni.gov/files/documents/1118/CLEANEDFinal%20USSID%20SP0018.pdf

NRO (National Reconnaissance Office) (undated). Sentient Programme white paper. Available at: www.nro.gov/Portals/65/documents/foia/declass/ForAll/051719/F-2018-00108_C05112980.pdf

NRO (National Reconnaissance Office) (2012). Declassified document on 'Sentient Program', 13 February. Available at: www.nro.gov/Portals/65/documents/foia/declass/ForAll/051719/F-2018-00108_C05113688.pdf

Oddity.AI (2023). The base rate fallacy, 25 November. Available at: https://oddity.ai/nl/blog/the-base-rate-fallacy/

ODNI (Office of the Director of National Intelligence) (2019). The AIM Initiative: a strategy for augmenting intelligence using machines. Available at: www.dni.gov/files/ODNI/documents/AIM-Strategy.pdf

Paletta, D. (2016). The CIA venture capitalist firm, like its sponsors, operates in the shadows. *Wall Street Journal*, 31 August. Available at: www.wsj.com/articles/the-cias-venture-capital-firm-like-its-sponsor-operates-in-the-shadows-1472587352

Posner, R. A. (2008). Privacy, surveillance, and law. *University of Chicago Law Review*, 75: 245–260.

Reuben, M. and Smart, W. (2016). *Privacy in human-robot interaction: survey and future work*. Paper presented at We Robot 2016: The Fifth Annual Conference on Legal and Policy Issues Relation to Robotics.

Rudder Baker, L. (1981). Why computers can't act. *American Philosophical Quarterly*, 18(2): 157–163.

Rusbridger, A. and MacAskill, E. (2014). Edward Snowden interview: the edited transcript. *The Guardian*, 18 July [online]. Available at: www.theguardian.com/world/2014/jul/18/-sp-edward-snowden-nsa-whistleblower-interview-transcript

Snowden, E. (2019). *Permanent Record* . London: Macmillan.

The Guardian (2013). XKeyscore Presentation from 2008, 31 July. Available at: www.theguardian.com/world/interactive/2013/jul/31/nsa-xkeyscore-program-full-presentation

Tokson, M. (2009). Automation and the Fourth Amendment. *Iowa Law Review*, 96: 581–649.

United Kingdom Government Office for Science (2015). Artificial intelligence: opportunities and implications for the future of decisionmaking. Available at: https://assets.publishing.service.gov.uk/government/uploads/system/uploads/attachment_data/file/566075/gs-16-19-artificial-intelligence-ai-report.pdf

United States Government Accountability Office (2022). Report to congressional committees: artificial intelligence: DOD should improve strategies, inventory process, and collaboration guidance. Available at: www.gao.gov/assets/gao-22-105834.pdf

United States v Turk, 526 F.2d 654 (1975).

United States v Jones, 565 U.S. 400 (2012).

Wooldridge, M. (2020). *A Brief History of Artificial Intelligence: What it Is, Where We Are, and Where We Are Going*. New York: Flatiron Books.

11

Locating Privacy: Geolocational Privacy from a Republican Perspective

Bryce Clayton Newell

Introduction

Mobile devices leave a great deal of geolocation data in their wake. As a form of digital exhaust, records of where we and our devices move in physical space accumulate automatically over time. People consciously choose to use apps and devices, such as smartphones, fitness trackers, and smart watches that track their location through a variety of means, including by onboard Global Positioning System (GPS), Bluetooth, cellular, and Wi-Fi sensors. We are also increasingly captured and located by visual and biometric sensors, such as video cameras, automated licence/number plate cameras, and biometric identification systems that recognize our presence and identify us by our faces, gait, or other biometric characteristics (Koops et al, 2019). These varied records of our location and movements over time are routinely collected, accessed, queried, and put to a variety of uses by commercial and governmental bodies. They are collected and stored by cellular providers, app developers, online platforms, website owners and their advertising partners, and network administrators. The data collected through these means are packaged and sold in commercial data markets, used to target advertisements at us, and are analysed by law enforcement during criminal investigations. As the *New York Times* reported in 2018, during 'every moment of every day, mobile phone apps collect detailed location data. ... And it's for sale' (Valentino-Devries et al, 2018). These realities, including the failure of law and regulation to meaningfully curb these commercial information practices or to stem the flow of personal data from private to public control, carry the potential to invade privacy on a massive scale and raise the spectre of domination by corporate and state actors.

Location data are useful to law enforcement and other government agencies because being able to locate a person, or a vehicle or electronic device such as a phone associated with that person, to a geographic or geospatial position at a particular point in time can provide important evidence in a criminal prosecution or, for example, in civil immigration cases. Aggregating such data over time also permits inferring or deriving additional information about a person and their (historical) movements and activities, including where they live, work, or other places they frequently visit. Processing geolocation data implicates important privacy interests (Koops et al, 2019; Roberts, 2024: 58). It does so, at least in part, because the collection, analysis, and use of geolocation information about people generate informational power for those who hold such data at the expense of the interests of the data subjects. Surveillance is all about accumulating informational power (Monahan, 2011: 495; Newell, 2021: 16). For Koops, the increasing surveillance of people as they move through space raises concerns about 'ubiquitous trackability' because these data are collected over time and aggregated with other datasets, making it possible to reveal additional 'aspects of private life' (2014: 259) through, for example, sophisticated data science and analysis techniques. Those with such power can come to dominate the people whose personal data they control, in the sense that they can manipulate, coerce, or otherwise interfere in those people's lives in arbitrary, highly invisible, and uncontrolled ways.

Linking republican theory and privacy

Republican political philosophy – as a political alternative to liberalism (and not to be confused with the similarly named political party in the US) – focuses intently on these questions of domination. For example, Lovett (2013: s. 1.2) argues that if political liberty is to be 'understood as a sort of structural relationship that exists between persons or groups, rather than as a contingent outcome of that structure', freedom is properly seen 'as a sort of structural independence – as the condition of not being subject to the arbitrary power of a master'. This approach differs from liberal theories of freedom that associate freedom with the absence of *actual interference*. Instead, Pettit (1996: 576–577) proposes that we view freedom as the opposite of 'defenseless susceptibility to [arbitrary] interference by another', or *domination*. The larger neo-republican research agenda promoted by Pettit, Lovett, and others is based on three primary tenets: (1) individual freedom (conceptualized as freedom as non-domination), (2) limited government power over its citizens based on a mixture of constitutionalism and the rule of law (with an emphasis on the importance of the free state promoting the freedom of its citizens without dominating them), and (3) a vigilant commitment by citizens to preserve the freedom-preserving structure and substance of their government through active democratic participation (Lovett and Pettit, 2009).

In the republican tradition, Roberts (2023: 39) argues, 'the value of privacy ... lies in its capacity to shield people from domination'. Conversely, the problem inherent in a loss of privacy 'is that others may acquire dominating power – the capacity to interfere in one's decisions on an arbitrary basis' (Roberts, 2015a: 321; Roberts, 2015b: 544), which is problematic even prior to any actual interference (van der Sloot, 2018). This republican theory of privacy is focused on privacy as instrumental to achieving the 'central ideal of modern republican theory – freedom as non-domination' (Roberts, 2015a: 321). On this view, privacy is valuable because it is instrumental to achieving other values, such as freedom, and to promoting human flourishing (Newell, 2015: 20; Newell, 2021: 56). It does so, at least in part, 'by making individuals less visible (more obscure)' (Newell, 2021: 56) to the state as well as other entities, which provides 'breathing room to engage in the processes of boundary management that enable and constitute self-development' (Cohen, 2013: 1906). And since 'freedom from surveillance, whether public or private, is foundational to the practice of informed and reflective citizenship' (Cohen, 2013: 1905), protecting people's privacy and related interests in data protection also serves important democratic aims.

A central theme within the republican tradition is that domination can exist absent actual interference. That is, domination exists when interference is possible, subject only to the exercised will 'or discretion of the interferer; interference that is uncontrolled by the person on the receiving end' (Pettit, 2012: 58). Additionally, not all interference constitutes domination (Capasso, 2022: 182), especially when the interference is non-arbitrary, controlled, or non-alien (Capasso, 2022: 182, citing Pettit, 1997, 2008, 2012). Thus, republican theory promotes the application of regulatory control in ways that reduce domination. Importantly, if we understand privacy as instrumentally valuable to achieving the republican idea of liberty (that is, non-domination), then we see that privacy must also be more than merely being *left alone*. Rather, privacy should take on characteristics of what Pettit (1996: 589) called 'antipower', enabling and empowering individuals and communities to 'command noninterference' by limiting the potential for arbitrary interference by others, including the state.

In this chapter, I outline and apply a republican theory of privacy to the intermingled location-related information practices of private companies and public law enforcement agencies and to the laws that regulate these information practices. These information practices, including data collection, use, and dissemination, or what I refer to collectively herein as 'data processing', constitute forms of surveillance that operate for a variety of normative and regulatory ends in themselves (Newell, 2023). Even though my primary interest is to situate the location-related surveillance of the state within a republican critique, the data processing practices of private companies and the laws regulating these practices are also important subjects of inquiry because much of the location data used in criminal investigations are initially collected by private companies and then subsequently shared with, or sold to, law enforcement. In bringing republican ideas to bear on this topic, I draw from the republican privacy theory of Roberts (2015a, 2018, 2023) as well as from the broader republican theory of freedom and non-domination offered by Pettit (1996, 1997, 2012, 2014). I summarize how data privacy laws in the United States (US) regulate (or fail to regulate) the transfer, sale, and dissemination of personal geolocation data to public law enforcement by private companies; briefly compare the US approach to that of the European Union (EU); and outline the privacy and data protection harms that flow from law enforcement access to commercial databases of personal geolocation information. I argue that a republican theory of privacy can adequately account for why data processing, and specifically the processing of geolocation data, causes harm that ought to be addressed by regulatory intervention, even when individuals may not experience actual interference in their lives or even notice that their location data have been processed or used by commercial or state actors.

Law enforcement access to location data

Law enforcement agencies have collected or obtained geolocation data for decades, both through their own direct surveillance activities as well as by requesting or purchasing data from private companies.

Law enforcement surveillance

In a pair of cases decided by the US Supreme Court in the 1980s, police investigators used tracking devices ('beepers') to track the location of containers placed in suspects' automobiles (Koops et al, 2019: 638, citing *United States v Knotts*, 1983, and *United States v Karo*, 1984). In the investigation underlining a more recent Supreme Court decision in *United States v Jones* (2012: 403), police installed a GPS tracking device to the bumper of a suspect's automobile and tracked the vehicle's movements for nearly a month, producing 'more than 2,000 pages of data' for the police and prosecutors to potentially use in trial. This surveillance connected the defendant, among other things, 'to the alleged conspirators' stash house' and resulted in a guilty verdict at trial (*United States v Jones*, 2012: 403–404). In another recent case, *Carpenter v United States* (2018: 2212), police obtained court orders to acquire cell-site location information (CSLI) from several suspects' wireless carriers, resulting in the acquisition of 127 days' worth of geolocation data related to the primary defendant's phone, or '12,898 location points cataloging Carpenter's movements – an average of 101 data points per day'. The investigators used this location data to create 'maps that placed Carpenter's phone near four of the charged robberies', and '[i]n the Government's view, the location records clinched the case: They confirmed that Carpenter was "right where the … robbery was at the exact time of the robbery"' (*Carpenter v United States*, 2018: 2213).

Law enforcement access to commercial databases

Law enforcement agencies have also sought location data from private databases as part of high-profile investigations into large numbers of possible suspects. For example, in the US Department of Justice's investigation into the breach of the US Capitol Building on 6 January 2021, the Justice department admitted to accessing and analysing 'location history data and cell tower data for thousands of devices present inside the Capitol' on 6 January (Grand Jury Action No. 21–20 (BAH), 2021: 3, 5). The government obtained these data 'from a variety of sources including Google and multiple data aggregation companies' (Shenkman et al, 2021; Grand Jury Action No. 21–20 (BAH), 2021). In the immigration enforcement context, multiple agencies within the Department of Homeland Security have contracted with private companies providing location data in efforts to locate and deport individuals present within the country without legal documentation (Shenkman et al, 2021: 12–13). Although these databases contain more than just geolocation data, geolocational data have been a primary target of such requests.

Private surveillance and data analytics tools are also so intertwined with state operations that some have referred to the private vendors who produce the databases, working under government contracts, as essentially 'building … surveillance systems' on the government's behalf (Lamdan, 2019: 255). US Immigration and Customs Enforcement (ICE), for example, has noted that its access to large commercial databases 'will allow the agency to quickly build a full picture of a person of interest through finding contact and location information, identifying associations, making connections between individuals, activities, locations, and more with the most recent and relevant information updated frequently' (Shenkman et al, 2021: 25). Additionally, research has shown that law enforcement and intelligence agencies have spent 'millions of dollars to gain access to private sector databases which often contain very sensitive and very personal information on individuals', including geolocation information (Shenkman et al, 2021: 5; see also Purshouse and Roberts, 2024: 11).

These efforts to purchase data – or access to databases – from private companies and data aggregation firms are seen by critics as 'exploiting loopholes in existing law' (Shenkman et al, 2021: 5). When acting as a consumer in an active commercial data marketplace (van Brakel, 2021: 229), police agencies have not always been subject to the typical procedural rules that would apply in the more traditional contexts of law enforcement investigations, such as those that would apply to, for example, searches of a suspect's home or digital devices or when requesting subscribers' geolocation data from a cellular phone service provider (especially after *Carpenter v United States* (2018)). Regardless of how and where law enforcement access geolocation data, however, privacy is implicated by these investigatory activities and the law ought to play an important role in limiting the sorts of information-induced harms that can flow from police use and analysis of such data.

Existing regulations on law enforcement access to commercial geolocation data

Data protection and data privacy laws typically provide some measure of protection for privacy or, at least, limit some uses of personal data without data subject consent or some other legal basis for processing. For example, the EU's General Data Protection Regulation (GDPR) regulates many forms of data processing outside the law enforcement investigations context, as do several state laws in the US, including the California Consumer Privacy Act (CCPA). Notably, at least 157 countries around the world have adopted some form of broadly applicable data privacy law (Greenleaf, 2022). Regulations on law enforcement access to commercial databases approach the problem in several ways.

On the one hand, some laws restrict the processing of personal information by law enforcement agencies directly. For example, the Law Enforcement Directive (LED), which was adopted alongside the GDPR in 2018, requires EU member states to regulate certain data processing activities of public police agencies for purposes of 'prevention, investigation, detection, or prosecution of criminal offences or the execution of criminal penalties, including the safeguarding against and the prevention of threats to public security' (Newell and Kosta, 2024: 212). However, the LED has not been transposed into domestic law of all EU member states in a timely fashion, meaning its provisions may or may not be adopted and enforced equally throughout the EU (Newell and Kosta, 2024: 212). In 2021, Senator Ron Wyden proposed a bill in the US Senate that would have directly regulated private sales of personal data (explicitly including location data) to law enforcement and intelligence agencies (Senate Bill, 1265). Congress did not enact Wyden's bill, but its proposal reflected the concern that existing law was not adequately regulating law enforcement access to personal information held in private databases. On the other hand, some laws regulate commercial data processing broadly, which has an indirect effect on the amount of information available to law enforcement from the commercial data market – that is, presuming these laws result in less data collection and processing activities overall. Most broad data privacy laws, such as the CCPA and the GDPR, fall into this second category since they regulate the processing of personal data by commercial data controllers but do not generally regulate processing by law enforcement.

Regulating government access to data in the US

Before California adopted the CCPA in 2018, commercial data collection and processing were almost completely unregulated under US law. The Federal Trade Commission (FTC) has played a limited but important role in the commercial data privacy space, but the scope of FTC regulation is limited by its authority to investigate unfair and deceptive commercial practices, not data collection and data processing more generally. The Stored Communications Act (SCA), which was enacted by Congress as part of the Electronic Communications Privacy Act of 1986, has played a role in regulating some law enforcement access to data. However, the SCA only regulates access to stored *communications* data and associated customer or subscriber data held by a company providing an 'electronic communication service to the public', which would include geolocation data sourced from a cellphone or other communications device but not geolocation data collected outside the communications context.

In *Carpenter v United States* (2018), the Supreme Court made the SCA even less relevant to questions of law enforcement access to historical location information collected by wireless carriers while also outlining why geolocation information attracts substantial privacy interests. In holding that law enforcement must obtain a warrant to acquire historical CSLI from wireless carriers rather than relying on the less stringent provisions in Section 2703 of the SCA, the Court noted that 'an order issued under Section 2703(d) of the Act is not a permissible mechanism for accessing historical cell-site records. Before compelling a wireless carrier to turn over a subscriber's CSLI, the Government's obligation is a familiar one – get a warrant' (*Carpenter v United States*, 2018: 2221). That is, because aggregated databases of geolocation information implicate such important privacy interests, the Fourth Amendment's warrant requirement should regulate law enforcement access to such data and take precedence over the SCA's more lenient procedural provisions. But whether the Fourth Amendment's prohibition on unreasonable (unwarranted) searches and seizures applies to law enforcement agencies purchasing personal data available on the commercial data market is still somewhat of an open question (Shenkman et al, 2021; Sobel, 2023; see also Solove, 2002).

This legislative lacuna has given rise to a vast commercial market in personal data in which data aggregators and data brokers buy and sell personal data to virtually anyone who wants to buy it, including to public law enforcement agencies. However, an emerging body of consumer data privacy statutes in the US is beginning to regulate some commercial processing of geolocation data. For example, recently enacted data privacy laws in California, Virginia, Colorado, Utah, Connecticut, and several other states consider geolocation information to be 'personal data' or 'personal information' (see, for example, Cal. Civ. Code § 1798.140), the regulatory targets at the centre of these statutory regimes, and several even define 'precise geolocation data' as a type of 'sensitive data' subject to some heightened protections and to several positive rights afforded to data subjects (see, for example, Cal. Civ. Code § 1798.140; Va. Code § 59.1-575; Utah Code § 13-61-101; Ct. Gen. Stats. § 42-515). Some of these laws also separately regulate data processing practices designed to 'evaluate, analyze, or predict ... an identified or identifiable natural person's ... location, or movements' as a form of profiling (VA Code § 59.1-575; see also Conn. Gen. Stats. § 42-515; Cal. Civ. Code § 1798.140; Colo. Rev. Stats. § 6-1-1303). However, these laws often specifically exempt data transfers to law enforcement from their regulatory reach and some even place positive obligations on data controllers to cooperate with law enforcement requests for data (see, for example, Cal. Civ. Code § 1798.145; Colo. Rev. Stats. § 6-1-1304).

The consumer-protection approach to data privacy in the US, with its focus on regulating data processing only within certain business-to-consumer contexts, has done little to directly regulate government access to personal data. As such, law enforcement access to commercial databases of personal information remains predominantly regulated by a patchwork of ageing, sectoral privacy laws at both the state and federal levels and by the prohibition on unreasonable police investigatory measures (searches and seizures) under the Fourth Amendment.

Regulating government access to data in the EU

In the EU, by contrast, the GDPR places broad limits on when data controllers can process personal data. Its reach is much wider than the more limited state-level data privacy laws in the US, regulating a broader range of entities and providing several additional data subjects rights, but it also does not reach the question of law enforcement access to personal data for purposes of criminal investigations (Newell and Kosta, 2024: 211). Filling this space, however, the LED 'applies when police and criminal justice authorities process the personal data of natural persons (including suspects, accomplices, victims, and informants) for law enforcement purposes in a domestic context, but it also applies to cross-border processing between member states' police and judicial authorities and to international transfers' (Newell and Kosta, 2024: 212). Article 3 of the LED specifically calls out location data as a type of personal data that can serve as an identifier – that is, data that make a natural person, or 'data subject', identifiable – for purposes of determining whether data are related to 'an identified or identifiable natural person'. Because location data can be personal data, the LED does provide some substantive limits on law enforcement access to and use of such data. However, the LED provides fewer substantive constraints on law enforcement than apply in the commercial context under the GDPR (Newell and Kosta, 2024: 212). While the LED demonstrates that personal data processing by public entities for criminal justice purposes is a viable regulatory option, even despite problems with full implementation and enforcement across all EU member states, the recent legislative movement across a growing number of US states to adopt consumer data privacy laws essentially fails to address these important questions.

The need for additional regulation

As outlined earlier, the US lacks a broad and generally applicable data protection law like the GDPR or a law enforcement-focused data privacy law such as the LED. Additionally, even in the US states with broad consumer data privacy laws, these state laws are more limited in their scope than the GDPR and primarily apply only within the consumer-protection context (Chander et al, 2021). This lack of broadly relevant data privacy law has opened the door for a robust commercial market in business-to-government data transfers or subscription-based access to commercial databases by law enforcement, which pose important problems for personal privacy. This data pipeline, in which personal data are collected by service providers, app developers, and others, and then re-packaged, shared, and sold to data aggregation firms and then again to public law enforcement agencies willing to pay for access, raises significant problems for traditional criminal procedure rules and the historical assumptions built into the laws that otherwise regulate law enforcement access to data, particularly within the US. The new wave of consumer data privacy laws in the US restrain commercial data processing practices to some degree, which potentially means that less data is available to law enforcement from these data providers. But there remains an untapped potential to build regulation into these laws that would address the sale or dissemination of (access to) personal data by commercial companies to public law enforcement agencies.

From the republican perspective, even the mere acquisition of informational power gives rise to concerns about domination. Where the liberal, non-interference view of freedom would not see an infringement on human liberty (and hence, privacy) unless and until a data controller acts on the informational power they have in a way that interferes with the life and choices of the individual, the republican position offers a more robust theory for why we should be concerned about informational power and domination even prior to interference actually occurring (Roberts, 2024: 58). Thus, the republican position is in direct support for restrictions on data collection itself, rather than only on other forms of downstream processing. As noted by Roberts (2024: 58):

> Republicans will say that to ensure they are not dominated by the police, citizens need to be able to dictate the terms that govern the use of such technology. Of course, the ultimate form of control over power is to prevent others from acquiring it, and commitment to ensuring that the use of intrusive technology does not lead to domination ought to mean that citizens determine whether certain technologies should be available to police.

These concerns are certainly more immediate in the US context than they are in the EU, since legislators in the US have done much less to regulate data collection in the first instance or put limits on the private-to-public pipeline of personal data enabled by robust commercial data markets, but that does not mean that the EU has a perfect regulatory system.

Resisting domination in the context of personal data processing is important because it ensures a greater measure of liberty and reduces the information-induced harm to which individuals and communities are subject. In broad strokes, the data-driven harms republicans argue should be avoided are those that flow from the arbitrary or uncontrolled power that data controllers may acquire as they collect, access, and analyse geolocational data related to humans. This also extends to geolocation data related to humans, but which arguably has been deidentified, or de-linked from identifiable individuals. Importantly, big data analytics has changed the game, making it possible for people to 'be profiled in actionable ways without being personally identified' (Taylor, 2016), meaning that information-induced harms or violations of privacy can accrue despite data being deidentified for analysis. From a critical data studies perspective, we ought to pay 'attention to subject formation within these data regimes, for a critical examination of where the interpellation of the individual emerges in algorithmic culture' (Dalton et al, 2016: 1). The mere fact that algorithmic systems (for example, those that employ artificial intelligence or machine learning techniques) generally operate by classifying and targeting individuals based on syntactic links between available data points (that is, at the syntactic rather than semantic level of information) implies a particular sort of subject formation in the creation of 'digital doubles' that prioritizes syntactic rather than semantic description. These syntactic analyses allow data controllers to draw inferences about the individual data subjects which may, in fact, be semantically accurate, even without any human intervention or interpretation, widening the scope of privacy-relevant harms beyond those inherent in more traditional privacy concerns rooted in the communication and interpretation of semantic information about people.

Even outside the republican tradition, Citron and Solove (2022) note that when geolocation data are accessed or used inappropriately, this can facilitate harassment and expose people to potential harm. Relatedly, in *United States v Jones* (2012), multiple justices on the Supreme Court expressed concerns about the ability of law enforcement investigators to draw inferences about a defendant based on their analysis of 28 days' worth of geolocational tracking data generated by GPS tracking devices attached to the defendant's automobile. Justice Sotomayor argued in a concurring opinion that geolocational tracking 'generates a precise, comprehensive record of a person's public movements that reflects a wealth of detail about her familial, political, professional, religious, and sexual associations' (*United States v Jones*, 2012: 415). Quoting a decision of the Court of Appeals of New York, she expressed concern that it 'takes little imagination' to detect or infer a range of sensitive information about a person from such data, including 'trips to the psychiatrist, the plastic surgeon, the abortion clinic, the AIDS treatment center, the strip club, the criminal defense attorney, the by-the-hour motel, the union meeting, the mosque, synagogue or church, the gay bar and on and on' (*United States v Jones, 2012*: 415, quoting *People v Weaver* (2009)). And because the data have already been collected, 'the government can … efficiently mine them for information years into the future' (*United States v Jones, 2012*: 415). This ability grants the government

> unrestrained power to assemble data that reveal private aspects of identity [and] is susceptible to abuse. The net result is that GPS monitoring – by making available at a relatively low cost such a substantial quantum of intimate information about any person whom the government, in its unfettered discretion, chooses to track – may 'alter the relationship between citizen and government in a way that is inimical to democratic society'. (*United States v Jones*, 2012: 416)

Besides selling the data to government actors, which implicates the particularly coercive powers of state law enforcement, geolocational data are also used to inform behavioural advertising and other commercial ends that seek to manipulate consumers – that is, 'to purposely influence and alter individuals' behaviours and beliefs' (Capasso, 2022: 180). Concerns about unregulated commercial data markets hinge on the fact that people's personal data are being *used* in ways that affect them (or target them) but that do not reflect their will. These are, in short, forms of domination. If 'privacy is valuable … because it shields the individual from domination and is a necessary condition for human flourishing' (Newell, 2021: 51) we must pay attention to enacting legislation that adequately addresses these forms of domination.

Conclusion

As Richards and Hartzog (2021: 962) explain, 'It wasn't supposed to be like this'. Although 'the internet promised human empowerment' (Richards and Hartzog, 2021: 964), the evolution of information technologies has enabled new and highly intrusive forms of surveillance. Even when private companies manage the collection of location data, the state often has ready access to these data through a variety of legal and extra-legal means. These demands for location-related data are based, at least in part, on the 'assumption … that if human mobility can be made more predictable, it also becomes more controllable' (Taylor and Meissner, 2020: 270). Yet, as Roberts (2023: 39) argues, 'the value of privacy … lies in its capacity to shield people from domination'. When a private company or public law enforcement agency tracks a person's location, it raises information privacy concerns due to the use or potential use to which such information is or could be put merely by virtue of its collection. From tracking suspects in narcotics investigations to identifying visits to abortion clinics or predicting future consumer behaviour, the analysis of geolocation data has the potential to tell important and sensitive stories about individuals' lives.

Typically, in the US, rules of criminal procedure provide a check on unbounded police investigations and the associated intrusion into people's private lives. However, when law enforcement agencies purchase personal data as a consumer in commercial data markets as a means of getting around limitations on police 'searches' or 'seizures' under the Fourth Amendment, the absence of alternative regulatory mechanisms such as law enforcement-focused data protection laws highlights problems with the US's existing approach to protecting personal data. These problems give rise to important concerns about information-driven domination that must be addressed to ensure individual and collective privacy is protected.

Within privacy, data protection, and surveillance studies scholarship, there is a growing body of literature that draws from, or is at least aligned with, the republican approach to privacy (see, for example, Hoye and Monaghan, 2018; van der Sloot, 2018; Ritsema van Eck and Houwing, 2021). For example, Julie Cohen's concept of 'semantic discontinuity' (Cohen, 2012, 2013) also frames privacy as related to liberty and human flourishing, enabling what she calls 'the play of everyday practice' (Cohen, 2013: 1932). This play, or freedom to choose our own life's path without the potential of arbitrary or uncontrolled interference in our choices, is enabled by instituting 'gaps and inconsistencies within systems of meaning' (Cohen, 2012: 224), which are essentially 'gaps in enforcement and in systems of surveillance and control'

(Balkin, 2012: 81). These opportunities are limited if data collection and subsequent processing occur but are not regulated to ensure limited arbitrary power flows to those who control or access such data. The notion of privacy as obscurity (Hartzog and Stutzman, 2013a, 2013b; Selinger and Hartzog, 2017: 119; Hartzog, 2018; Newell, 2021) is similarly relevant to addressing republican concerns about the collection, use, and analysis of databases including geolocation information related to people, because it highlights the need to reduce the informational power wielded by those who control or have access to data about people.

In the end, US data privacy law must do much more to protect individual privacy and more robustly protect people from the possibility of *informatic domination*, or the state of affairs made possible by the ability of an agent to use or process information relating to a natural person in an arbitrary or uncontrolled way and that could meaningfully affect or influence the behavioural choices or range of available choices available to an individual or group of individual persons. The affordances that existing US laws provide to commercial data controllers and law enforcement agencies, in relation to the location-tracking tools, technologies, and data-sharing arrangements at their disposal, promotes the continued consolidation of informational power within corporations and state institutions, resulting in the potential for domination and the loss of individual and collective freedom. Legislators should approach regulatory reform by looking for ways in which privacy and data protection law could better promote antipower and reduce the possibility of informatic domination. This, in turn, can better protect privacy and data protection as fundamentally important rights instrumentally linked to personal and collective freedom. We ought to look to more robust regulatory systems, like those adopted in the EU, for some inspiration, but certainly more can be done to improve upon those designs as well.

Acknowledgements

This chapter was written with funding from the European Research Council (ERC) under the EU's Horizon 2020 research and innovation programme (grant agreement No. 716971), awarded to Nadezhda Purtova for her project 'Understanding information for legal protection of people against information-induced harms' (INFO-LEG). The chapter reflects the author's views, and the ERC is not responsible for any use that may be made of the information it contains. The ERC was not involved in study design, or in the collection, analysis, and interpretation of data, in writing the report, or in the decision to submit the chapter for publication. The author is grateful to the organizers of the Beyond Privacy Workshop in Copenhagen on March 23–24, 2023 – Sille Obelitz Søe, Jens-Erik Mai, Rikke Frank Jørgensen, Bjarki Valtysson, Tanja Wiehn, and Johan Lau Munkholm – for funding attendance at that workshop, and to the organizers and other participants at the workshop – including Beate Roessler, Marjolein Lanzing, Simon Willmetts, Paško Bilić, Karen Louise Grova Søilen, and Taina Bucher – for insightful commentary and feedback on an earlier draft of this chapter.

References

Balkin, J. M. (2012). Room for maneuver: Julie Cohen's theory of freedom in the information state. *Jerusalem Review of Legal Studies*, 6: 79–95.

Capasso, M. (2022). Manipulation as Digital Invasion: A Neo-Republican Approach. In F. Jongepier and M. Klenk (eds) *The Philosophy of Online Manipulation*, pp 180–198. New York: Routledge.

Carpenter v United States, 138 S. Ct. 2206 (2018).

Chander, A., Kaminski, M. E. and McGeveran, W. (2021). Catalyzing privacy law. *University of Minnesota Law Review*, 105(4): 1733–1802.

Citron, D. K. and Solove D. J. (2022). Privacy harms. *Boston University Law Review*, 102(3): 793–863.

Cohen, J. E. (2012). *Configuring the Networked Self: Law, Code, and the Play of Everyday Practice*. New Haven, CT: Yale University Press.

Cohen, J. E. (2013). What privacy is for. *Harvard Law Review*, 126(7): 1904–1933.

Dalton, C. M., Taylor, L., and Thatcher, J. (2016). Critical data studies: a dialog on data and space. *Big Data & Society*, 3(1): 1–9.

Grand Jury Action No. 21–20 (BAH). (2021). In re Capitol Breach Grand Jury Investigations within District of Columbia. 339 F.R.D. 1, United States District Court, District of Columbia, 16 July 2021.

Greenleaf, G. (2022). Now 157 countries: twelve data privacy laws in 2021/22. *Privacy Laws & Business International Report*, 176(1): 3–8.

Hartzog, W. (2018). *Privacy's Blueprint: The Battle to Control the Design of New Technologies*. Cambridge, MA: Harvard University Press.

Hartzog, W. and Stutzman, F. (2013a). Obscurity by design. *Washington Law Review*, 88(2): 385–418.

Hartzog, W. and Stutzman, F. (2013b). The case for online obscurity. *California Law Review*, 101(1): 1–50.

Hoye, J. M. and Monaghan, J. (2018). Surveillance, freedom and the republic. *European Journal of Political Theory*, 17(3): 343–363.

Koops, B.-J. (2014). On legal boundaries, technologies, and collapsing dimensions of privacy. *Politica e Società*, 2014(2): 247–264.

Koops, B.-J., Newell, B. C., and Skorvánek, I. (2019). Location tracking by police: the regulation of 'tireless and absolute surveillance'. *UC Irvine Law Review*, 9(3): 635–698.

Lamdan, S. (2019). When Westlaw fuels ICE surveillance: legal ethics in the era of big data policing. *N.Y.U. Review of Law & Social Change*, 43(2): 255–293.

Lovett, F. (2013). 'Republicanism'. In E. N. Zalta (ed) *The Stanford Encyclopedia of Philosophy* (Spring 2013 edition). http://plato.stanford.edu/archives/spr2013/entries/republicanism/

Lovett, F. and Pettit, P. (2009). Neorepublicanism: a normative and institutional research program. *Annual Review of Political Science*, 12: 11–29.

Monahan, T. (2011). Surveillance as cultural practice. *The Sociological Quarterly*, 52(4): 495–508.

Newell, B. C. (2015). *Transparent Lives and the Surveillance State: Policing, New Visibility, and Information Policy*, doctoral dissertation, University of Washington, Seattle.

Newell, B. C. (2021). *Police Visibility: Privacy, Surveillance, and the False Promise of Body-Worn Cameras*. Oakland, CA: University of California Press.

Newell, B. C. (2023). Surveillance as information practice. *Journal of the Association for Information Science and Technology*, 74(4): 444–460.

Newell, B. C. and Kosta, E. (2024). Apples, Oranges, and Time Machines: Regulating Police Use of Body-Worn Cameras in Europe and the United States. In A. Roberts, J. Purshouse, and J. Bosland (eds) *Privacy, Technology, and the Criminal Process*, pp 196–221. New York: Routledge.

People v Weaver, 12 N.Y.3d 433 (2009).

Pettit, P. (1996). Freedom as antipower. *Ethics*, 106(3): 576–605.

Pettit, P. (1997). *Republicanism: A Theory of Freedom and Government*. Oxford: Clarendon Press.

Pettit, P. (2008). Republican Liberty: Three Axioms, Four Theorems. In C. Laborde and J. Maynor (eds) *Republicanism and Political Theory*, pp 102–130. Oxford: Blackwell.

Pettit, P. (2012). *On the People's Terms: A Republican Theory and Model of Democracy*. New York: Cambridge University Press.

Pettit, P. (2014). *Just Freedom: A Moral Compass for a Complex World*. New York: Norton.

Purshouse, J. and Roberts, A. (2024). Introduction: Criminal Justice, Technology, and the Future of Privacy. In A. Roberts, J. Purshouse, and J. Bosland (eds) *Privacy, Technology, and the Criminal Process*, pp 1–17. New York: Routledge.

Richards, N. and Hartzog, W. (2021). A duty of loyalty for privacy law. *Washington University Law Review*, 99(3): 961–1022.

Ritsema van Eck, G. J. and Houwing, L. (2021). A Republican and Collective Approach to the Privacy and Surveillance Issues of Bodycams. In B. C. Newell (ed) *Police on Camera*, pp 223–230. New York: Routledge.

Roberts, A. (2015a). A republican account of the value of privacy. *European Journal of Political Theory*, 14(3): 320–344.

Roberts, A. (2015b). Privacy, data retention and domination: Digital Rights Ireland Ltd v Minister for Communications. *Modern Law Review*, 79(3): 522–548.

Roberts, A. (2018). Why privacy and domination? *European Data Protection Law Review*, 4(1): 5–11.

Roberts, A. (2023). *Privacy in the Republic*. New York: Routledge.

Roberts, A. (2024). Police Use of Intrusive Technology: Freedom, Privacy, and Political Legitimacy. In A. Roberts, J. Purshouse, and J. Bosland (eds) *Privacy, Technology, and the Criminal Process*, pp 39–65. New York: Routledge.

Selinger, E. and Hartzog, W. (2017). Obscurity and Privacy. In J. C. Pitt and A. Shew (eds) *Spaces for the Future: A Companion to Philosophy of Technology*, pp 119–129. New York: Routledge.

Shenkman, C., Franklin, S. B., Nojeim, G., and Thakur, D. (2021). Legal loopholes and data for dollars: how law enforcement and intelligence agencies are buying your data from brokers. Center for Democracy & Technology [online], December. Available at: https://cdt.org/wp-content/uploads/2021/12/2021-12-08-Legal-Loopholes-and-Data-for-Dollars-Report-final.pdf (accessed 17 July 2023).

Sobel, A. (2023). End-running warrants: purchasing data under the Fourth Amendment and the state action problem. *Yale Law & Policy Review*. Available at: https://ssrn.com/abstract=4480782 (accessed 21 July 2023).

Solove, D. J. (2002). Digital dossiers and the dissipation of Fourth Amendment privacy. *Southern California Law Review*, 75(5): 1083–1168.

Taylor, L. (2016). Safety in Numbers? Group Privacy and Big Data Analytics in the Developing World. In L. Taylor, B. van der Sloot, and L. Floridi (eds) *Group Privacy: The Challenges of New Data Technologies*, pp 13–36. Cham: Springer.

Taylor, L. and Meissner, F. (2020). A crisis of opportunity: market-making, big data, and the consolidation of migration as risk. *Antipode*, 52(1): 270–290.

United States v Jones, 565 U.S. 400 (2012).

United States v Karo, 468 U.S. 705 (1984).

United States v Knotts, 460 U.S. 276 (1983).

Valentino-Devries, J., Singer, N., Keller, M. H., and Krolik, A. (2018). Your apps know where you were last night, and they're not keeping it secret. *New York Times* [online], 10 December. Available at: www.nytimes.com/interactive/2018/12/10/business/location-data-privacy-apps.html (accessed 17 July 2023).

van Brakel, R. (2021). How to watch the watchers? Democratic oversight of algorithmic police surveillance in Belgium. *Surveillance & Society*, 19(2): 228–240.

van der Sloot, B. (2018). A new approach to the right to privacy, or how the European Court of Human Rights embraced the non-domination principle. *Computer Law & Security Review*, 34(3): 539–549.

Index

References to endnotes show both the page number and the note number (231n3).

INDEX